Published in conjunction with
the British Association of Social Workers

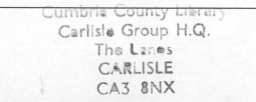

...an important stage in its development. The ...acing fresh challenges to work flexibly in fast-changing ...nd organizational environments. New requirements for training ...e also demanding a more critical and reflective, as well as a more highly skilled, approach to practice.

The British Association of Social Workers (www.basw.co.uk) has always been conscious of its role in setting guidelines for practice and in seeking to raise professional standards. The concept of the *Practical Social Work* series was conceived to fulfil a genuine professional need for a carefully planned, coherent series of texts that would stimulate and inform debate, thereby contributing to the development of practitioners' skills and professionalism.

Newly relaunched, the series continues to address the needs of all those who are looking to deepen and refresh their understanding and skills. It is designed for students and busy professionals alike. Each book marries practice issues and challenges with the latest theory and research in a compact and applied format. The authors represent a wide variety of experience both as educators and practitioners. Taken together, the books set a standard in their clarity, relevance and rigour.

A list of new and best-selling titles in this series follows overleaf. A comprehensive list of titles available in the series, and further details about individual books, can be found online at: www.palgrave.com/socialworkpolicy/basw

Series standing order ISBN 0–333–80313–2

You can receive future titles in this series as they are published by placing a standing order. Please contact your bookseller or, in the case of difficulty, contact us at the address below with your name and address, the title of the series and the ISBN quoted above.

Customer Services Department, Macmillan Distribution Ltd, Houndmills, Basingstoke, Hampshire RG21 6XS, England, UK

Practical social work series

Editor: Jo Campling

New and best-selling titles

Terence O'Sullivan

Decision making
in social work

Second edition

palgrave
macmillan

First edition 1999 (published outside the Practical Social Work series)
Reprinted eight times
Second edition 2011

Published by
PALGRAVE MACMILLAN

Palgrave Macmillan in the UK is an imprint of Macmillan Publishers Limited, registered in England, company number 785998, of Houndmills, Basingstoke, Hampshire RG21 6XS.

Palgrave Macmillan in the US is a division of St Martin's Press LLC, 175 Fifth Avenue, New York, NY 10010.

Palgrave Macmillan is the global academic imprint of the above companies and has companies and representatives throughout the world.

Palgrave® and Macmillan® are registered trademarks in the United States, the United Kingdom, Europe and other countries

ISBN 978–0–230–22359–2

This book is printed on paper suitable for recycling and made from fully managed and sustained forest sources. Logging, pulping and manufacturing processes are expected to conform to the environmental regulations of the country of origin.

A catalogue record for this book is available from the British Library.

Library of Congress Cataloging-in-Publication Data

O'Sullivan, Terence.
    Decision making in social work / Terence O'Sullivan. — 2nd ed.
        p. cm. — (Practical social work series)
    ISBN 978–0–230–22359–2 (pbk.)
    1. Social case work. 2. Decision making. 3. Social service. I.
    Title.
HV43.O894 2010
361.3'2—dc22   2010032636

10 9 8 7 6 5 4 3 2
20 19 18 17 16 15 14 13 12

Printed and bound in China

Contents

List of figures and tables

Figures

Tables

To Teresa

Preface to the second edition

The first edition has been extensively revised and extended to reflect developments and changes in social work practice and its contexts. The framework for decision making in social work practice has generally stood the test of time, and with the revisions here I seek to give more emphasis to themes already present in the first edition. This second edition reflects the increased importance of service user involvement, collaborative and integrative working, knowledge-based practice, emotional competence, being reflexive about framing situations and analysing options, managing risk, constructing well-reasoned arguments and using supervision. Key aims in the revisions have been to maintain the accessibility of the original text and more explicitly to show the book's focus on practice. Chapters 1 and 7 have been rewritten, Chapter 8 replaced with an entirely new chapter on supervision and the others extensively revised.

Chapter 1 now lays the groundwork for the rest of the book by taking a preliminary look at some key concepts including problem solving, ethics, risk, power and reflexivity. Service-user movements have been added to the practice contexts outlined in Chapter 2, with the other contexts being updated and revised. Chapter 3 has been revised to give more emphasis to the importance of service-user decision making and the role social workers can have in helping them make informed life choices. In this context I now discuss strengths and capacity building and the Mental Capacity Act 2005. Chapter 4 has been revised to reflect more explicitly the importance of collaborative and integrated working amongst frontline professionals. Chapter 5 retains its emphasis on the importance of thinking and emotional competence but now more fully reflects the role and importance of knowledge in sound decision making. Chapter 6 gives more extensive treatment to how framing processes can distort as well as facilitate the understanding of decision situations. Chapter 7 has been rewritten to show how ethical theory, risk theory and decision theory can be used to analyse options, manage uncertainty and make decisions. It now also includes a section on constructing arguments to justify decisions. Chapter 8 is a new chapter on the potential role supervision has in helping, supporting and guiding frontline workers in making decisions.

TERENCE O'SULLIVAN

Introduction

When a child is killed by a parent, a passer-by murdered by a mentally disordered person or the dead body of an older person has lain undetected in their dingy flat for weeks, the social workers involved can be accused of errors of judgement or incompetence. Sometimes this criticism may be warranted, but often it is unfounded, appearing to fulfil a need to hold somebody responsible for the failings of society. Subsequent attempts to improve social work decision making can be divided into two categories: those that focus on restructuring services and providing procedures to follow; and those that endeavour to strengthen professional social work by developing the knowledge and skills of social workers, and providing them with a supportive organizational environment. This book falls into the latter category and is rooted in the belief that social workers need high levels of skill, knowledge and organizational support to manage the complexity of the situations they work with. As Gibbs (2009: 297) suggests, the focus needs to be on the nature of the professional challenge rather than the failure of individuals.

There are a number of reasons why social work decision making requires high levels of organizational support, professional knowledge and skill. Social workers are involved in making difficult judgements and decisions in emotionally fraught situations in which they need to take into account a large number of interacting factors operating on different levels of analysis, ranging from the personal to the societal. Social workers need to be able to think clearly and manage their emotions, while balancing risk and safety to enable people to manage their lives and achieve the outcomes they want. They need to manage and cope with uncertainty by keeping an open mind while still making plans and taking action, even though outcomes cannot be predicted with certainty. They need to involve service users at the highest level and work closely with other professionals, carers, community members and relatives to assess situations, analyse options, anticipate consequences and make decisions.

This book provides a framework for making decisions in social work practice that will aid the development of the required knowledge, skill and support. The framework is set out in nine chapters, with Chapter 1 introducing some key ideas, concepts and issues that run through the subsequent chapters. Chapter 2 considers the practice context within which decisions are made. Chapters 3 and 4 explain how service users can be effectively involved and the different stakeholders work together. Chapter 5 explores processes of using knowledge, thinking and emotional competence, while Chapters 6 and 7 look at two central aspects of decision making, the framing of the decision situation (Chapter 6) and the analysing of options to make ethical and informed decisions (Chapter 7). Chapter 8 considers the role of effective supervision in supporting and guiding decision making. Finally, Chapter 9 concludes by considering why sound decision making does not always lead to good outcomes.

The underlying processes of decision making are illustrated in each chapter by a practice scenario. These should not be considered case studies of practice, since they fall short of giving a full account of decision making in the specific situations. They focus on particular decision points whereas social work practice invariably involves a continuous process of making a series of decisions. The framework is a general one, applicable across the broad range of social work; however, in trying to make the chapters more accessible, they may at times come to reflect the particular concerns of the case scenario. The terminology used to denote those who engage, receive or use the assistance of a social worker remains an issue. None of the available terms are ideal and for reasons of consistency and common usage the term 'service user' is used throughout, with the exception of the terms 'primary' and 'secondary clients'.

It also needs to be remembered that the purpose of the following chapters is not to examine the issues of the specific fields of social work from which the case scenarios are drawn, but to explore a particular aspect of decision making. For example, the purpose of Chapter 1 is not to examine child protection investigations, which happens to be the illustrative example, but to lay the groundwork for building a framework for decision making in social work. In this way the different aspects of making decisions are considered chapter by chapter, so that by the end of the book a framework for decision making in social work practice will be complete.

The content of the book has strong links to all Six Key Roles of The National Occupational Standards for Social Work, including:

- **Key Role 1, assessment and supporting service user decision making:** Chapter 3 'Involving Service Users and Carers' will help the reader support service user decision making (Unit 2). Chapter 6 'Framing Situations' explains the underlying processes involved in assessing and analysing situations (Unit 3). Chapter 7 'Analysing Options' is directly relevant to recommending courses of action (Unit 3).

- **Key Role 2, planning and carrying out plans:** Understanding the underlying processes of decision making depicted in this book will lay the foundations for planning with service users (Unit 6).

- **Key Role 3, preparing for decision making forums:** Chapter 4 'Working Together' will assist the reader to participate effectively in decision making forums (Unit 11).

- **Key Role 4, assessment and management of risk:** Chapter 7 'Analysing Options' is directly relevant to managing risk and uncertainty (Unit 12).

- **Key Role 5, using supervision and working in multidisciplinary networks:** Chapter 8 'Using Supervision' will help the reader to use effectively supervision and support; Chapter 4 'Working Together' concerns multidisciplinary and multiorganizational work (Unit 17).

- **Key Role 6, using knowledge and managing dilemmas:** Chapter 5 'Using Knowledge and Managing Emotions' will enable the reader to use different sources of knowledge in practice and to reflect critically on the emotions generated in practice (Unit 20). Chapter 7 'Analysing Options' is relevant to resolving dilemmas (Units 18 and 21).

The book will help readers to enhance their own decision making and improve the support they give to the decision making of others. As such it will have broad appeal to students, newly qualified social workers, more experienced practitioners and frontline managers. Students on undergraduate and postgraduate social work degrees will find the book an invaluable resource for a wide range of modules, particularly in the way it relates theory to practice in an accessible way. Newly qualified social workers will find it helps them to make better use of support and supervision in their assessed year in employment. Practitioners on post-qualifying courses will value the breadth and depth given to the underlying processes of decision making in both adult and children services. The text will be of value to frontline managers who are looking for ways to improve the support they can give to frontline practitioners and their decision making.

1 | Making decisions

Decision making is a core professional activity at the heart of social work with much of what social workers do involving making decisions with others. All the various tasks involved in social work processes, no matter how they are divided, involve the making of decisions. This includes referral/inquiry, allocation, assessment, planning, plan implementation, review and closure decisions. If social workers are to increase the chances of achieving their professional aims of promoting human welfare, social justice and preventing human suffering, the decisions made within social work will need careful attention. Munro (2002: 107) points out that a reluctance of social workers to make decisions shows up both in avoiding decisions altogether and a tendency to procrastinate so that decisions are made in reaction to a crisis rather than as a long-term plan. This book is about how social workers can become more proactive in their decision making practices and this first chapter takes a preliminary look at some key ideas, issues, concepts and questions that will lay the foundation for the rest of the book.

practice scenario

One Friday afternoon, an anonymous telephone call is received at a local office claiming that a four-year-old child has been badly injured by her mother at a particular address. The office had received a number of anonymous calls recently concerning families on this estate, which on investigation turned out to be hoaxes. The two duty social workers, unable to find out any further information about the family, consult with their team manager and police colleagues. Together they decide that the best way of proceeding is to carry out a home visit as a preliminary enquiry, to see if there are any grounds for a full investigation. At the address the two social workers identify themselves ↘

to a young woman who answers the door. They establish that she is the mother of a four-year-old child who is asleep upstairs. They explain that an anonymous caller has made an allegation and ask to see the child. At this point the woman becomes indignant, stating that she was not going to let them wake her daughter just because of some malicious person and slams the door. The two social workers return to their car to decide what to do next.

Child protection agencies receive referrals from a variety of sources concerning children who may need protection from harm, some of which will be filtered out very quickly, while others need to be further investigated (Gibbons *et al.*, 1995: 51). One of the many problems faced by these agencies is how to respond to referrals from members of the public who do not give their name. The majority of these will turn out to require no further action, but they do need careful screening as calls of this nature do at times contain important information (Wattam, 1995: 172). They also require sensitive handling, as being implicated in harming your child, even without any foundation, is a traumatic experience for families.

If the two social workers in the car that Friday afternoon do not systematically think through the decision situation and the options available to them, there is a danger that a child will be further harmed or, alternatively, that an innocent family will be traumatized by unwarranted intrusion. Social work decisions are often problematic balancing acts, based on incomplete information, within time constraints, under pressure from different sources, with uncertainty as to the outcome of different options, as well as a constant fear that something will go wrong and the social worker will be blamed. To be able to find their way through this labyrinth, social workers need to be critically aware of the processes involved in making sound decisions, so as to be able to participate proactively and not be swept along by events.

What is decision making?

Decision making is surprisingly difficult to define without involving a particular theory as to how decisions are made. To decide is to make up one's mind and typically involves making a choice. Decision making can be simply defined as the process of *making* a choice when there is some degree of recognition of a need or desire to choose. It would be relatively straightforward to confine decision making to making a deliberate choice from the options available but this would neglect the fact that some choices are intuitive and are made without conscious thought. These non-deliberated intuitive decisions are particularly important in social work (England, 1986) and will be discussed at some length in Chapter 5. Such decisions are based on expertise built up through experience. Notwithstanding the importance of intuitive decisions in professional work, deliberation is required when decision situations need careful analysis and when working with others.

Decision making varies in a number of important ways. Firstly, decisions vary as to how much deliberation they are given; some decisions being given extensive deliberation, whereas others are made with scant deliberation and others still no deliberation at all, as in the case of intuitive decisions. Very little progress would be made if social workers were to analyse every decision in detail, but on the other hand there are certain decision points that justify detailed consideration of the different options. Secondly, decisions vary as to their perceived consequences and so the amount of pressure experienced. Some decisions are viewed as important because, for example, they are perceived to have life and death consequences, whereas others are thought to have minimal consequences. Thirdly, the intensity of emotion that decision makers experience can vary. For example, making a particular decision may generate high anxiety, while another can be taken with little emotion.

Although there are well-recognized decision points, such as reviews, for the most part it is difficult to delineate where decision making starts and finishes. Rather than thinking of decision making as having a clear beginning and end, it is more appropriate to think in terms of chains or sequences of decisions taken over time, each feeding into the next. The links in the chain can be thought of as the choices made, the chain starting at the point of referral and ending at the point that the case file is closed, as shown in Figure 1.1. The developing chains of decisions endeavour to take decision situations in particular directions, either in incremental steps or by making major changes. The practice scenarios used in this book feature particular points in time within particular decision chains. In this chapter's example, the chain is at the enquiry stage, a number of decisions have already been made, and after the two social workers have decided what to do, others will follow.

Whose decision?

When considering decision making in social work, there is a danger that only the decisions taken by social workers will be focused on. It is important to remember that decisions in social work are rarely taken by one person alone and different people have different roles and perspec-

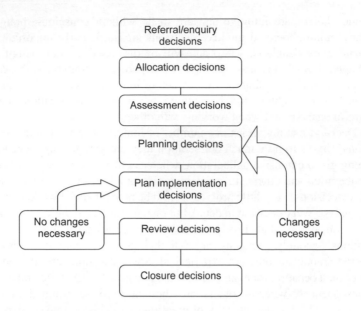

Figure 1.1   Decision chains in social work

tives to take within chains of decisions. Many decisions are made by service users or jointly with others or with the guidance and support of others. In the example, the two social workers, the child and the mother are not the only stakeholders in the situation. There are a number of other potential stakeholders – including other family members, the social workers' supervisor, the person who made the anonymous call, the receptionist who took the call, the team manager, the health visitor, the GP, the staff at the nursery school and the police. Each has had, or potentially will have, decisions and inputs to make at various points in time. The focus in this book is the decisions made within social work; its subject matter relates to the decisions and inputs of service users and the other stakeholders as much as social workers.

The term 'stakeholder' will be used to denote all those who have some interest or concern in the decision being made. This interest will vary in nature, sometimes being a professional or agency interest, while with others it will be a personal, family or life interest. Sometimes the interest can be central and intense, while at other times it may be more marginal and low key. Stakeholders will also vary as to their position in society and their relationship with the agencies involved, with some being in a relatively powerful position, while others may be relatively powerless. Not all the stakeholders will necessarily be decision makers, some, for example, could be providers of information or services.

Social workers have a number of roles within decision making, which can change between and within decision situations. At any particular point in time social workers need to be clear as to what their role is in relation to the decision being taken. Four distinct roles can be identified:

● facilitation of service-user decision making;
● collaborative decision making with others;
● making professional judgements;
● making recommendations to others.

These are not mutually exclusive but rather different aspects of the social work role. At times service users and carers have important life decisions to take and seek the help of social workers who can have a valuable role in helping them make an informed decision. Many of the decisions in social work are collaborative ones made jointly or in consultation with other stakeholders both inside and outside decision-making forums. At times social workers have to make professional judgements and come to conclusions when there are no clear-cut answers and there is uncertainty about what is happening. Also social workers make recommendations both orally and in written reports, based on their information gathering and analysis, for example, to managers, courts, conferences or panels.

Decision making and problem solving

Klein (1999: 141) claims there is more overlap than difference between decision making and problem solving, with one being regarded as a subset of the other, or vice versa. This close association between decision-making and problem-solving processes means that a book on 'decision making in social work' will also be about 'problem solving in social work'. In their day-to-day work social workers help adults, children and families solve problems and overcome difficulties: the definition of social work developed by the International Federation of Social Workers (IFSW) and the International Association of Schools of Social Work includes the term 'problem solving in human relationships'. The IFSW states that:

> the social work profession promotes social change, problem solving in human relationships and the empowerment and liberation of people to enhance well-being. Utilising theories of human behaviour and social systems, social work intervenes at the points where people interact with their environments.

Principles of human rights and social justice are fundamental to social work. (IFSW, 2000)

However, the term 'problem solving' needs to be used with caution, as it can be depicted in negative terms, being associated with particular approaches to professional work with people, including problem-focused approaches (particularly those that focus on deficits to the neglect of strengths), unthinking, reactive, quick-fix approaches that emanate from worker anxiety, and attempts at fixing problems for people. Ruch (2007a: 376) points out that 'all too often in practice, practitioners repeatedly try to come up with practical solutions to entrenched chronic situations without endeavouring to understand their own behaviours, those of the people they are trying to help and the other professionals involved'. However, this superficial, frantic, anxiety-driven approach contrasts sharply with, for example, the joint problem solving described by Folgheraiter (2004: 201). Hence the term 'problem solving' can simply refer to processes involved in solving problems which can take many forms, including when proactive, deliberative and thoughtful workers recognize the strengths and problem-solving capacities of service users. Such solution-focused, proactive, capacity-building approaches to problems can be referred to as 'solution building', a term borrowed from Berg and De Jung (1996). Solution building can take the form of 'co-production' when frontline workers and agencies respect service users as assets, who can provide mutual support and deliver services to produce their own solutions (Boyle et al., 2006; Carr, 2008: 13).

Decision making and ethics

Most would agree that the decision making that takes place within social work should be ethical decision making as opposed to unethical, but what 'being ethical' involves is contested. Ethics relates to the study of what is to be regarded as good conduct and concerns what are 'right or wrong' behaviours or actions. It is concerned with what we ought to do in particular situations and how we ought to act towards others. The question whether a course of action is morally right is often a contested one. Bowles et al. (2006: 55) identify three modes of ethical thinking: virtue-based ethics, deontological ethics and consequentialism, all of which are important in social work decision making and action. Bowles et al. state that:

all of the traditional approaches capture some aspect of the truth of ethical complexity, and all of them, if properly balanced, contribute to successful resolution of real problems. (Ibid.: 56)

A person using these different modes of ethical thinking would ask different questions when making a difficult decision. Virtue ethics would ask what virtues are required in this situation and concentrates on what characteristics decision makers should possess. Deontological ethics would ask which course of action accords with universal principles and ethical rules, for example, self-determination. Consequentialist ethics would ask which option is most likely to produce a good outcome.

Banks (2006: 13) points out that deciding what to do in social work is not solely a technical matter, a legal matter or an ethical matter, but a combination and interaction of all three, and the importance decision makers place on 'ethics' in a particular situation will depend on their perspective. As Banks states:

> what is a technical matter for one person (simply applying the rules) may be an ethical problem for another (a difficult decision but it is clear what decision should be made) or a dilemma for a third person (there appears to be no solution). (Ibid.)

Ethics has relevance for all the chapter topics of this book. For example, professional ethics is an important part of the practice context (Chapter 2). Involving service users to the highest level (Chapter 3) is put forward as an ethical principle. Working together (Chapter 4) introduces the imperatives of 'discourse ethics' by which a climate of open communication can be achieved. Emotional competence (Chapter 5) raises the question of whether it is ethical to override strong emotions. The discussion of personal beliefs in Chapter 6 raises the question of whether the intrusion of personal convictions into professional work is to be regarded as an unethical distortion or the ethical use of the whole 'self'. The different ethical theories of making a choice (Chapter 7) can be used to argue that a particular course of action is the best in the circumstances. Whether to share with one's supervisor sensitive information given in confidence can also be an ethical issue (Chapter 8).

Decision making and power

'Power-sensitive practice', a term used by Beckett (2006: 126), is used here to mean 'being sensitive to power dynamics, relations and differences'. The ability to influence or determine a decision is likely to be unequally distributed amongst stakeholders, hence the importance of 'power' in understanding processes of deciding what course of action to take. However, Taylor and White (2000: 115) highlight the need to ask different and better questions, 'rather than assuming the professionals have power in their encounters with service users simply because they are professionals'. This would mean that the power dynamics of situations need to be analysed using a more nuanced, subtle, complex and dynamic view of power than sometimes has been the case. There is a danger that, in understanding the way that society is structured, power dynamics between, for example, professionals and service users are seen as inevitably a straightforward one of domination of the latter by the former.

Power not only needs to be understood at the structural level of analysis but also at the level of the face-to-face situation. Stakeholders bring their capacities and resources to face-to-face interactions, and these may be unequal, but no one is completely powerless or completely powerful. Each face-to-face encounter is negotiated with the possibility that the seemingly less powerful exert influence and determine decisions. Authority is a certain kind of socially sanctioned power that stems from holding a particular position, which can only be legitimately used within the limits of some role. The social workers in the practice scenario have authority to investigate the allegation, but they need to do so within ethical, legal and procedural rules, and at least at this stage the mother has the power to refuse them entry.

Tew's (2006: 41) 'Matrix of Power Relations' concerns the ways power is exercised and it helps us to understand and analyse power dynamics. It consists of two dimensions of power: 'the productive power/limiting power' dimension and the 'power over/power together' dimension. Table 1.1 presents this Matrix of Power and shows four types of power: protective, cooperative, oppressive and collusive.

Good professional practice involves productive modes of power; however, there is a danger that oppressive power and collusive power come into the picture. The concept of power has some relevance for all the chapters of this book. In Chapter 2, part of the practice context is the power structures embedded in society. In Chapter 3, power is involved in service-user empowerment. In Chapter 4, a barrier to working together is the power differentials between stakeholders. In Chapter 5,

Table 1.1 *Matrix of power*

	Power over	*Power together*
Productive modes of power	Protective power	Cooperative power
Limiting modes of power	Oppressive power	Collusive power

Source: Adapted from Tew (2006: 41).

power can come from holding certain types of knowledge. In Chapters 6 and 7, power can be used to determine the way decision situations are framed and options chosen. In Chapter 8, an important feature of social work supervision is the power dynamics between supervisor and supervisee.

Decision making and risk

Both options identified by the two social workers in the practice scenario involve 'risk', a term theorists and others have used in a number of different ways and which unfortunately is sometimes poorly conceptualized. Stalker (2003: 216) having reviewed the literature states that 'the theories [of risk suggest] that social work theorists and practitioners should adopt a critical approach to their understanding of and response to risk'.

Two discourses of 'risk' can be detected within the helping professions. There is 'risk' as danger, concerned with safety, and there is 'risk' as chance, concerned with uncertainty and risk taking. Parton (2001) argues that there has been a comparatively recent tendency for 'risk' to be exclusively associated with the assessment and avoidance of danger, which has led to practice becoming more defensive and preoccupied with safety and the need to avoid blame. This book endeavours to take a balanced approach to 'risk', which will be associated with uncertainty of outcomes and chance, rather than solely the assessment and management of danger.

The concept of 'risk' has relevance to all the chapters of the book. In Chapter 2, an important part of the cultural climate in which social work practice takes place is a preoccupation with the management of risk and holding someone to account when things go wrong. In Chapter 3, an important role of social workers is helping service users manage risks and make life decisions to achieve the outcomes they want. In Chapter 4, anxiety about risk is both a motivation and impediment to working together. In Chapter 5, an aspect of emotional competence is the management of the anxiety generated by risk and uncertainty. Chapter 6 explains how a preoccupation with risk can mean assessments being skewed to the negative side of people's lives and how care is needed to include strengths as well as problems. Chapter 7 discusses the management of risk through risk assessment, hazard reduction, capacity building, providing support and services. Chapter 8 emphasizes the important role supervision has in providing support and guidance to frontline workers to contain the emotions generated by risk and thinking through assessments and plans.

Decision making and reflexivity

D'Cruz *et al.* (2007) identify a number of ways the term 'reflexivity' is used within the social work literature and explains how it is often used loosely and left undefined. Here the term refers to practitioners becoming critically aware of the assumptions and processes that underlie how they make sense of practice situations, make choices and act. The argument is that decision making in social work requires reflexivity, that is, when making decisions, social workers need to be reflexive about their beliefs, emotions, thinking, reasoning and actions. In the literature the terms 'reflexivity' and 'reflection' are often used interchangeably (Fook, 2002: 43). However, the terms can be used to draw an important distinction between different processes. Within this perspective 'reflexivity' is similar to but different from 'reflective practice'. Reflective practice is commonly seen as a learning process, akin to Gibbs's reflective learning (Gibbs, 1988) within the cycle: practice; reflection on that practice; planning changes to future practice; implementation of those changes. This is learning by looking back on practice and practice incidents, and adjusting future practice on the basis of these reflections. Reflective learning is particularly important in supervision where frontline practitioners can think about what is going on rather than simply reacting to problems (Gibbs, 2009: 296).

Reflexivity involves bending one's thinking back on itself and includes examining the ways knowledge is being constructed and used to frame decision situations and make choices. To be reflexive is to take a critical stance towards one's own cognitive and emotional processes and is sometimes referred to as 'metacognition'. It involves being critically aware of and critically analysing one's thought processes with the purpose of having them under a degree of critical control (Eraut, 1994: 106). This would include our production and use of knowledge, our emotional impulses to act, and our thinking about the situation and how to respond. The term 'critical' is used here to mean taking a questioning stance towards our knowledge, thinking and emotions, including our beliefs, assumptions and interpretations. This includes scrutinizing that knowledge, the ways we are using it and the ways it has been constructed, particularly in terms of hidden biases and distortions.

If social workers do not take this reflexive approach to their work there is a danger that they remain unaware of unfounded assumptions and have mindsets that mean that they do not properly think through situations and decisions. This can lead to mistakes and lost opportunities that negatively impact on their practice and people's lives. Each chapter in turn will endeavour to promote within the practitioner a critical questioning stance towards: their thinking about the practice context (Chapter 2); their approach to involving service users (Chapter 3); the way they work with others (Chapter 4); their emotions and thinking and the knowledge they are using (Chapter 5); the ways they frame decision situations (Chapter 6); the ways they analyse options (Chapter 7); and the way they give and receive supervision (Chapter 8).

What is sound decision making?

The aim of sound decision making is to achieve good outcomes; however, it is not possible to know whether a decision has been effective until after it has been implemented. This is why a distinction is made between 'a sound decision' and 'an effective decision'. Sound decision making concerns *processes*, whilst effective decisions relate to *outcomes*. A sound decision is one that has been *made* appropriately, while an effective decision is one that achieves the decision makers' goals. The purpose to making a sound decision is that at some point in the future it will prove to have been an effective decision. Sound decision making is the subject of this book. However, what are regarded as 'sound decision making processes' is open to question, but I will define them as:

● being critically aware of the practice context;
● involving service users and carers to the highest level;
● working collaboratively with others;
● using knowledge, thinking clearly and managing emotions;
● framing decision situations in a clear and accurate way;
● analysing options and basing choices on reasoned analysis;
● making effective use of supervision.

Uncertainty means that at the time of the making of a decision it is not possible to be certain which option will be effective in achieving the identified goals. Sound decision making increases the chances of decisions being effective; however, given the uncertain, complex, unpredictable nature of social situations, achieving good outcomes cannot be guaranteed.

Figure 1.2 gives the framework that forms the structure of the book and which reflects a systemic and contextualized understanding of decision making in professional practice. There is a chapter on the six processes of making a decision, namely 'involving service users', 'working together', 'using knowledge and managing emotions', 'framing situations', 'analysing options' and 'using supervision'.

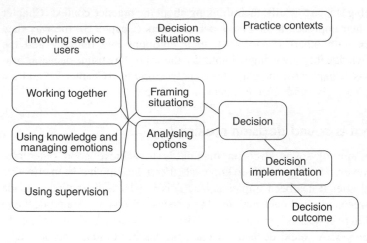

Figure 1.2   A decision-making framework

Chapter 2 sets out the 'practice contexts' within which frontline practitioners work, and each chapter gives a specific 'decision situation' in the form of a practice scenario. The concluding chapter will briefly discuss the relationships between 'decision', 'decision implementation' and 'decision outcome'.

There now follows a brief preview of the elements of the framework, given in terms of the issues faced by the two practice scenario social workers.

Being critically aware of the practice context

The practice scenario social workers will need to be critically aware of the practice context, for example of relevant legal requirements and agency procedures. They have an in-depth knowledge of the relevant law and know that there is a statutory duty to investigate where they 'have reasonable cause to suspect that a child ... is suffering, or likely to suffer, significant harm' (Children Act, 1989, Section 47(1)(b)). Government guidance is clear that if they do have reasonable cause to suspect, they are 'required to take steps which are reasonably practicable either to obtain access to the child themselves, or to ensure that access to him is obtained on their behalf by someone who is authorised by them for a purpose' (Department of Health, 1989: 61). The nature of the call and its context has caused the social workers to be cautious; they want more information before deciding whether a full investigation is warranted. Their team manager regards the current status of their work as a preliminary enquiry to gather information, but the failure to engage the child's mother is preventing them obtaining sufficient information. Neither the law nor the agency procedures give specific guidance about what to do next and they will have to decide with others what to do.

Involving service users to the highest level

The social workers in the example regard the unseen child as their primary client and the mother as a secondary client. The difference between primary and secondary clients will be discussed in Chapter 3 but the terms do not necessarily indicate who most face-to-face contact is with. Four levels of involvement will be presented in that chapter: being told, being consulted, being a partner and being in control. If the level of involvement were to be *being told*, the social workers would insist on seeing the child with the aid of a court order if necessary. If it was *being consulted*, the social workers would speak to the mother again, listen to what she had to say and take this into account in making the decision about what to do next. If the level was *being a partner*, the social workers would negotiate with the mother until they both could agree on a course of action. Finally, if the level of involvement was *being in control*, the mother, in possession of all the information, would decide what to do. A key issue for the social workers is that the level of involvement fits with the nature of the particular situation.

Working collaboratively with others

The social workers in the practice scenario are endeavouring to work collaboratively with the mother, the police and their supervisor, and they will have checked records and databases for the involvement of others. At this particular point in time, within the series of decisions, many of the potential stakeholders remain unknown to the social workers. There could be a health visitor, a nursery teacher or grandparents that have an appropriate interest in the decision situation. Depending on what the result of their initial enquires are, social workers could be involved in working collaboratively with the family alongside other professionals.

Using knowledge, thinking clearly and managing emotions

The two social workers' professional intuition tells them that the referral was another malicious call, but they consider whether it is a decision that should be the subject of detailed analysis. They do not want to be either too hasty in dismissing the call as a hoax or in asking for police assistance. They are aware that involving the police, at this stage, may spiral into getting an order to gain entry to the property, possibly with the use of force. The ability of the two social workers to think clearly and vigilantly may be affected by the emotions, stress and exhaustion they are both experiencing. They feel compassion for the woman who opened the door who was obviously shocked and angry about their intrusion. They have had a busy and harrowing week and were looking forward to the weekend; now they find themselves experiencing internal conflict. On the one hand they do not want to subject the mother to further intrusion, but on the other they need to see the child to establish that she is safe. They are using their knowledge of law, policy and procedures, as well as of human psychology and interaction, to determine what the next step is and how best to take it.

Framing decision situations in a clear and accurate way

Through framing processes the available information is shaped and organized into a picture of the situation, including key factors, outcome goals and a set of options. The two social workers endeavour to identify the key factors of the situation and consider what weight to give to the fact that most of the anonymous calls the office receives are unfounded. They consider their shorter-term decision goal as getting to see the child, in the context of the longer-term goal of promoting the child's overall development within her family. They consider how they should frame the immediate options and think in terms of two possible courses of action: call at the house again and use as much professional skill as they can muster to persuade the mother to allow them to see the child; or return to the office to consult further with the team manager and police.

Analysing options and basing choices on reasoned analysis

The social workers analyse the options in terms of their likely consequences and the likelihood of them being successful. In making the choice they endeavour to balance the risk of using up more valuable time, in the vain attempt at persuading the mother to let them see the child and in the process aggravate her further, with the danger of being unnecessarily heavy-handed in the situation they believe should be resolved by the use of professional skill.

Making effective use of supervision

Sound decision making requires appropriate support and guidance to be available to frontline workers. The two social workers briefly consulted their supervisor before leaving the office and are about to ring for further guidance. One option is to return to the office and have a face-to-face discussion. Frontline workers need this support and guidance in both thinking through difficult decisions and managing their emotions. Frontline managers need the capacity and space to give such supportive supervision; and frontline workers need the attitudes and skills necessary to effectively use it.

It may be frustrating to leave the social workers at this point facing their dilemma, but it highlights the uncertainty they face and the fact that the subject matter of this book is the process of making sound decisions whose further exploration needs to await subsequent chapters. At some point in the future the social workers or another party may come to evaluate the decision taken that afternoon. Decision makers may be aware at the time that they are making a critical decision or it may only become clear some time afterwards. If the social workers satisfactorily resolve the situation, it is likely that little further thought will be given to their decision. But if it is subsequently found that they failed to protect a child from further harm or they become the subject of a complaint about being heavy-handed, their decision could come under critical scrutiny. Some time in the future when the outcome of their decision is known, a judgement can be made as to whether or not it was an effective decision that achieved their identified goals.

chapter summary

In this chapter we have had a preliminary look at some ideas, issues and questions that have relevance to subsequent chapters of the book. I have explained how it was difficult to define 'decision making', but that a simple working definition was 'the processes of making a choice' and how there was a strong overlap between the processes of decision making and those of problem solving. Decision making in social work was identified as a collaborative exercise involving others, with the role of social workers varying depending on the situation. The importance of ethical decision making, the recognition of power differentials and a critical approach to risk and risk taking was stressed. The concept of reflexivity and its importance in sound decision making was ↘

explained. I made clear the distinction between sound decision making and effective decisions and how sound decision making is believed to increase the chances of decisions becoming effective decisions that achieve good outcomes. The chapter finished with a preview of the decision-making framework to be introduced in the subsequent chapters.

key practice points: making decisions

Social workers making and supporting decisions need to:

- work collaboratively with both service users and other professional workers;
- be ethical, both in terms of the underpinning principles, the outcomes sought and the qualities required;
- be sensitive to power differentials and dynamics;
- take informed and well-managed risks;
- be reflexive towards their thinking and emotions.

putting it into practice

1. What do you think are the key factors that the social workers in the practice scenario should take into account in deciding what to do next?
2. If you were one of the social workers what would you be inclined to do next and why?
3. Choose one of the concepts 'reflexivity', 'risk', 'power', 'ethics' or 'problem solving' and explain its importance to the social workers in deciding what to do next.

Recommended reading

Chapter 8 'Empowering Relationships', in R. Smith (2008) *Social Work and Power*, Basingstoke: Palgrave Macmillan. This chapter focuses on power dynamics, relations and negotiations between social workers and service users.

Chapter 9 'Ethical Decision-making', in W. Bowles, M. Collingridge, S. Curry and B. Valentine (2006) *Ethical Practice in Social Work: An Applied Approach*, Buckingham: Open University Press. This chapter explains how ethical decision making involves a number of different elements.

Chapter 4 'Risk and Protection' by V. E. Cree and S. Wallace (2009), in R. Adams, L. Dominelli and M. Payne (eds) *Practising Social Work in a Complex World*, Basingstoke: Palgrave Macmillan. This chapter presents a balanced view of risk as presenting opportunities as well as dangers in social work and people's lives.

2 | Practice contexts

Social workers need to be critically aware of and take into account the contexts in which decisions are being made. What is meant by 'context' can be problematic, but here it will be taken to refer to the way society and social welfare is structured. This includes expectations, requirements, structures and conditions surrounding decision making. The contexts depicted in Figure 2.1 will be outlined, including service-user movement, professional, societal, legal, policy, organizational and interprofessional contexts of decision making. These changing, interlocking and sometimes contradictory contexts together form the background of professional practice. They are important because, while they potentially influence decision-making practices, workers may not always be consciously aware of the possible positive and negative impacts they can have and how they can present both opportunities and constraints.

The contexts can be seen as sources of pressure to act in certain ways, both in the interests of service users and against their interests. Having a

Figure 2.1   Practice contexts

critical awareness and understanding of the contexts enables social workers to see the wider picture and positively respond in a way that keeps the interests of service users to the forefront. However, the contexts themselves may be beyond the immediate influence of individual workers, who can be considered to have a professional obligation to join with others to bring about necessary changes.

practice scenario

Emily is a 14-year-old young woman who lives in a children's home known as Woodside. She is looked after by the local authority and has a history of self-harm, illegal drug use, being sexually exploited and absconding. There is mounting concern about the increasing severity of her self-harm injuries. She is excluded from school and is receiving support from the local child and adolescent mental health service. Leroy, Emily's key worker, is a residential social worker. Emily recently absconded from Woodside and not for the first time has ended up in hospital having seriously cut herself. She is now back at the home and the staff team are having a weekly meeting with her to discuss the previous week, plan for the next week and review her general progress. Emily's absconding and self-harm behaviour is raising a question mark over the suitability of Woodside to meet her needs. Leroy believes that some of his colleagues have a very low tolerance of risk and their thinking has become dominated by Emily's possible transfer to a secure children's home. Despite her persistent absconding, Emily says she wants to stay at Woodside as the staff are trying to help her.

Service-user movements

Service-user and carer movements are now a major part of a changing practice context and have the potential to transform the organization and design of agencies and services. They have presented bottom-up challenges to the established ways of doing things, with the aim of transforming the ways services are organized and delivered, including professional attitudes and practices. Carr (2007: 266, 268) states, 'on many levels traditional power relations are being unsettled' and 'many statutory and non-user controlled service providers are beginning to feel the larger effects of power devolution and showing signs of resistance'.

At the same time, Beresford and Croft (2004: 62) argue that, while the service-user movement's achievements should not be overstated, they should equally not be underestimated. Achievements include changes in legislation, policy, service organization and social work practice, including the participation of service users and carers in all aspects of social work education and training.

Emily and the other young people have regular meetings with staff to discuss the running of Woodside. The actual impact of such service-user participation on the organization and design of services and professional practice is unknown. A Social Care Institute for Excellence (SCIE) review of the impact of user participation on change and improvement in social care services states that:

> seen within a larger framework defined by stages, it seems that the first stage of establishing the principles of service user participation and developing participation processes has been reached. The research ... points to a transition from this first adaptive stage to a second stage of transformational change. (Carr, 2004: 28)

The research found that often service users do not know what agencies are doing with the views collected through participation exercises. However, 'despite the overall lack of research or data on the relationship between user participation and service change and improvement, the review shows strong indications why change may not be occurring' (ibid.: 13). These indications include managers, professionals and service users wanting different things from service-user participation with agencies favouring consultancy to partnership.

The SCIE Report (Carr, 2004) suggests that Emily's participation is likely to have more impact if the policy makers, managers and frontline staff have the political will to make changes and pay attention to the ideas that young people see as important, recognizing that these may well be different from those of adults. It states that participation should not be an end in itself, but a means to change, with the implication that participation needs to be ongoing and not a one-off event. It is argued that this will entail developing a participatory culture and moving beyond one-off consultation exercises, which are often seen as tokenistic. More informal means of participation are needed that are embedded in the actual organization and delivery of services and staff practices. The report identifies a degree of professional anxiety about sharing power and responsibility with children and young people and suggests that 'adults should recognise that encouraging participation does not mean handing over responsibility for decision making to children.

Children themselves are clear that while they want to be able to express their views, they do not necessarily expect to have control over final decisions' (ibid.: 16).

One of the stumbling blocks to the transformation of services and professional attitudes is the power differentials and dynamics between service users, policy makers, managers and frontline workers. However, if these power differences are openly acknowledged, opportunities do exist for alliances between services users and frontline professionals. Beresford and Croft (2004: 53) argue that social work is unlikely to develop a more emancipatory role unless social work practitioners develop these closer links and alliances and gain more support from managers to play a role in service-user participation. However, a new professionalism is needed based on a transformed expertise. Not the expertise of 'knowing what is best' but rather the expertise of enabling people to have control over their own lives and services so that they can achieve the outcomes they want.

Professional context

An important practice context for Leroy in his work with Emily is his professional identity as a social worker. Leroy has undergone professional training and education, is registered with the General Social Care Council (GSCC) and is required to uphold the GSCC Code of Practice. This context includes what it is to be a professional social worker and the influence that social work theory, ethics and values have on what Leroy does, thinks and believes. The professional aim of social work can be summarized as the promotion of human well-being, social justice and the prevention of human suffering. Three aspects of achieving this aim can be identified:

1. asserting certain values;
2. developing systemic understandings of people and their social situations;
3. acting in ways that foster human well-being.

To take asserting certain values as an example, a professional expectation on Leroy would be that he holds certain values and that he would stand up for these values in his practice, particularly in situations in which they are being denied or contradicted. Written statements of professional values of social work show there is a large degree of agreement on what these values are, although not necessarily on their detail, expression or interpretation. Banks (2006: 83) states that the majority of codes of ethics in social work have similarities which start with a list of values and principles, 'which generally include variations on: respect for the unique value of the individual person; service user self-determination; social justice and professional integrity'.

For example the British Association of Social Workers' *Code of Ethics for Social Work* (BASW, 2002) has the stated aim of expressing the values and principles which are integral to social work, and it gives guidance on ethical practice. It states that social work is committed to five basic values: human dignity and worth; social justice; service to humanity; integrity; and competence. The code explains that 'social work practice should both promote respect for human dignity and pursue social justice, through service to humanity, integrity and competence'. The code also gives guidance on ethical practice by applying the values and principles to social work practice. For example, it gives guidance on self-determination by service users and states that:

> social workers will help service users to reach informed decisions about their lives and promote their autonomy, provided that this does not conflict with their safety or with the rights of others. They will endeavour to minimise the use of legal or other compulsion. Any act which diminishes service users' civil or legal rights must be ethically, professionally and legally justifiable. (BASW, 2002)

Banks (2006: 100) argues that how useful social workers find codes will depend on what they want from them. They will not find detailed guidance of how to act in particular situations. However, she goes on to state that they have an important role in defending the profession from outside attack, of maintaining professional identity and of setting some general benchmarks against which to judge agency policies and practice and emphasizing that social workers have a responsibility over and above just doing their job and following agency rules.

Social workers carry out difficult and contradictory tasks on behalf of society, which by their very nature can involve both the care and control of service users. Webb and Wistow (1987, cited in Bamford, 1990: 160) suggest that society and the social work profession have different objectives and different interests. At times 'society' may be more interested in social control and providing a service of last resort at minimum cost than the enhancement of human well-being and self-determination. Leroy is concerned that the use of compulsion is minimized, but there are genuine concerns about Emily's welfare and safety and how best to meet her needs. The agency management is presenting the suggestion that Emily be placed in a secure children's home as being in her best interests, but

Leroy fears that she is being sacrificed to ease the burden on the staff team and to fill the gap in local child mental health services. In Leroy's view the management team are placing more value on the smooth running of Woodside than on Emily's future well-being.

Societal context

Decision makers need to be critically aware of the nature of the society in which they practice and where the decision situation is located, yet its everyday familiarity can make this difficult. In an approach that Mullaly (1997) termed 'structural social work', individual and family problems have been produced by society and their complete resolution and prevention are dependent on the reform of society. A number of different social groupings exist in society reflecting dimensions of difference such as poverty, gender, ethnicity, 'race', sexuality, disability and age. The dimensions of difference are also dimensions of oppression in the form of ageism, disablism, heterosexism, racism, ethnocentrism, sexism and economic inequality. A feature of most societies is the manifest inequality of wealth and income that exist, which form divisions between those who live in poverty and those that do not, between the socially excluded and the socially included.

Two interlocking dimensions of society will be considered: the social structure and the cultural climate. Both of these are complex areas of study in their own right and it is beyond the scope of this book to give more than a brief sketch of how they form a context for decision making in social work. The impacts societal contexts can have on social work practice and service-user lives will be illustrated through the examples of: the poverty Emily was brought up in; the structural changes in households, family life and gender roles; and the potential impacts that media portrayal of social work can have on frontline workers and management.

Structure of society

Social structure is a contested term that is associated with the organization of social life, particularly in terms of the complex patterns and relations within a society (López and Scott, 2000). Service users tend to be located at the bottom of hierarchical structures of inequality and oppression. In such circumstances, the enhancement of human well-being is a challenge. For example, the poverty Emily and her mother lived in has had a profound effect on their lives and made positive changes difficult to achieve. Kempson (1996: 30) found that life on a low income impacts on family life and 'can result in poor diet, lack of fuel and water, poor housing and homelessness, debt, poor physical health, and stress and mental health problems'.

The estate they lived on is highly stigmatized, the level of unemployment high, the housing stock in poor condition, and the general environment bleak, with high levels of crime, scanty community facilities and under-resourced schools. Ghate and Hazel (2002: 235) identify a key finding of their research into parenting in poor environments as the extent to which 'stressors are multiple, overlapping and cumulative in their adverse effect, with risk factors in one domain almost always highly associated with risk factors in another'. If Emily is to grow into a well-adjusted adult, she has many adverse circumstances and experiences to overcome and Leroy's work with her needs to be seen in a context of lack of opportunity and negative environment.

Some approaches to social work emphasize the need to tackle the causes of social problems rather than just ameliorating their symptoms (Mullaly, 1997). This can be seen either as a rival approach to individual and family focused work or as its logical extension. While many social workers would agree with the analysis that the problems service users face have their root cause in the structure of society, they point to the lack of practical strategies emerging from this analysis. As Leonard (1996: 16) states, structural approaches are 'stronger in critique than in prescriptions for action'. However, an influential perspective remains that social workers need to play an active part in bringing about societal changes and work with service users and other citizens to reform society.

Emily and her parents live in a society in which deep social changes are occurring in the ways people live their lives. Emily has grown up at a time of changing institutional structures, including patterns of gender roles, family life and household structures. Many children and young people positively manage changes in household and parenting arrangements; however, others can experience difficulties that are not easy to overcome. Adult members of society and social provisions can be ill prepared for such social changes and there can be 'gaps in parenting offered to children following family break-up' (Gorell Barnes, 1991: 145). When Emily's parents separated a number of years ago, they were unable to continue to work together as parents and Emily was drawn into the antagonism between them. She responded by behaving in ways that her mother found challenging. Her mother found herself isolated and under stress while she struggled to keep control of her daughter. Emily gradually lost contact with her father and increasingly resented her mother's new partner and now dreams of one day finding her father and going to live with him. Leroy cannot undo the social changes that were part and parcel of Emily's parents' breakup; rather, he sees himself helping her to find better ways of coping with her strong emotions and finding a path forward in her life.

Cultural climate

The term 'culture' is commonly used to denote the values, beliefs and practices dominant in a particular society. Prevailing values and beliefs about what is a problem, what causes it or who is to blame and how it can be overcome form an important backdrop to decision making in social work. One characteristic of society is that from time to time it can be beset by a panic over a particular social issue which impacts on the cultural climate for its duration. At such times, decision makers need to consider whether they are being unduly influenced by the current focus of societal concern. In the midst of professional or public unease it may be difficult to distinguish between a misinformed social panic and the development of awareness of a legitimate cause for concern. For example, in a series of steps during the latter part of the twentieth century, the different ways children can be abused were increasingly recognized, with a progressive understanding that children can be harmed – physically, sexually and emotionally – within differing contexts by individuals and organized groups. Moral panics are by definition disproportionate reactions to perceived threats (Critcher, 2006: 2) and in their midst there is a danger that it becomes difficult to distinguish between a considered response and an overreaction.

The mass media plays a role in reflecting and developing social concerns and at times can produce a hostile climate in which to make decisions. Although there has been attention to various aspects of the relationship between the mass media, the general public and social work (Garrett, 2001; Mendes, 2001; Zugazaga *et al.*, 2006), comparatively little attention has been paid to the impact of media coverage on social workers themselves and their practice. There is a danger that when social workers and their agencies feel under attack from the mass media and the general public they can become defensive in their work, producing an excessive concern with safety and a corresponding unwillingness to take risks. Leroy believes his managers are currently being overly defensive in relation to Emily's situation for fear of criticism in the light of a recent suicide of a looked-after person living at another of the agency's establishments. This had received extensive negative coverage in the local press, and there is a need for critical self-awareness in relation to the current climate and conscious efforts need to be made to avoid engaging in defensive reactive practices and being swept along by heightened anxieties.

Legal context

The law forms an important context for making decisions in social work, as it gives agencies and workers powers and duties, and citizens rights and safeguards. The law plays a part in a number of different ways, with some decisions having a strong legal dimension, whereas others have no specific legal requirements. It provides a statutory framework for compulsory intervention in people lives, for example the use of secure children's homes is a highly regulated area since it concerns the restriction of liberty. In comparison, some other decisions are relatively unregulated, for example whether it is time for the work with a service user to come to an end. Social workers need a good knowledge and understanding of the relevant statutes and regulations and have available to them legal advice if they are to be critically aware of the legal requirements and use the law positively.

Discussion at Woodside has tended to revolve around its unsuitability for Emily and how she meets the legal criteria for her to be placed in secure accommodation. While accepting that the level of assessed risk is high, Leroy believes that professionally the question is much wider. He believes that the available secure children's home placement is totally unsuitable for Emily, that rejecting her is the worst thing they could do and that they need to stick with her during this difficult period in her life. Leroy has found that his participation in the deliberations about Emily's future placement has required a clear understanding of the legal provisions and safeguards concerning the restriction of her liberty. He is aware that the care of Emily comes under the Children Act 1989, that a court would consider an application to restrict her liberty in relation to section 25 of that Act, and that a children's guardian would be appointed and Emily legally represented.

Amongst other things, section 25(1) sets out the criteria which need to apply for a court to make an order. The court cannot make an order authorizing that a child be kept in secure accommodation unless it appears '(a) that (i) he has a history of absconding and is likely to from any other description of accommodation; and (ii) if he absconds, he is likely to suffer significant harm; or (b) that if he is kept in any other description of accommodation he is likely to injure himself or other persons'.

Emily meets these criteria. Indeed many young people may fall within the criteria but whose circumstances, from a professional point of view, would not justify the restriction of their liberty. Leroy knows that the local authority have a duty to avoid the need for children to be placed in secure accommodation (Brammer, 2007: 318) and he fears that this will not be carried out.

Law and social work

The exact position of the law in relation to social work has been disputed, between it being *the* central determining focus and it being *one* of a number of important considerations (Braye and Preston Shoot, 2010: 4). There is a spectrum of views of the role of the law in social work. One extreme is that the law is the sole basis of social work, the other is that the law at times can be the antithesis of social work. Blom-Cooper's statement in the report into the death of Jasmine Beckford represents the former. Blom-Cooper (1985: 12) states that 'we are strongly of the view that social work can in fact be defined *only* in terms of the functions required of its practitioners by their employing agency operating within a statutory framework'.

The other end of the spectrum is the view that social work values should always take precedence over the law when there is a contradiction between the two. Indeed there are aspects of many laws that appear to contradict social work values and concerns. Dalrymple and Burke (2006) give the examples of immigration, mental health and youth justice legislation. On the other hand legislation increasingly reflects social work values and concerns. For example, Preston-Shoot *et al.* (2001: 16) give the examples of access to files and direct payments to users of community care services. The problem may not be with the law but the adequacy of service provision; for example, it has not been so much criticism of the law that surrounds the 'welfare route' into secure children's homes but policy makers not having geared the establishments to meet the needs of young people like Emily (O'Neill, 2001; Simmonds, 2008).

A common view is that the law is an important basis of social work; however, it does not define the full extent of professional social work and has some well recognized limitations. Brammer (2007: 12) argues that, while accepting that law shapes social work practice, it is necessary to recognize its limitations. One limitation is that it does not always provide clear direction, but rather sets boundaries, and so allows discretion within limits. Also it is often open to interpretation, may not keep pace with practice developments and, crucially for the subject matter of this book, may not help social workers decide when to act. An important issue is how to achieve an appropriate balance between recognizing the important role law plays in social work and not letting this develop into an overemphasis on legal matters to the exclusion of others. As Olive Stevenson states:

> the image of the social worker as 'agent of the law' is ... partial and dangerous. For it encourages a view of professional competence which rests solely

or mainly on an ability to interpret and execute legal requirements, whereas, in fact, such competence rests on far wider abilities in which that elusive but crucial element of professional judgement is central. (Stevenson, 1986: 503)

The emphasis needs to be on the positive use of the law, within good professional practice. Statutes and regulations can promote what professional workers regard as good practice and which can be used to benefit and empower service users. Dalrymple and Burke (2006: 58) argue that 'despite the complexity of the relationship between the law and ... social care practice, using the law alongside professional codes and guidance can contribute to the development of good practice which is beneficial, supportive, and promotes anti-oppressive values'. The relationship between the law and social work is summed up by Brayne and Broadbent (2002: 64) when they state that the law is at one and the same time a 'defining mandate [and] an insufficient mandate to reflect the complexity both of practice and of service users' lives'.

Policy context

Over the years social workers and other human service professionals have been on the receiving end of many policy changes. What is meant by the term 'policy' is by no means straightforward or agreed (Hill, 1997: 6). In what follows, the term will be used to denote the existence of a set of previous decisions about objectives and actions to be taken in response to particular problems, issues, needs or desires. The intention of having a policy is usually to guide future actions and decisions. The existence of policy can lessen the role of professional discretion and judgement, but having a policy can bring consistency to decision making and enable policy makers to achieve their aims. Usually policy makers and policy implementers are different sets of people and hence those charged with implementing policy inevitably have to interpret it in the light of the particular circumstances of specific situations. Policies are rarely made in sufficient detail so as to dictate what to do in a particular situation; and for them to do so is neither feasible nor desirable.

Governments and social care agencies are among the most important policy makers for social workers, although frontline teams can have policies as well as individual workers. However, a top-down approach to policy making is being increasingly questioned, with demands for the involvement of more local, and a wider range of, stakeholders. What impact policy has on social workers' attempts to enhance human well-being has to remain an open question depending on the content and nature of the policy and how it is interpreted and implemented.

Government policy

Laws are often supplemented by written practice guidance in which relevant government departments set out how the law should be implemented. There has been a proliferation of such guidance including directions, practice guidance, circulars and codes of practice, all of which supplement statutes. The boundary between statutes and government practice guidance is becoming increasingly blurred. For example, the government guide to interagency working to safeguard and promote the welfare of children *Working Together to Safeguard Children* (HM Government, 2006) is divided into two parts. Part 1 is 154 pages (1–154) of statutory guidance, while Part 2 is 42 pages (155–97) of non-statutory practice guidance.

Government guidelines can add strength to professional arguments. For example, the *Children Act 1989: Guidance and Regulations, Volume 4: Residential Care* states that:

> restricting the liberty of children is a serious step which must be taken only when there is no appropriate alternative. It must be a 'last resort' in the sense that all else must first have been comprehensively considered and rejected – never because no other placement was available at the relevant time [or] because of inadequate staffing. (Department of Health, 1991: 118)

However, a critical reading, rather than a mechanical application, of government guidance is needed to promote an opening-up rather than a narrowing of possibilities in decision making. Government guidance can be seen as promoting good professional practice, but it is also a means of controlling what social workers do. Payne (1997: 388) argues that the sometimes enthusiastic acceptance on the part of social workers of this guidance indicates 'a pact between government and social workers in the UK' under which the government can implement its policy objectives by giving guidance and workers can protect themselves from criticism by following government advice.

Agency policy

The distinction between government policy and agency policy is at times hard to maintain as the two are inextricably linked to each other. Agencies are, after all, charged with implementing government policy. Even though central governments may strongly influence or even determine agency policies, there is always considerable scope for agencies to formulate their own policies within the context of laws, regulations and guidance. The agency's policies may be set out in general statements but more usually they are reflected in detailed procedures and protocols.

The availability of resources is perhaps one of the most important contextual factors constraining policy formation and implementation. In order to gate keep an expensive resource, agencies tend to develop policy in terms of restrictive eligibility criteria. For example, an authority may have its own criteria for secure accommodation that is tighter than the one contained in the Children Act 1989 (Harris and Timms, 1993: 90–1). In this particular instance professional social work may welcome an agency's tight restrictive criteria, since it is likely to restrict the inappropriate use of secure children's homes. However, an inflexible policy may not allow practitioners and their managers to use positively such homes when a suitable placement with appropriate services is available. There is a tension between the need to ration expensive resources, handle high risk situations and meet service-user need. Resources do need to be rationed, but the balance achieved between financial considerations and the needs of service users will impact on whether agency policy is a constraint or an opportunity to enhance human well-being.

Organizational context

The way human services and social care agencies are organized, structured and managed is an important context of professional social work practice. In particular the culture and climate of an agency can either support or undermine professional decision making and there can be various degrees of friction between social workers and agency managers. From social work's earliest history there has been recognition of a tension between achieving the professional aims of social work and agency function. From a professional perspective social workers are not mere functionaries of agencies but members of a profession who are employed by agencies, who as frontline workers retain considerable discretion. However, how social workers experience their work environment, and the existence, nature and availability of support, are crucially important in relation to enabling difficult and complex decisions to be made.

Structure of human services

An important aspect of the organizational context of practice is the way services are organized and structured and the degree to which they are subjected to change. Since their inception in 1948, the welfare and health systems of the UK have been the subject of continual change and reform. In particular, structural change has been a continuing theme in the organization of agencies that employ health and social care workers and deliver services. The aim has been the provision of flexible services from an integrated system in order to place the service user at the centre of service planning and professional practice; however, there have been fundamental difficulties in structuring human services to achieve this goal – for example, whether or not to organize services on the basis of individual user groups, families or communities, life course groups or categories of need. No matter how human services are structured, human need is so wide ranging and diverse that some fragmentation in one form or another is likely to exist. Whatever way services are structured, professional social work needs to have the confidence to see its enduring features having continuing relevance and the capacity to adapt and succeed. Some structures, however, may fit better with social work's 'whole person in their environment' perspective than others.

There is no reason to doubt that structural change will continue; the early twenty-first century in the UK is a good example of continuous attempts to tackle the challenge of how best to structure human services. Each of the countries of the UK have their own distinctive structures and in England and Wales, the successful implementation of changes required by *Independence, Well-being and Choice* (Department of Health, 2005), *Every Child Matters* (DfES, 2004) and the Children Act 2004 are likely to complete the move to separate 'children services' and 'adult services'. Blewett (2008: 243) states that:

> across adult and children's services [there] has been structural reform that has sought to 'join up' services working with specific service groups. As a result the unified social services departments in which social work was prominent have been replaced by new configurations of services. In children's services, therefore, there has been a move toward integrating education and social care into unitary children's services departments. In adult services the integration process between health and social care that began in the 1990s has continued to be greatly extended.

Glasby (2005) argues that despite changes in context the underlying ideas and aims set out in all the post-1948 reforms show significant consistency over time and he sees no reason why the reforms of the early twenty-first century will succeed when previous ones have failed.

Whether the services received by service users will be enhanced or degraded in an integrated children's service and an integrated health and social care service remains an open question, as does just how 'integrated' these services will actually turn out to be in terms of frontline practice. However, in the words of Blewett (2008: 250),

The early twenty-first century is a period of challenge for social work. That is to say, it is a period in which social work has enormous opportunity but also a period in which it faces a significant threat to the integrity of the profession. The social work profession has a strong case to make. Its defenders can draw with confidence on considerable evidence from research and service user feedback in order to argue convincingly that social work makes a valuable contribution to the process of improving the lives of the most vulnerable members of society.

In Leroy's area, services are organized into children's services and adult services, a division which has benefits as well as drawbacks. It is hoped that collaboration with Emily's school will be enhanced; however, family members continue to see a number of workers and experience services as fragmented. For example, Emily's mother has mental health difficulties and is a service user of the adult mental health team located at a local health trust, while the Child and Adolescent Mental Health Service continues to be part of another health trust. Despite efforts to work closely, the family and its members continue not to be seen as a whole.

Social care organizations

Social workers work in many different types of organizations, including statutory, voluntary, not-for-profit and for-profit agencies, while there is a growing number of independent practitioners and independent practices. Seden (2008) states, 'an organisation is commonly defined as a way of arranging a set of people and resources together to achieve certain goals'. She explains that whatever kind of organization social workers are based in, to be effective they must understand how the organization works and their own role and the roles of colleagues within it. Despite the diversity of operational structures, a typical agency is hierarchical, with a number of layers each accountable to the one above. There can be successive layers of management above frontline social workers, with a distinction needing to be made between the upper management, middle management and the frontline management.

In organizational theory this arrangement is referred to as 'bureaucracy', a term that denotes a particular type of structure, not a pejorative adjective used to describe a rigid, rule-obsessed organization bound with red tape. Based on Weber's classic work on bureaucracy, Coulshed and Mullender (2006: 30) give the main characteristics of bureaucratic organization as a division of labour with specialist functions and tasks, a formal administrative hierarchy, rules and procedures, the exclusion of personal consideration from the conduct of official business, and employment based on technical qualifications.

Organizational structures are neither 'good' or 'bad' in themselves but 'good' or 'bad' in relation to the degree they fit the organization's purpose. There have always been doubts about the appropriateness of the bureaucratic structure for social work; however, social work could be more accurately described as being situated within 'street-level bureaucracies', a term used by Lipsky (1997) to denote an arrangement where professional practice is located in public bureaucracies. There have been claims that street-level bureaucracy no longer exists and that the growth of managerialism and the introduction of a new public service management has led to the curtailment of professional discretion. For example, Dustin (2006: 303) argues that:

a professional role requires professional discretion and the capacity to make professional judgements. A managerialized role, conversely, requires following procedures and meeting targets set by managers. Increasingly, procedural and managerialized systems are intended to minimize professional discretion and thereby, perhaps, creativity.

However, there continues to be considerable debate about the reality of the ending of professional discretion. Evans and Harris (2004) argue that the death of discretion has been exaggerated, that too simple a view of 'discretion' has dominated the debate and that street-level bureaucracy continues to exist. Their argument is first that:

the proliferation of rules and regulations should not automatically be equated with greater control over professional discretion; paradoxically, more rules may create more discretion. Second, discretion in itself is neither 'good' nor 'bad'. In some circumstances it may be an important professional attribute, in others it may be a cloak for political decision makers to hide behind or it may be an opportunity for the professional abuse of power.

Third, that discretion needs to be understood as graduations of freedom to make decisions and not as an all or nothing phenomenon.

Organizational culture and climate

Gibbs (2009: 296) stresses the importance of the way frontline workers experience organizational cultures and points to how the culture needs to legitimize and normalize worker feelings of anxiety, uncertainty and ambivalence. In particular she points to the capacity of organizations to support and enable workers to manage the demands of their work and the negative consequences for workers and their frontline managers if they are exposed to an unhealthy culture which is low in emotional capital and high on task completion.

Hemmelgarn *et al.* (2006) identify culture and climate as two dimensions of an organization's social context. They state that culture refers to shared norms, beliefs and expectations that drive behaviour and communicate what is valued in the organization, and that organizational climate exists when there are shared perceptions of the psychological impact of the work environment on well-being. Glisson and Hemmelgarn (1998) found a good organizational climate (including low conflict, cooperation, role clarity and personalization) is the primary predictor of positive outcomes for service users. In many agencies there is a need to distinguish between the cultures within frontline teams and the ways members of those teams experience the wider agency culture. The former shapes the immediate context of social workers' work, while the latter shapes an environment in which frontline teams operate, with frontline managers being sandwiched between the two.

How well social workers can get on with what they see as their job can depend on how well managers manage and coordinate people, systems and resources. Farnham and Horton (1996: xiii) view 'managing' as 'involving a complex set of human and technical activities which take place within specific organizational settings and environments'. For social workers to be effective, social care agencies need to be well organized and well managed. However, Coulshed and Mullender (2006: 3) point out that 'in common with professionals in most other disciplines and human services, social work practitioners tend to hold negative attitudes towards the administrative and managerial aspects of their organizations'. There can be a tendency to complain about 'management' and see it as inevitably a bad thing. There is a need to recognize the difference between 'good' and 'poor' management, though what these terms mean can be contested. Coulshed and Mullender (2006: 5) identify 'virtuous management' as combining efficiency, effectiveness and economy with 'compassion, integrity and determination to uphold the humane purpose of social welfare organisations'.

Interprofessional context

An important part of the practice context is the way practitioners actually work together locally with members of other professions and agencies, both inside and outside their team, rather than how they should in theory. There will be a particular set of relationships and attitudes locally. The Department for Education and Skills (DfES, 2004: 5) states that:

> a central part of the Every Child Matters: Change for Children programme is addressing the weaknesses in how we work together … We know that the picture on working together is inconsistent. Too much is dependent on local relationships and there is too little implementation of what we know is good practice.

Notions of good practice and government policy are that agencies and professions should collaborate with each other and work in an integrated way to the benefit of the service user. The aim is to achieve integrated, joined-up and seamless services built around service users and provided by multidisciplinary teams made of professionals from a range of agencies or based together in the same agency or team. A number of agencies and professions are involved with Emily and her situation in addition to Leroy's agency, including the child and adolescent mental health service, the police, the school psychological service and the local secondary school. This means a range of professional workers are involved with her in relation to her health, education and welfare. Leroy realizes that it is crucial for him to have a positive working relationship with the child mental health and education workers, though this has proved difficult at times. Part of the difficulty has been the history of suspicion and distrust between services and professions.

Hudson (2002) identifies two different perspectives on the prospect of different agencies and members of different professions being able to work positively with each other for the benefit of service users. The first is a 'pessimistic tradition' that members of differing agencies and professions will not be able to effectively work with each other because of issues of professional identity, status, discretion and accountability. The other is an 'optimistic hypothesis' that, given the right conditions and will, members of different professions and agencies will be able to work with each other effectively. From his research, co-location and trust were included in the factors that promoted interprofessional collaboration.

Territories and boundaries

Whether interagency and interprofessional collaboration actually happens in practice can hinge around how frontline practitioners manage boundaries between the agencies and professions and the nature of the dynamics between individual practitioners and teams. Given the nature of the situations frontline practitioners deal with, there is a tendency for agencies, professions and individual workers to endeavour to maintain a boundary around what they regard as their territory, resulting in points of tension. Disputes can occur over whose responsibility a service user is or whose job it is to carry out a particular task. This can take the form of a perceived encroachment into another agency's or profession's role, seeing the other as reneging on its responsibilities or making strenuous efforts to keep boundaries tight so as not to be swamped by external demands. Woodhouse and Pengelly (1991: 185) found that maintaining boundaries was one way of defending against anxiety, when workers managed 'the fear of being swamped with human problems for which there was no solution [by having] a dour persistence and painstaking thoroughness within the limits of the narrowly defined task'.

There is a lack of agreement as to how to achieve effectively interagency and interprofessional collaboration. Axelsson and Axelsson (2009: 324) state that professional and organizational territoriality can be a serious barrier to interprofessional collaboration and argue that in order to overcome this the professional groups must be able to see beyond their own interests, be more flexible and give up parts of their territories if necessary. Rushmer and Pallis (2003) argue that an emphasis on the blurring of professional boundaries, with individuals working flexibly across demarcated professional lines, is mistaken. Rather, effective integrated working depends more on individuals having distinct roles with clear boundaries, having positive attitudes and appropriate expectations, respect for the role of others and not acting beyond their levels of competence. A study of a multidisciplinary adult community mental health team (Sserunkuma and Sin, 2010: 12) gives some support to the latter position, showing that the social workers were clearer about their roles than their nursing colleagues and as a consequence were more positive about the changes. Whatever the merits of these arguments, tensions are likely to remain where there are overlapping skills, a confusion about roles and competing philosophies.

Relational dynamics

Situations involving difficult decisions can evoke anxiety which can give rise to a tendency to draw in as many other agencies as possible, to share the risk, or alternatively to find an agency on which to offload difficult situations. In our practice scenario, there has been a history of suspicion, mistrust and some hostility between Leroy's agency and the local child and adolescent mental health service. The social workers in children's services have tended to see the adolescent mental health service as unhelpful and too selective about the situations they choose to get involved in, while they in turn have often perceived the social workers in children's services as not doing their job properly.

Workers need to be aware of these dynamics and endeavour to work towards positive working relations and not to let destructive dynamics interfere with their practice. One agency can be seen as negatively impacting on the work of another and may become a scapegoat onto which negative emotions can be deposited. For example, the decision by Emily's school to exclude her has had a profound impact on the work of the Woodside staff. Emily is now around the home all day, and only receives three hours of personal tuition a week. Woodside staff believe the school should have been more tolerant of Emily's behaviour, while the school staff feel that Leroy and his colleagues do not fully appreciate that they have to be concerned about the education of *all* their pupils, not just Emily.

chapter summary

Practitioners need to be critically aware of the changing, interlocking and sometimes contradictory contexts in which they work and positively respond in ways that keep the interests of service users to the forefront. Each of these changing contexts in its own way can have a significant impact on what social workers do. Service-user and carer movements are transforming social work practice and the organization and design of agencies and services. These changes require a new professionalism based on an expertise of enabling people to have control over their own lives and services so that they can achieve the outcomes they want. However, service-user opportunities for change are at least in part shaped by the nature of the society in which they live, and social workers need to join with others to reform society. Laws, regulations and official guidance need to be used positively by social workers and not be allowed to exclude all other considerations. The nature of the organizations that social workers practise in has a direct and influential impact on their morale and practice, and they need to be organized and structured to support frontline practice. The relationships between local agencies can positively or negatively impact on the quality of service and regardless of local circumstances, frontline practitioners need to make resolute efforts to have positive working relationships with one another.

key practice points: being aware of the practice context

Practitioners need to be critically aware of the wider practice contexts in which they work so they can:

- positively respond to the aspirations of service users' and carers' movements;
- use social work theory, skills, ethics and values to promote human well-being and social justice and to prevent human suffering;
- bring to the attention of the general public and government how social inequalities negatively impact on people's lives and contribute to the problems they experience;
- positively use laws, regulations and policies;
- contribute to the transformation of the organizations they work within;
- proactively promote interprofessional collaboration in their own practice.

putting it into practice

1. Which contexts identified in the chapter do you believe are having the most positive and the most negative impact on Leroy's practice?
2. With reference to at least three of the practice contexts identified, discuss the arguments for and against Emily remaining at Woodside.
3. Can you think of any practical ways Leroy could develop more positive working relations with the staff at Emily's school and the local child and adolescent mental health service?

Recommended reading

'Towards practising social work law', Chapter 1 of S. Braye and M. Preston-Shoot (2010) *Practising Social Work Law*, 3rd edn, Basingstoke: Palgrave Macmillan. This chapter examines the contested relationship between law and social work.

J. Blewett (2008) 'Social work in new policy contexts: threats and opportunities', in S. Fraser and S. Matthews (eds), *The Critical Practitioner in Social Work and Health Care*, London: Sage. This chapter considers major developments in social welfare policy and concludes that they give social workers opportunities to make important and unique contributions to human welfare.

J. Seden (2008) 'Organisations and organisational change', in S. Fraser and S. Matthews (eds), *The Critical Practitioner in Social Work and Health Care*, London: Sage. This chapter argues that in order to be effective, social workers need to understand the organizational contexts they work within.

3 | Involving service users and carers

The focus of this chapter is on individual decisions concerning service users' and carers' own life situations and the services they receive. It should be clear from the previous chapter that the full involvement in these decisions is only one aspect of service-user and carer participation in health and social care services, the other being collective participation in policy decisions, planning and delivery of services. In various guises a core value of social work has been that service users should have direct involvement in decision making (Payne, 1989), but this has not always been put into practice. As Beresford and Croft (2004: 57) argue, 'the formal professional ideology of social work has long been associated with self-determination, self-development and autonomy'. However, this has too often remained at the level of rhetoric and the challenge remains to turn aspirations into actual practice. Three aspects of service-user and carer involvement are discussed: identifying network members and their relationships with each other; distinguishing between different levels of involvement; and promoting service-user and carer involvement. The aim is for service users to achieve the life outcomes that they want and for the service-user experience to be empowering rather than disempowering.

---

practice scenario

Ann is a 37-year-old single parent caring for her two daughters, Kate, aged 13, and Karen, aged 10. The children see their father, who no longer lives in the family home. Ann has been suffering from anxiety and depression and four months ago her GP referred her to the multidisciplinary community mental health team. Sandra, a social work member of the team, has been working ↘

with Ann for three months, focusing on her low self-esteem and depression. Zena, Sandra's colleague in children's services, is also working with the family because of concerns about Ann's elder daughter, Kate, who has been experiencing problems at school. Sandra's manager is reviewing the care plan and there are differing views as to what should happen. Ann wants the current focus of work to continue, as she feels she is still not ready to tackle wider issues. Sandra believes that Ann has made sufficient progress to refocus the work on returning to employment and building supportive social networks of her own. There have been tensions between Sandra and the team manager over the allocation of resources for preventative work, with the manager questioning the need for further work and wanting the case closed to allocate resources to a higher-priority one.

Who is the client?

Human systems are complex and multifaceted, and it is not uncommon for there to be more than one person in a decision situation, so careful consideration needs to be given as to who the network members are and what their relationships are with each other. As well as service-users and carers, there can be relatives, friends and others who are part of the service user's life situation and who are also to be regarded as stakeholders. A 'person in their environment' perspective sees people as embedded within human systems consisting of a number of connected individuals, for example a family, social network or neighbourhood. When taking this whole systems approach it is important to be clear about the answers to a number of questions, including:

- Who are the service users?
- What is the scope of the work, for example is it focused on an individual, a dyad (two people, for example, a couple or a father/daughter dyad), a group or a whole system?
- Whose welfare is the primary objective?
- Are there members whose welfare is an important secondary objective?
- Who has decision-making responsibility, and for which decisions?
- Who is the face-to-face contact with?

The way the community mental health team and Sandra have framed their work, Ann is the sole service user and the focus of the work, but they could have framed the situation in other ways. For example, they could have focused on the family group, the household or a wider network, possibly including Ann's two daughters, her boyfriend and the children's father. In contrast, Zena sees Kate as the service user, and the focus of her work is the relationship between mother and daughter.

Primary and secondary clients

At times, both in children's services and adult services, it may be helpful to make a distinction between primary clients and secondary clients. Primary clients are the person or persons whose welfare is the central objective. Secondary clients are the person or persons who have a central role in the life of the primary client and whose welfare is an important but secondary objective. The welfare of primary and secondary clients are often bound up with each other, and being a primary or secondary client does not necessarily reflect decision-making responsibility or who the face-to-face work is with, but what the prime objective of the work is. Sometimes all the service users in a situation may best be regarded as primary clients, while in others it may be helpful to distinguish between primary and secondary clients. As Zena is working for children's services, she regards all the children as her primary clients and Ann as her secondary client. She is clear that if there are conflicts of interest her primary clients are the children. Ann is a secondary client, being the children's parent, and has a central part to play, as do family functioning and relationships. The children's welfare intertwines with their mother's welfare and she and the children's father have parental responsibility for making decisions in respect of them. When a child provides 'care' for their parent, both may be primary clients of different agencies, though workers will need to see the individuals and their relationship as part of a wider system (Aldridge, 2008: 256).

In adult services there may be a clearly identifiable person who is the primary client, in the sense that his or her well-being is the central objective. However, there are often other people pivotally involved, possibly in caring or supporting roles, who may be regarded as secondary clients. Lloyd (2003) highlights the dangers of narrow conceptualizations of 'carers' and 'service users' as separate groups and advocates a relational approach that stresses diversity, reciprocity and interdependence within networks of care in which the actions of one can impact on the welfare of the other, with a whole-system perspective often being appropriate. So although potentially primary and secondary clients can have competing needs, their lives and welfare are linked. The carer's welfare can be affected by their caring role and the welfare of the primary client can impact on the welfare of the carer, who may have support needs of his or her own, something recognized by carers' legislation, including the Carers (Recognition and Services) Act 1995, as extended and amended by the Carers and Disabled Children Act, 2000 and the Carers (Equal Opportunities) Act 2004 (Brammer, 2007: 448).

Promoting involvement in decision making can be more complicated in situations considered to have more than one person involved, whether they are all primary clients or whether some of them are considered secondary clients. Negotiations can be difficult and agreement harder to reach since there are a number of people to be included. There needs to be recognition that there are different parties involved and there may not be agreement between them as to what is the best course of action. When the focus of work is a family group, community group or network, important differences between group members may exist, with power relations and group dynamics entering the picture. These issues are dealt with in more detail in the next chapter, when working together is discussed.

Why involve service users and carers?

As we saw in the previous chapter, service-user and carer movements have campaigned for more involvement in decision making. This is not only in the reform of services but in decisions concerning individual service users, and how they live their lives and the services they receive. Service users want to be fully involved in decisions that concern them and consider that they have the right to such involvement. In addition there are other reasons why social workers need to involve service users in decision making, including requirements of ethical practice, effective practice and law and policy. Although presented as neat categories there can be considerable overlap between them.

Ethical practice

Service users can be considered to have the moral right to the fullest involvement in decision making, unless there are good reasons that justify limiting the extent of their involvement. For example the British Association of Social Workers' *Code of Ethics* includes the obligation to:

> respect service users' rights to make informed decisions, and ensure that service users and carers participate in decision-making processes. (BASW, 2002)

One aspect of involvement is consent. A service user's consent is required to implement any plan, unless there is a statutory basis for imposing a decision. The British Association of Social Workers' *Code of Ethics* includes the following statement about informed consent:

> Social workers will not act without the informed consent of service users, unless required by law to protect that person or another from risk of serious harm. Where service users' capacity to give informed consent is restricted or absent, social workers will as far as possible ascertain and respect their preferences and wishes and maintain their freedom of decision and action, whether or not another person has powers to make decisions on the service user's behalf. Where the law vests the power of consent in respect of a child in the parent or guardian, this in no way diminishes the social worker's duty to ascertain and respect the child's wishes and feelings, giving due weight to the child's maturity and understanding. (Ibid.)

The notion of informed consent entails that service users know what they are consenting to and that their consent is freely given and not entered into under undue duress.

Effective practice

There is general acceptance that the more involved a person is in the making of a decision, the more likely they are to be committed to its successful implementation. For example, Braye (2000: 16) recognizes 'in many arenas of professional practice the goals of intervention are enhanced by participation, or indeed that participation is essential to their achievement'. If people feel workers have not consulted them or given them an opportunity to influence decisions or imposed a decision on them or not fully explained one to them, they are less likely to become positively involved in its implementation. It is understandable that in such situations service users may become uncooperative or actively sabotage plans they have had no part in making.

Legal and policy basis of practice

In both adult and children's services there are legal and policy bases for involving service users in decision making. For example, Article 12 of the United Nations Convention on the Rights of the Child states that 'parties shall assure to the child who is capable of forming his or her own views to express those views fully in all matters affecting the child, the views of the child being given weight in accordance with the age and maturity of the child'. The Children Act 1989 states that before making any decision with respect to a child whom they are looking after, or proposing to look after, a local authority shall give due consideration to the child and their parents' wishes and feelings. Within children's services the required minimum level of involvement is often relatively low at the 'being consulted' level, but there is a strong commitment to working in partnership with children, young people, parents, families and carers.

It is government policy to transform adult care services in England so service users have choice and control over the support they need to live the lives they want (Department of Health, 2008). If this personalization of services is achieved it will give service users the highest level of involvement, that is 'being in control'. The intention is that all individuals eligible for publicly funded adult social care have a personal budget and, either through direct payments, individual budgets or an agency managed budget, have choice and control of the services they receive. The Department of Health has issued guidance to support service-user independence, choice and risk taking (Department of Health, 2007). The document endeavours to set out common principles that encourage an approach that supports people to make decisions about their lives and manage any risk in relation to those choices.

There are a number of good reasons why service-user and carer involvement should be central to practice; however, it is helpful to distinguish between different levels of involvement. Such distinctions are likely to increase rather than decrease service-user involvement in decision making because there is a danger that notions of involvement remain vague and at the level of rhetoric, with the possibility of professionals believing that service users are being fully involved, when in fact they are not.

Levels of involvement

There are different levels of service-user involvement which are clearly demonstrated by Arnstein's (1969) influential eight-rung ladder of citizen participation. Here a more succinct model of service-user and carer involvement will be put forward that consists of four levels: being in control, being a partner, being consulted and being told. Levels of involvement relate to specific decisions, not to individuals, so in any particular situation there can be different levels of involvement in relation to different decisions. Each of the participants, including managers, frontline workers, service users and carers, can place limits on the level of involvement that is considered appropriate in relation to particular decisions.

The argument is that there should be a presumption that service users have the right and capacity to make decisions for themselves, unless there are valid reasons for believing otherwise: there needs to be an assumption that service users have control over their own lives and services, unless there are specific justifiable reasons why this should not be the case. So rather than considering what allows for the higher levels of involvement, the focus needs to be on what prevents a higher level of involvement. When working with service users, social workers need to identify explicitly the level of involvement and be clear about the reasons why a higher level of involvement is not feasible and subject these reasons to critical examination.

Being in control

The highest level of involvement is 'being in control' which entails respecting service users' capacities to make decisions for themselves. Carr (2004: 11) considers the government's introduction of direct payments in 1996 as the start of meaningful advances in the extent that service users are entitled to exercise control over the support they are given to live independent lives. When the level of involvement is 'being in control' the social worker needs to be clear as to who the control is actually falling upon, as it may not always be the primary client but a particular family or network member, which may or may not be appropriate (Lupton, 1998).

Social workers can have an important role in helping service users to achieve control over their own lives. Sometimes the most valuable service a social worker can offer is to support service users to make informed decisions that achieve the outcomes that they want. At times all human beings face tricky decisions in their lives and may welcome help in thinking through a decision, including the options and their possible outcomes. The aim would not be to influence service users' choice of option but to help them make an informed decision that they are less likely to regret, through knowing they have systematically thought through all the options. Service users 'being in control' is likely to become more common as the personalization agenda in adult social care enables people to live their own lives as they wish (Department of Health, 2008). If the decision in the practice scenario was to be made on a service-user 'being-in-control' basis, Ann would review the service she is receiving and decide what form it should take in future.

Being a partner

The next level of involvement is 'being a partner'. This is when parties jointly make decisions by reaching agreement through open dialogue and negotiation. An aspect of 'being a partner' is that each of the partners, in theory at least, has a veto over the final decision and shares accountability and responsibility for the decision. Working together in partnership is highly regarded in social work, though this often includes a far wider range of practices but less equality than what here is being referred to as 'being a partner'. The 'being a partner' level of involvement in decision making specifically entails achieving jointly agreed decisions.

If the parties in the case example made the decision on a joint basis, Sandra, her team manager and Ann would jointly agree to continue or discontinue the work. They would negotiate with each other in order to reach agreement, though each is looking for a different decision. The team manager wants the case closed; Sandra wants the work refocused, while Ann wants the present focus to continue. When the parties have different starting positions, negotiation becomes a key process which involves recognizing the right of each party to his or her own position and making concerted efforts to reach agreement. Within this perspective each of the partners would have a veto over the decision concerning the future service Ann receives.

A crucial question pertinent to the 'being a partner' level is what happens if the parties cannot reach an agreement. The level of involvement can be seen as going up to the service user 'being in control' or down to 'being consulted', depending on whether the agency or service user has the power to take the decision in his or her own right, which includes leaving the matter undecided or 'walking away' from the situation. In relation to the allocation of resources, agencies tend to have most power, though service users are likely to hold the balance of power in relation to their own life decisions – however, their power is considerably reduced when they want or need something that the agency controls or when they fear compulsory intervention in their lives.

Recording agreement in writing can bring greater clarity as to what has been agreed (Aldgate, 1989), but service users need to have been involved in deciding what goes into the written agreement, not feel obligated to sign and be fully aware of what they are agreeing to. Written agreements can work against service-user involvement when used to maintain agency control (Dalrymple and Burke, 1995: 68) and when service users feel under pressure to sign, despite reservations. Allowing external pressure to force an agreement is not only bad practice but counter-productive, since the nature of the agreement reached will impact on the degree of commitment to the agreed decision.

The notion of agreement can be problematic, with it being questioned whether service users, carers and social workers can be meaningfully referred to as reaching agreement in the context of differences in power. The issues are similar to those of giving consent, in that agreement needs to be informed, given freely and not entered into under undue duress. At the very least, workers need to recognize that there are different degrees of agreement, including resignation, acquiescence, acceptance, consent, consensus or enthusiasm. What form the agreement takes will depend on the amount of common ground and the concessions or compromises made and the extent to which a new viewpoint has developed. Furthermore, the degree to which participation is voluntary and agreement is freely given will determine whether it is partnership or coercion.

At the 'being a partner' level the question is: why can't the service user be in control? There is a tendency for agencies and workers to consider service users as having control over some decisions and not others (Cupitt, 1997). The principle of self-determination gives service users control over their own bodies and their own ways of life, as long as they are not harming other people or, in some circumstances, themselves. However, agencies do not usually extend this principle of service-user control to deciding the level of resource. It is important that workers do not confuse the allocation of a particular quantity of resource with deciding what services that quantity of resource provides. If Sandra had been allocated a 'personal budget' she would have control over the nature of the service, but the agency would still make the decision about the size of her budget based on an assessment and the application of an eligibility criteria involving levels of need.

Being consulted

The next level of involvement is that of 'being consulted', where service-user and carer opinions are taken into account when deciding what to do, a process familiar in the context of one professional consulting another (Brown, 1984) and managers consulting staff about changes. Consultation can provide a valuable degree of participation when workers carry it out well, though it remains a relatively low level of involvement, with professionals or agencies taking decisions. As a general principle agencies and workers should at the very least consult all service users about decisions that affect their lives and the services they receive. This includes people assessed as not having the capacity to make a particular decision. Even when professionals impose decisions to protect other people, consultation about aspects of the decision are often feasible, because consultation takes into account but does not necessarily act upon the opinion of the service user.

If the decision in the practice scenario was to be made on a 'being consulted' basis, Ann would be asked her opinion, this would be listened to and taken into account when taking the decision. The weakness of consultation is not only that it is a relatively low level of involvement but that it can easily be a sham, with the motions gone through but the principles of consultation not upheld. As consultation can so easily become tokenistic, workers need to take active steps to ensure that it is genuine. When professional workers and agencies judge that they cannot take on board what service users say, it can be difficult for the service users to know whether or not they have been genuinely consulted. That is, whether they have been listened to with an open mind and that what they have said has genuinely been taken into account, with value placed on fulfilling their wishes and respect given to their understanding of their situation. Agencies and workers need to inform service users explicitly and specifically of what aspects of their opinions they took on board and those they did not and the reasons why.

At the 'being consulted' level the question is: why can't the decision be a jointly agreed one? There are a number of potential reasons why joint decision making may not be feasible. As we have seen workers and service users may endeavour to make joint decisions, but, despite their best efforts, they may not reach agreement, leaving the agency or the service user to make the decision, depending on whether the level goes up or down. If there is acceptance that agencies need to ration resources to sustain services, there are substantial problems with Ann having a veto over the amount of resource allocated to her. The argument is that Ann is not in a position to balance the competing claims on resources and that if she is allowed a veto the higher-priority case could remain inappropriately unallocated.

Being told

The lowest level of involvement is 'being told' the result of decision making without being consulted. In most decision situations consultation is feasible, but for it to be authentic the person being consulted needs to have a potential influence on the decision. 'Being told' is more honest than a sham consultation, where social workers find themselves in situations in which management has already taken the decision or that consultation would have endangered others. The belief that a decision is in the best interests of the service user is no justification for 'being told', as even a paternalistic approach allows for consultation. 'Being told' represents virtually no involvement at all; but even at this level there are still important issues of good practice, including whether the service user is clearly and explicitly informed as to what the decision was, who took it, on what grounds it was taken, why he or she was not consulted and what are the means of redress, appeal or complaint. It is important to remember that unfortunately there are worse practices than 'being told', when service users or carers are not informed of a decision that affects them.

If in the practice scenario the decision was to be made on a 'being told' basis, Ann would not be consulted or invited to the review, but informed of what the decision was after it had been taken. At the 'being told' level the question is: why can't the service user be consulted? The team manager has agreed to take the decision after consulting Ann at the review, but for a while Sandra was worried that despite her protests the team manager would direct her to terminate her work with Ann immediately and take on the new case. A number of thoughts went through Sandra's mind when she wondered what she would do if this happened. She imagines explaining to Ann that it was a management decision, which in the end she was unable to influence. In her mind's eye she sees Ann getting angry with her, threatening to turn her own case into a high-priority one.

Limits on the level of involvement

The barriers to service-user involvement fall into two categories: those regarded as necessary but problematic limits and those regarded as removable limiting factors. Potentially legitimate limits on the service user's involvement could include: service users being a danger to themselves or to others, the age and understanding of children, a service user's lack of capacity to make a particular decision, and the need to distribute limited resources fairly. Other barriers are unnecessary impediments that social workers and service users should work towards removing. Workers need to remember that they are required to act within the law and professional ethics and that informed consent is necessary for the implementation of any plan, unless there is a statuary basis to do otherwise.

Being a danger to others

A major source of tension in statutory social work is decisions concerning the danger that a person poses to others. There may be times when the argument is that service users cannot determine courses of action because they are a danger to others. A key issue in preventing the service user from harming others is the reliability of the assessment that he or she is such a threat. There will always be a degree of uncertainty as to whether the fears will materialize, and it has become increasingly popular to think in terms of assessing the likelihood of feared outcomes happening by means of risk assessment tools. These collect information on known risk factors and have both benefits and limitations (Maden, 2003). Whether these tools provide a sound basis for making predictions remains a contested issue, and there is general agreement that workers use them in combination with professional judgement. If Ann was at risk of harming others and refused a service, she could easily find herself in a reversal of her present situation. For example, if professionals believed that through her mental ill health there was a danger of her harming her daughters, they may force her to receive a service in the form of compulsory detention under the Mental Health Act 1983.

Being a danger to self

At other times it might be thought appropriate for services users *not* to determine courses of action, because they are considered a danger to themselves. People often used the term 'paternalism' in a pejorative way but within moral philosophy it means going against the expressed wishes of the service user for his or her own good (Gert and Culver, 1979). A common dilemma for social workers is whether paternalistic interventions to protect service users from themselves can be justified or whether people should have autonomy to live their lives as they wish, no matter what dangers they put themselves in (Abramson, 1985). Clark (2000: 182) concludes 'that paternalism is [only] justified when the intended beneficiary is at significant risk of serious harm: *and* when he has irremediably defective knowledge and understanding of the situation'.

Paternalism is when, despite consultation, workers or others oppose service users' expressed wishes on the grounds that they know better than them what is in their best interests. Social workers always need both legal and moral authority to act in this paternalistic manner. Where there is no such authority, the implementation of decisions without the explicit consent of the service user is unethical and may be illegal. There needs to be a clear recognition that service users have the right to take risks that do not unduly expose others to harm and that potentially social workers have a role in helping them make informed decisions about taking and managing risks.

Age and understanding of children

The level of involvement of children in decision making may vary as to what is regarded as their level of understanding. Adults often wish to protect children, believing that they know what is in a child's best interests. They may find it hard to make the necessary adjustments as children grow older and become more independent. The 'being consulted' level is a matter of good practice and will often be a legal requirement (Department of Health, 1990: 12). However, higher levels of involvement are often appropriate. The term 'Gillick competent' came into use after the court decision *Gillick* v. *West Norfolk and Wisbech Areas Health Authority* [1986] AC 122 stated that when a person under the age of 16 is of sufficient understanding that person may give consent to treatment in the absence of parental consent and it is not necessary to notify the parent (Brammer, 2007: 192). The term is now being used more generally to denote children who are competent to make decisions for themselves, independent of their parents and other adults. It still remains an adult's decision as to whether a child has sufficient understanding to make a particular decision. Brammer (ibid.) notes that 'courts have demonstrated that they are prepared to overrule the wishes of "Gillick competent" minors and their parents in order to reach the decision which is in the child's best interest'.

Despite some commentators referring to The Children Act 1989 as a children's charter, it gave children few decision rights, as opposed to participation rights. Brandon *et al.* (1998: 28) argue that even the right to participate is not consistently applied throughout the Act, with it depending on the child's age, level of maturity and the issue at stake. The question for day-to-day practice is: when can children move beyond the 'being consulted' level and become partners or be in control? With adults the presumption is that they have the capacity to make life decisions for themselves unless others can make a case that they do not. There may be a reversal of the situation for children, with the onus being on establishing that they have sufficient understanding to make particular decisions for themselves.

Mental capacity

Adults with severe dementia, a severe learning difficulty, a severe mental health problem or neurological damage may not have the capacity to make certain decisions for themselves or to negotiate decisions in a partnership. There is a danger that workers and others see mental incapacity as a global attribute, rather than only appertaining to a particular decision. It may be that others need to take a specific decision for a person, if he or she lacks the capacity to make that particular decision, while remaining capable of making other decisions. In England and Wales the Mental Capacity Act 2005 provides a statutory framework for when a person over the age of 16 years lacks the capacity to make a decision for themselves. Within the Act and its accompanying Code such a person is one 'who lacks the capacity to make a particular decision or take a particular action for themselves at the time the decision or action needs to be taken'. It is stressed that people may lack the capacity to make some decisions for themselves, but have the capacity to make other decisions. Those who act 'in a professional capacity for, or in relation to, a person who lacks capacity' have a legal duty to 'have regard to relevant guidance in the Code of Practice' that accompanies the Act (Department of Constitutional Affairs, 2007: 2).

The Act sets out what the inability to a make decision consists of. Section 3 of the Act states:

> For the purposes of section 2, a person is unable to make a decision for himself if he is unable – to understand the information relevant to the decision, to retain that information, to use or weigh that information as part of the process of making the decision, or to communicate his decision (whether by talking, using sign language or any other means).

It is worth stating five key principles in the form they appear in Section 1 of the Act, as they have a wide applicability:

1. A person must be assumed to have capacity unless it is established that he lacks capacity.
2. A person is not to be treated as unable to make a decision unless all practicable steps to help him to do so have been taken without success.
3. A person is not to be treated as unable to make a decision merely because he makes an unwise decision.
4. An act done, or decision made, under this Act for or on behalf of a person who lacks capacity must be done, or made, in his best interests.
5. Before the act is done, or the decision is made, regard must be had to whether the purpose for which it is needed can be as effectively achieved in a way that is less restrictive of the person's rights and freedom of action.

The Act created the Independent Mental Capacity Advocate Service to help make important decisions when a person who lacked capacity had no appropriate family or friends to consult. Under the Act the responsible body, either an NHS body or a local authority, must instruct an

Independent Mental Capacity Advocate (IMCA) to support and represent the person when he or she is making decisions about serious medical treatment or changes in accommodation. The Code of Practice (Department of Constitutional Affairs, 2007: 178) states that 'IMCAs will work with and support people who lack capacity, and represent their views to those who are working out their best interests'. The implementation of the Act has meant that social workers need to establish new ways of working with IMCAs and to accept the shifts in advocacy and negotiation roles (Manthorpe *et al.*, 2008: 158). There is a general belief that the Act has been a considerable advance in providing a framework for working with people who lack the capacity to make a particular decision for themselves. Many of the principles set out in the Act and its accompanying code fit well with the general principles of sound decision-making practices featured in this book.

Fair distribution of limited resources

The need to distribute limited resources fairly is another potential reason for placing limits on levels of involvement. There is common acceptance that resources are finite and, when demand exceeds supply, some form of rationing needs to take place and that agencies should do this on a fair and equitable basis. It is important to distinguish between different methods of rationing, including explicit formal mechanisms and hidden informal ones. Waiting lists are a more or less hidden form, whereas written eligibility criteria are an example of explicit rationing. It is not uncommon for formal and informal rationing to occur in combination with each other. When the provision of the service is means tested, it is important to keep a clear distinction between 'eligibility criteria' and any 'assessment of financial contribution'.

Eligibility criteria define the level of need a person requires for agencies to allocate a resource or access a service. Such criteria are often formally set out, but in certain areas of practice they can remain on an informal and often unspoken level. National and local criteria may exist for determining eligibility in some areas of practice, for example in adult social care. They usually involve qualifying thresholds, possibly consisting of a number of bands, at which agencies allocate resources, for example direct payments or access to a specific service. Policy makers and agencies usually base thresholds on the level or degree of unmet need, exposure to risk or barriers to achieving life outcomes. They raise complex issues about what constitutes need, risk and quality of life and how policy makers should operationalize them. Additionally, written criteria will always require a degree of interpretation and so allow for some level of discretion.

Space does not permit detailed discussion here, but it is useful to distinguish between three ways of establishing needs: 'service-user defined need' by asking the service user; 'professionally defined need' by professionals using their professional judgement; and 'bureaucratically defined need' by applying agency criteria or some combination of these. Social workers often find themselves in an intermediary position, applying agency rules, while wanting to fulfil either service-user defined need or professionally defined need or some negotiated consensus between the two. Social workers may perceive that they have no choice but to accept reluctantly the level of resources that politicians have made available to them, and so the necessity of rationing, and do the best they can with these, while actively campaigning for increases in the total amount of resources made available by governments and agencies.

The argument has been that the starting point for any consideration of level of involvement should be that service users have control over their own lives. A move down from the 'being in control' level needs to be explicitly justified and will only be appropriate when based on a sound well-reasoned critical argument. Workers should critically examine each proposed lower level as to why a higher level is not possible. They need to ask a series of questions depending on the proposed level. When the proposed level is 'being a partner', social workers need to ask: why is the service user not in control? When the proposed level is 'being consulted', they need to ask: why is the service user not a partner? When the proposed level is 'being told', they need to ask: why are they not consulting the service user?

Service users and carers will have their own views about what level of involvement in decision making they wish to have or are entitled to. A dilemma for Sandra is that Ann is not keen on attending the review. Sandra knows that she will have to draw her work with Ann to a close, unless during the course of the review the team manager changes her mind. Sandra has come to believe the work should continue on a refocused basis, but has been unable to convince her team manager. She has advocated on behalf of Ann without success and has come to believe that the only hope is for Ann to make a convincing case for herself at the review. Sandra is aware that there is a danger that if Ann competently presents herself at the review she may well undermine her own case for support, while at the same time any encouragement from Sandra for Ann to argue her own case may subject her to too much pressure too soon. Sandra very much believes in an open non-patronizing approach and reminds herself that she should respect Ann as an adult. She believes that with preparation for the review Ann could be enabled to have control over her own participation and together they consider the various sources of disempowerment operating and how these could be overcome – but in the last analysis it will be for Ann to decide whether to attend the review, whether to speak and if she does what she says.

Service-user disempowerment

In this chapter I have stressed how social workers should involve service users to the fullest level in decision making. Participation in decision making involves communication and relationships between people, and to be successful service users need to be in a position to get involved. All the higher levels of involvement (being consulted, being a partner and being in control) may prove impossible without the service user feeling empowered to involve him- or herself in the decision making – but empowerment is by no means a straightforward or unproblematic idea. 'Empowerment' is a contested concept with many issues around what people mean by the term and how service users become empowered and for what purpose.

Adams (2008: 17) defines 'empowerment' both as capacity and process: as 'the capacity of individuals, groups and/or communities to take control of their circumstances, exercise power and achieve their own goals, and the process by which, individually and collectively, they are able to help themselves and others to maximize the quality of their lives'. There is concern about the role of professionals in relation to service-user empowerment with the danger that service users become the victims rather than the beneficiaries of professional empowerment practice (Bristow, 1994).

When professionals see their role as empowering the service user there is a danger of this becoming a patronizing and controlling process. Much of the controversy is around the appropriateness of one relatively powerful individual seeing him- or herself as empowering another and whether social workers can or should see themselves as empowering service users. What is objected to is seeing the process as some sort of transfer of power or anointing of the powerless by the powerful. Statements like 'I empowered the service user to make the decision for himself' can be associated with an arrogant and patronizing attitude. It may be more appropriate or more accurate to refer to 'social workers enabling service users to be fully involved in decision making'. While service-user self-empowerment remains the goal, professionals have an important contribution to make by changing their practices and those of the agency, providing information and opportunities, and working in a way that recognizes strengths and builds capacity.

Many service users will want to and feel able to be fully involved in decision making, though others may feel insufficiently prepared or reluctant for a variety of reasons. Many service users live in poverty or have lived a life under oppression of one sort or another, or experienced social exclusion or problems of living, and may find the process of getting involved more disempowering than empowering. A great deal of what counts as 'empowerment' in social work may involve social workers ceasing to do those things that service users find disempowering. This means implementing the basic principles of good professional practice, including listening to what service users say and giving this due respect. Going beyond these basic principles includes taking a strengths-recognition and capacity-building approach.

Strengths and capacity building

As well as being concerned with the way society, agencies and professional practice can oppress and disempower service users, social workers also need to be concerned about how service users can overcome the effects of past and present oppression. Professionals need to address a number of issues if service users are to participate effectively in decision making, which may include whether they have the information they need, sufficient emotional energy, confidence in their ability and belief that they can make a difference. The importance of recognizing strengths is being increasingly accepted as an important part of social work, and a capacity-building approach recognizes that service users like all human beings have unused, hidden or underdeveloped capacities. Such an approach entails enabling service users to develop their capacities so as to be able to participate fully in decision making.

Postle and Beresford (2007) argue that service users or carers carry out such capacity building within their own groups and state that such groups often welcome the support of social workers. They argue that 'a key feature in the development of user-controlled organisations has been capacity building: the development of skills and confidence enabling group members to feel stronger and increase their capacity' (ibid.: 146). Service users like Ann can effectively overcome disempowerment, obtain information, get support, build confidence and regain hope as a member of a service-user-controlled group. However, Sandra is working with Ann on an individual basis, which may not be as effective as her joining a group with others in a similar position (Mullender and Ward, 1991). There is also the issue of whether it would be better if Ann had an independent advocate to speak for her at the review rather than the capacity-building and self-advocacy approach preferred by Sandra in which she helps Ann to speak for herself.

Worker expertise and service-user disempowerment

One of the contexts of involving service users in the making of decisions is the role given to experts in society, with there being a trend of increased regulation by experts of more and more aspects of people's lives (Illich *et al.*, 1977). Despite Sandra's best efforts, Ann may continue to perceive her as possessing power and expertise, and so place her in a position of authority. The mass media may have established the image of professionals as authority figures long before Sandra came into contact with Ann, who continues to see Sandra as an expert from whom she seeks a solution to her problems. In these circumstances, an integral part of the work involves service users, carers and workers liberating themselves from these beliefs. Professionals need to recognize and limit the negative impacts of perceived or real 'authority' of the professional role.

The need for information

The adage 'information is power' is at least partially true with service users needing information if they are to be effectively involved. For example, people will not always know what is possible and may content themselves with the familiar. Service users need accessible information about services, life issues, policy and procedures to be able to take an informed view of their situation and the options available. What is meant by an informed view can be problematic, with one person's informed view being another person's biased or mistaken view. The social worker has a responsibility to increase service users' awareness of what could be available, though where they then get their information can be an issue. The agency has a responsibility to provide accessible information, but the service users may also need access to independent sources of information, advice and advocacy services.

Recognizing and working with emotions

Workers need to take into account 'the emotional cost of a life which has been directed by other people or fashioned by uncontrollable circumstances' (Barber, 1991: 35) which may result in an understandable reluctance to be involved (Croft and Beresford, 1993: 30). Service users may feel emotionally drained and actually want decisions made for them, feeling already overburdened by life, without the further burden of being involved in decision making. The social worker needs to be cautious about rushing in to take responsibility, as there is a danger that this will only confirm the service user's self-image as 'inadequate' or as not being able to cope. Inexperienced social workers may mistakenly see their role as solving service users' problems for them rather than working with them to enable them to regain some control over their lives. Ann decides to be present at the review but gets anxious about speaking and would rather Sandra spoke on her behalf. Sandra resists the temptation to take over and sees her role as supporting Ann, without further disempowering her, and arranges with her to prepare for the review.

Building confidence

Service users may lack confidence in their own ability to contribute to the making of decisions – something they may trace back to low self-esteem and lack of opportunity to develop participatory skills. They may have had life-long experiences of being discounted and ignored, and may have missed out on the opportunities to develop themselves. In the case example, Ann left school at the earliest opportunity without any qualifications and has been undermined all her life by male partners and her father. As a consequence she lacks confidence in her own ability to present her case at the review. Some compensatory action in terms of confidence building and skill development may be needed to overcome the impacts of these negative experiences to enable service users to gain confidence in themselves. Small steps can sometimes make a big difference, for example anxiety can increase when faced with the unfamiliar – Sandra takes care to show Ann the room in which the review will take place and introduces her to the team manager and rehearses with her what will happen at the review and what she wants to say.

Restoring hope

Hope is an ingredient in effective participation in decision making and its absence can be a symptom of disempowerment. Webb (2007: 73) associates hope with a person's belief that a positive outcome is possible, coupled with uncertainty that it is achievable. Lazarus (1991: 283) argues that hope can have positive consequences, such as 'when it sustains constructive efforts'. Hope and the lack of it relate to both the service user's psychological state and/or his or her perception of external conditions which may more or less relate to how things actually are. For example, Ann's lack of hope may relate to her realistic appraisal of current agency practices, leaving the restoration of hope dependent on these changing. In other circumstances, lack of hope may relate more to the service user's emotional outlook on life, with the gaining of hope dependent on these changing. In many decision situations the combination of internal and external factors may contribute to a lack of hope. One possible issue in the restoration of hope is the danger of kindling false hope. At present Ann has little hope that the team manager will change her mind and Sandra is in two minds about Ann becoming more hopeful about the outcome of the review. Sandra believes that false hope can be destructive and she examines the basis of her own hope that there will be an authentic consultation at the review. She believes that her team manager is still open to influence and has not closed her mind to the possibility of the preventative work continuing with Ann.

The team manager does not change her mind but Ann gets a certain amount of satisfaction from putting her own case forward and feels she has made the first crucial step in gaining some control over her life. In the end pressure from higher-priority work determined the result with a negotiated agreement proving unattainable. The level of involvement turned out to be 'being consulted', with the team manager carefully taking into account the arguments put forward by Ann and Sandra. Sandra is disappointed with the decision of the review and wonders whether it is worth struggling on, facing setback after setback in her quest to promote preventative work. She feels undermined by her team manager, who she believes could have taken greater account of what Ann had to say and could have given more respect to her own professional judgement. She hopes Ann maintains her recovery, but fears that the team will be seeing her again, but then as a high-priority referral.

chapter summary

In this chapter I have argued that service users and carers are entitled to full involvement in decision making and that a distinction between primary and secondary clients may sometimes be necessary. It was argued that a presumption should be made that service users have the right and capacity to make decisions for themselves, unless there are strong valid reasons for believing otherwise. Distinctions were made between four levels of service-user involvement and how these are influenced by factors such as paternalism, the protection of others, the lack of mental capacity and the need for agencies to ration resources. I have explained ➘

⬎how practitioners need to cease disempowering practices so as to enable service users to be fully involved. I finished by considering the importance of the strengths-recognition and capacity-building approaches.

key practice points: involving service users and carers

To involve service users, practitioners need to:

● ensure service users have the highest level of involvement in decision making;
● make the presumption that service users are 'in control' of their own lives and decisions;
● be able to justify explicitly lower levels of involvement in relation to specific criteria;
● take a strength-recognition and capacity-building approach and be critically aware of how their own practices may be experienced as disempowering.

putting it into practice

1. Do your think Sandra is justified in identifying Ann as the sole primary client?
2. What level of involvement should Ann have had in the practice scenario decision? Give reasons for your answer.
3. What, if any, are the potential justifications for limiting Ann's level of involvement?
4. Identify some practical ways Sandra could help Ann to build her capacity to participate effectively at her review.
5. Do you think Ann should have had an advocate with her at the review? Give reasons for your answer.

Recommended reading

S. Braye (2000) 'Participation and involvement in social care', in H. Kemshall and R. Littlechild (eds), *User Involvement and Participation in Social Care,*

London: Jessica Kingsley. This chapter explores the contested territory of participation and involvement in social care.

S. Carr (2007) 'Participation, power, conflict and change: theorizing dynamics of service user participation in the social care system of England and Wales', *Critical Social Policy*, 27(2) 266–76. This journal article explores some of the dynamics of service-user participation.

'Power', Chapter 4, in J. Fook (2002) *Social Work: Critical Theory and Practice*, London: Sage. This chapter takes a critical look at the notion of empowerment and discusses how it can be disempowering to be 'empowered' by a more powerful other.

4 Working together

A characteristic of sound decision making is working together to achieve good service-user outcomes. There is no reason to believe that the long history of failures to work together depicted by inquiry reports is representative of practice generally (Stanley and Manthorpe, 2004: 10). However, it is commonly accepted that working together across boundaries is easier said than done. Responses to failures have tended to include exhortations to work together, reorganization of services and the introduction of more detailed procedures. But it is increasingly recognized that working together also requires effective communication between stakeholders and that many barriers can exist to such communication taking place (Reder and Duncan, 2003). When professionals and service users work together there is contact between people with different identities, who inhabit different worlds. Such work requires all professionals to be aware of both the construction of their own professional identity and the identity of other professions, as well as how the different professions relate to service users. Social work practice needs to be geared to facilitating stakeholders to work together in constructive ways, though divisions can mean that achieving the full benefits of working together can be a challenge.

practice scenario

Ellen is a social worker about to attend a core group meeting in respect of Paul, a four-year-old child who is the subject of a child protection plan. Paul lives with his mother Gail, aged 20 years, and father Bob, aged 21. A child protection conference was held a week ago, after a series of incidents in which Paul was left home alone by his parents and was assessed to be suffering from general neglect, including frequent visits to the local hospital with minor injuries, language development delay, sporadic atten- ↘

dance at nursery school and concern about lack of nurturing. The conference identified the core group members as Paul's parents, Ellen as the lead worker, the health visitor and nursery teacher. The outline child protection plan is to work with the family to build the parents' capacity to provide Paul with good enough care while monitoring his development and the standard of care he is receiving.

Meeting together

Working together invariably involves meeting together in one form or another, though this does not necessarily mean *effectively* working together. Stakeholder meetings are forums in which service users, carers, professionals and others meet together with the aim of working together in the interests of the service users. The different participants form a group with its own dynamics in which internal relationships impact either positively or negatively on the way group members work together. Such meetings play an important part in decision making and problem solving by formulating and reviewing assessments and plans, and making decisions and recommendations. Social workers have a valuable contribution to make to such groups, bringing systemic perspectives, contextualized understandings of problems and commitment to social justice – and they often play an important role in being the lead workers or having particular responsibilities.

Meetings can be divided into more formal meetings, like reviews, conferences, committees and panels, and less formal meetings, like network meetings, family meetings and core group meetings. Sometimes meeting together is part of a more formal procedure that needs to be complied with, while at other times one of the stakeholders can be proactive in drawing the others together to discuss the situation. In the practice scenario the core meeting is being held under the official guidance for interagency working to safeguard and promote the welfare of children, *Working Together to Safeguard Children* (HM Government, 2006), which makes clear that the intention is that it falls into the category of a less formal meeting between stakeholders. *Working Together* states that:

Core groups are an important forum for working with parents, wider family members and children of sufficient age and understanding. It can often be difficult for parents to agree to a child protection plan within the confines of a formal conference. Their agreement may be gained later when details of the plan are worked out in the core group. (105)

As well as the degree of formality, such groups have a number of other basic features that impact on the nature of meetings and their dynamics, including group size, membership and attendance. There is increasing sensitivity to the importance of group size in promoting participation as there can be a tension between the need to be inclusive and the need to create the conditions in which constructive discussions can take place. Large meetings can be intimidating, have demotivating effects (Baron *et al.*, 1992) and offer less opportunity to make a contribution. Who actually attends is another factor in shaping what happens and it is not uncommon for important members of the professional or family network to be unable or unwilling to attend a meeting. Leadbetter (2008: 204) found that a source of tension between workers occurred when competing priorities prevented a group member from attending key meetings or contributing to planning.

Although identified as a member of the core group, Bob has said he is unable to attend – there is now a danger that he will become a convenient scapegoat on which to project negative feelings. The core group have agreed that Paul is too young to attend, though even the attendance of older children at reviews and conferences can be an issue and the subject of some disagreement. For example, Minty (1995: 49) argues that it is insensitive to make 'it a rule that older children participate in large meetings, such as case conferences, where the inadequacies of their families may be publicly exposed'.

Benefits of working together

Working together represents a significant investment in enabling service users to receive effective services that provide protection, care or support in overcoming life's difficulties and achieving good life outcomes. The intention is that the practice scenario core group meetings result in significant changes in the care of Paul so that his development is no longer being impaired and that indeed he starts to flourish. Stakeholder meetings have the potential to enable participants to work together in an integrated way, resulting in sharing information, a fuller picture, integrated assessments and plans, a commitment to carrying out plans, and taking coordinated action.

Sharing information

An important benefit of working together is the sharing of information, though there are tensions and controversies involved (Hudson, 2005). There is an important distinction between the sharing of information through the development of large electronic databases and frontline workers sharing personal information on a case-by-case basis in accordance with legal, ethical and professional obligations. The professional cultures and values of the different professions may play a role in shaping attitudes to interagency information sharing in frontline practice, with some professions being more reluctant to share than others (Richardson and Asthana, 2006: 664). There can be conflicting pressure on practitioners to both share information across professional boundaries and protect the privacy of service users and the confidentiality of their personal information.

Richardson and Asthana (2006: 660) identify four information-sharing models of frontline practitioners: the ideal model, the over-open model, the over-cautious model and the chaotic model. The ideal model involves knowing when it is appropriate to both share and withhold information. To promote appropriate information-sharing HM Government have provided practitioners with 'seven golden rules' (HM Government, 2008), including that they should: remember that the Data Protection Act is not a barrier to sharing information; be open and honest with service users from the outset about when information will be shared and with whom; consider safety and well-being; and seek consent to share when appropriate.

Developing a fuller picture

Sharing information is one thing, but using this information to build a fuller picture is another. Each stakeholder comes to the meeting with his or her own partial view, and simply sharing information will not be enough for the full benefits of working together to be realized. Differing views and perspectives need combining to form a new synthesis, which is more holistic and systemic than simply adding pieces of information together. With appropriate facilitation and good professional practices a meeting between stakeholders can produce a much richer and more valid picture of the decision situation, reflecting a systemic understanding of the different domains and levels of interacting influences. This will help to develop fuller understandings of the nature of the difficulties, building solutions and identifying sources of support. When stakeholders put the bits of the jigsaw together to form a coherent picture, it is more likely that they will plan and take effective action.

Developing coherent and integrated plans

Integrated working involves members of different professions and agencies respecting and collaborating with each other to bring their own skills and expertise to planning services and interventions with service users. Many situations require joint and coordinated plans involving a number of people. Health, social care and educational workers need to be able to work together in coordinated and integrated ways that dovetail with each other, each being supportive of the other. Stakeholders working together means people making sure that what they do fits in with what the others are doing, thereby giving more chance to implement the plan successfully. This involves the development of a coherent overall plan, with stakeholders being clear of their roles and the roles of others. Professional members of the core group need to place their work with Paul and his family in the context of an overall plan in which his parents have an active role. Paul's child protection plan has implications for all members of the core group, and their active participation in discussions will increase the chances of effective implementation.

Engendering commitment

One of the potential benefits of meeting together is that the various stakeholders can come to share a commitment to a plan. Gail will play an important role in the child protection plan, and if she remains unconvinced of its merits she may comply with it but have no commitment to it. Compliance without commitment increases the danger that the motions are gone through but the aims are not achieved. Commitment stems from feeling a party to the decision rather than having it imposed, and if the nursery teacher's point of view is listened to and taken into account, she is more likely to be committed to what is decided. Mere presence is not enough for this to take place – actual participation is needed. It is known from research that individuals tend to have more commitment to carrying out a decision if they declare their intention publicly rather than keeping it to themselves (Janis and Mann, 1977: 281). So if the details of the child protection plan are agreed, and the various stakeholders publicly express their agreement, there is likely to be greater commitment than if this did not happen.

Integrated action

Meeting together will make it more likely that stakeholders will act in joined-up ways, with their actions combining together to form a coherent intervention. However, once the meeting is over, they may have varying degrees of contact with each other before the next meeting, and there is a danger that they all go their separate ways and do their own thing. It is important that Ellen carries out her role as the lead professional and actively coordinates the implementation of the plan and keeps it under review. She will need to have contact with the other stakeholders and they need to contact her if there are changes in the situation. It may also be appropriate to set up specific monitoring processes that operate between meetings to check that the plan is being implemented as agreed. The implementation of the plan will need to be reviewed at the next meeting and any necessary adjustments made.

Working together effectively

There are a number of individual and group processes that increase the chances of effective communication and open dialogue between stakeholders. The absence of these processes may mean that participants make unsound decisions, that their investment of time and energy is wasted and that an opportunity has been lost. Through their own individual practices each stakeholder can make a contribution to creating a supportive and cooperative group climate in which open and effective dialogue produces sound decisions and plans.

Preparing

The more stakeholders have prepared for a meeting, the more likely they are to successfully work together. Preparing for a meeting involves getting oneself ready to participate effectually. This can involve a number of tasks, including reading any notes or minutes of the previous meeting, particularly in relation to any action points; reading any reports or other documents to be discussed; thinking about issues to be examined; being clear why the meeting is taking place and what its purpose is; preparing any reports required for the meeting; and having pre-meeting contact with others if necessary. Preparatory work can be helpful if service users or other non-professional stakeholders are likely to feel intimidated or overwhelmed at the meeting. When children or young people attend a meeting it does not necessarily mean talking on their behalf, but may involve preparing with them anything they wish to say and making sure they understand that they do not have to speak (Scutt, 1995: 238). Practitioners need to ascertain accurately the views, wishes and feelings of non-attending children before the meeting so that participants can respect them as important contributors.

Communicating effectively

Working together requires stakeholders to communicate with each other, though there is an important distinction between effective and ineffective communication. Communication can be seen as a process of both sending and receiving messages and the creation and interpretation of meaning. Effective communication is when the participants attach similar meanings to the messages exchanged (Gudykunst, 1998: 26; Reder and Duncan, 2003: 85). However, a message can be 'constructed and sent' and 'received and interpreted' without the receiver attaching a similar meaning to the one intended by the sender. There are many factors that can influence the outcome of an episode of communication (Reder and Duncan, 2003: 89), which include the two complementary processes of 'explaining clearly' and 'listening vigilantly'. For example, Ellen is explaining her draft proposed child protection plan and the other stakeholders are listening to her. Whether she is able to communicate effectively her intended meanings will at least partly depend on how clearly she explains the plan and how vigilantly the other stakeholders listen to what she is saying.

Trevithick (2000: 120) states that 'explaining' is a core skill in social work that has tended to be a taken-for-granted activity and that is covered very little in social work texts. Brown and Atkins (2006: 196) state that the original root of the word 'explaining' is 'to make plain'; defining the term as an attempt to provide understanding of something to others. They see 'understanding' as seeing connections which were previously not seen. They divide explaining into three types: (i) interpretative explanations that address the question 'What?', for example 'What is the nature of the neglect?'; (ii) reason-giving explanations that address the question 'Why?', for example 'Why is the neglect happening?'; (iii) descriptive explanations that address the question 'How?', for example 'How do we turn neglect into nurturing?'. They go on to explain that to understand an explanation, explainers need to construct the message considering not only what they want to explain, but also the knowledge and characteristics of the intended recipients.

'Listening' involves receiving messages and interpreting their meaning. This includes not only the verbal content of messages but the accompanying non-verbal information. There is a danger that the listener has a mindset, having already made up his or her mind, and so is not really listening to what the other person is saying. Effective listening involves having an open mind while endeavouring to achieve an understanding of the other person's view. The chances of understanding the intended meaning of a message are increased when a listener has a critical self-awareness of his or her 'own frame of reference' and that of the sender. However, stakeholders should not take the intended message at face value but rather be vigilant and scrutinize the views put forward and challenge any inconsistencies.

Promoting participation and discussion

The purpose of attending meetings is not to observe the proceedings but to be a participant. To participate is to make a contribution that the others listen to and, in turn, to listen to the contributions of others. A question remains as to how far Gail will be a participant. It is her choice if she wishes to speak, but she does need to have the opportunity and to feel that what she has to say will be respected and listened to. Whether Gail is able to put her point of view forwards may depend on a number of factors, including her degree of confidence, how prepared she has been for the core group meeting and the degree of skill others can bring to bare to enable her participation. Professional workers' participation may also need facilitation, for example, if the health visitor keeps her concerns to herself many of the benefits of meeting together will be lost. Exploratory questions may enable and encourage non-contributing stakeholders to express their views if the general atmosphere is one of each of the stakeholder's contribution being valued.

It is through discussion that potentially an in-depth picture of the decision situation is constructed and a full range of appropriate options identified and evaluated. Discussion involves the exchange of ideas, perspectives and opinions and may need to be encouraged to build different and more systemic ways of understanding the situation. It is through the process of discussion that views are modified, abandoned, clarified or confirmed. Discussion may at times be a taken-for-granted process, but productive discussion is by no means inevitable. If stakeholders are to make progress, discussion needs to be focused on the issues at hand and to take place in a logical sequence. While there may be no shortage of discussion, much of it can be off the point. The chair has a particular role of keeping the group focused on relevant issues and not being sidetracked onto irrelevancies, but there is a balance to be struck between a stifling tight control on what is discussed and re-establishing the focus when the discussion drifts off course.

Constructive management of conflict

A climate of cooperation, collaboration and mutual support needs to be created if stakeholders are to work together constructively. Establishing and emphasizing a common purpose may help to create such a climate. For example, Ellen emphasizes that they all share the goal of promoting Paul's welfare, while there may be differences about how this can best be achieved. Differences are important from a decision-making point of view, but whether conflict takes place in a cooperative or competitive atmosphere will largely determine whether the conflict is constructive or destructive. There is a difference between healthy exchanges of differing opinions, in the context of endeavouring to achieve a consensus, and individual stakeholders or factions being embroiled in personal feuds involving in-fighting and win/lose arguments. Members can foster a positive group climate by enabling stakeholders who hold differing views to see each other as partners seeking consensus, rather than opponents trying to win an argument.

Johnson and Johnson (1982: 325) identified three negative and three positive strategies used by individual stakeholders to manage conflict. The three negative strategies are win–lose, rejection and avoidance. Win–lose involves viewing differences of opinion as an opportunity to win an argument at the expense of the other person. Rejection involves perceiving a member's disagreement as a personal rejection and so withdrawing from the discussion, feeling hurt. Avoidance is evading arguments whenever possible. The three positive strategies are confirmation, perspective taking and problem solving. Confirmation involves confirming the other person as a valued person who you happen to disagree with on a particular point. Perspective taking involves seeing differences of opinion as opportunities to gain a different perspective on the issue. Problem solving involves endeavouring to bring differing perspectives together to build more systemic understandings. It is through these positive strategies that conflict can be creative.

Skilful chairing

The chair of a meeting plays a crucial role in facilitating stakeholders to work together in a constructive and vigilant way. This involves enabling participants to discuss the decision situation and to maintain positive working relationships with one another. Chairs can carry out their role in a variety of ways, and for the effective functioning of groups they require a number of skills, including interpersonal and group skills, conflict management skills, and an understanding of group and emotional dynamics. For example, there is a strong emotional dimension to the decisions made within social work and an important role of chairs is enabling emotions to be expressed without the group being disabled by them. The chair will need considerable skill enabling participants to express strong emotions, like anger, without this causing the premature closure of the discussion.

Even a relatively informal meeting like a core group meeting can benefit from having an identified chair, though there is an issue about whether one of the stakeholders can be an effective chair or whether an independent chair is required. Having an independent chair has both advantages and disadvantages. There is a danger that the existence of an independent chair increases the formality of the meeting. However, an independent chair is more likely to have the appropriate skills to manage the meeting well. If a stakeholder chairs the meeting there is a danger that his or her own participation will be impaired. Harlow and Shardlow (2006: 68) found that social workers tended to chair core group meetings and that the other professional members tended to see chairing as the social workers' responsibility, even though there was a local decision to rotate the chair. They give the example of a participant who stated that she refused to help with chairing on the grounds that this would impede her own participation in the meeting, with no reference to the possibility that the social worker's participation might also be impeded.

Overcoming barriers

Stakeholders working together entails members of different social, economic and professional groups coming together to collaborate with each other. However, there are a number of potential lines of division within stakeholder groups which potentially form barriers to effective cooperation. These include 'the divisions within society', 'divisions between service users and professionals', 'divisions between different professions' and 'divisions within families'. All these divisions reflect societal structures of power and operate simultaneously in any situation and, as was made clear in Chapter 1, how they play out in any particular situation will depend on the circumstances and how interactions are negotiated.

Divisions within society

To the extent that stakeholders working together form a microcosm of the wider society, there is likely to be a replication of dominant social structures within stakeholder groups, with members and non-members of oppressed groups being present. Potentially, members of socially dominant groups can discriminate against those stakeholders who are perceived to be different. Individual stakeholders may hold racist, sexist, ageist, ethnocentric, homophobic, heterosexist or ablest beliefs and make discriminatory comments. The beliefs contained within the discourses of heterosexism, ageism, racism, ablism, sexism and ethnocentrism can dominate stakeholders' meetings through their taken-for-grantedness and 'naturalness'. In the long term these attitudes and beliefs may need to be confronted, but it will depend on the actual circumstances of a meeting as to if, when or how such discrimination is challenged and by whom (Thompson, 2003: 226).

Mullaly (2002: 84) argues that one major way in which the dominant groups reinforce their positions of power and privilege is through the use of stereotypes which he describes as biased and over-simplified conceptions of social group members. He goes on to explain how members of dominant groups can project their own experience and culture as representative of humanity, often without realizing it, and how groups perceived as different become the 'Other' and are marked by negative stereotypes that reinforce notions of group superiority. These stereotypes permeate society and become so ingrained that they are seldom questioned by members of the privileged group themselves. Stakeholders need critical awareness of when meetings come under the influence of hegemonic ideas and stereotypes and how they can appropriately challenge them.

Service-user–practitioner relations

The division between those that hold official positions and those that do not is potentially one of the sharpest within stakeholder groups. The power differential between the two can form a barrier to service users and professionals working together. Considerable power and status comes from holding an official position within an agency which is further enhanced if this is accompanied by professional status. Service users are not totally powerless and professionals are not all powerful, though professionals generally do hold more power and service users can often perceive them to hold more power than they actually do. Practitioners need to acknowledge power differentials and develop practices that do not disempower service users. They need to be aware of the possibility that they hold stereotypes of service users that impact on the way they behave towards them.

There is a danger that professional workers leave service users and other non-professionals as observers rather than participants at the meeting. Gail feels at a disadvantage amongst the professionals and may be inhibited from expressing her opinions. In these circumstances, anti-oppressive practice and enabling practice have important roles to play in achieving the goal of participation. This would include careful choice of venue, the use of non-technical language, avoiding acronyms, putting people at their ease, fully explaining procedures and encouraging people to participate. Chapter 3 has shown how considerable preparatory work may be required before service users feel able to become involved in working together with other stakeholders. A fear is that certain individuals, subgroups or interests will dominate a meeting and that service users will not have an effective say. A key aim of social work practice is to enable all stakeholders to participate, despite differences in power. If this aim is to have a chance of being achieved professional workers need a clear understanding and sensitivity towards dynamics of power that can operate when working together.

Professional workers can at least partially bridge the barriers between themselves and service users through empathic listening to what service users have to say. Forrester *et al.* (2008: 47) sees empathic listening as listening with an open mind, endeavouring to understand the service user's position and point of view. He found that even when raising concerns, empathic listening reduced resistance and increased disclosure, but not at the expense of clarity over concerns, and may have contributed to greater agreement over what would happen next. He states that 'of particular importance was that workers who raised concerns empathically were able to challenge parents about concerning behaviour while retaining a positive relationship with them' (ibid.: 49).

Divisions between professions

The different professions and occupations have historically developed to focus on different domains of life, for example the domains and subdomains of law, health, education and social welfare. Different challenges require different sets of skills, knowledge and perspectives, and one function of professional education is for students to develop a distinct professional identity. The division of labour between the different occupational groups has advantages and it is likely that there are many examples of members of different professions working together collaboratively. However, professional groups can create their own boundaries which may form barriers to working together.

These boundaries operate on a number of different levels. For example, having different professions with different sets of skills, knowledge and perspectives on approaches to problems and solutions can get in the way of effective communication (Reder and Duncan, 2003: 92). There is a danger that rivalry and destructive conflicts develop that prevent working together in a constructive way. Harlow (2004) identifies a number of explanations of why the different professions may not work together productively. For example, difficult situations tend to generate intense emotions within the professional network and there is a danger that unwanted painful emotions are projected onto a member of another 'professional group' (ibid.: 35). Also, conflicted group dynamics can develop when different members of the professional network identify with particular family members (ibid.: 36).

Relations between the different professions are ideally based on mutual respect for each other's particular expertise. Unfortunately, this may not always be the case as certain professions can occupy dominant positions, potentially leaving some stakeholders feeling either intimidated or without influence. Smith (2008: 115) claims there is a consensus that there are power and status differentials between the different professions, as well as those operating between practitioners and service users. The perspectives of the different professions can carry different weights, for example, male professions being given more weight than female professions (Ferguson, 1987; Stevenson, 1989: 185; Hugman, 1991: 11; Smith, 2008: 115). This does not relate to the gender of individual members of these professions, but rather their professional ethos which is rooted in the histories of the different professions. Medical perspectives and legal perspectives (both of which have a predominantly male ethos) can carry more weight than social work perspectives or nursing perspectives which have a more female ethos. Professional ethos may be counter-balanced by other factors, such as a worker's agency being the lead agency or the controller of resources.

There is a need for members of all professions to develop collaborative skills and values to give central place to listening to the service user and providing an effective service. Clark (1997) identifies the need for dual professional socialization into both an individual disciplinary identity and the norms of collaborative practice. This would involve developing an identity as a member of a profession as well as an interprofessional team member (Spafford et al., 2007: 173). Professionals should learn to be team players that recognize both the importance of their own professional identity and the necessity of collaboration to provide effective service to the service user, appreciating each has a different professional voice and perspective which is equally valid and valued.

Ellen, the health visitor and the nursery teacher positively work together most of the time, each respecting the other's role and expertise, though there are tensions around the availability and control of resources, the sharing of responsibility and tasks, the tolerance of risk, and the thresholds for intervention. Barrett and Keeping (2005) state that to contribute effectively to decision making within interprofessional teams, professional workers need to have a commitment to working together, a confidence in their own role, be able to set aside stereotypes and to give explicit acknowledgement of each profession's unique contribution to collaborative working.

Divisions within families

It is not uncommon for there to be power differentials and lines of division within families and other social networks. Divisions of gender, age, generation, ethnicity, religion and family of origin can result in discord between family members. For example, intrafamilial conflict can occur between different generations and sides of a family, or can be structured around gender difference. There can be matriarchal or patriarchal figures that hold considerable influence within the wider family or social network. There is considerable conflict between Bob's family of origin and Gail's, to such an extent that this is a major source of tension between the couple. Bob has a good relationship with his mother, who endeavours to support Gail with the care of Paul, but Gail sees this as interference and an undermining of her parenting. Such family dynamics can form a barrier to working together and may need to be addressed before progress can be made.

Power differentials can mean that one family member has a degree of control over another and feels entitled to dominate. Because of these dynamics a family member can feel prevented from expressing him or herself freely. There is a danger that professionals collude with the more powerful member, particularly when there is a threat of violence, though, at least in some situations by the clear establishment of ground rules and structures, a context may be created in which all stakeholders feel able to speak their views. In the context of family medication, Flynn (2005: 411) refers to active power balancing where ground rules, the use of the procedural power and the raising of questions enable all family members to speak without being coerced. In using the term 'procedural power' Flynn (2005) is referring to the capacity of the mediator to actively balance power relations between the parties in the way he or she implements the procedures of the meeting. From their research, Holland et al. (2005) argue that 'family group conferences', with their provision of 'private family time', potentially can have a role in democratizing family relations. They found that children felt more listened to, although not necessarily more influentially, and that men were more likely to attend, compared with child protection conferences. They report that except in a small minority of cases men did not use the forum of family group conferences to coerce women or children. In three of seventeen conferences fathers who were normally domineering were described as being restrained by the style of the conference and the presence of children.

Seeking agreement

Before discussing 'seeking agreement' it needs to be made clear that not all stakeholder meetings have the aim of reaching a joint view. For example, the service user may have a right or responsibility to take the decision during or after the meeting. Service users can benefit from hearing what other stakeholders have to say but there is a danger that they will experience pressure to conform to the wishes of others. For example, a worker may arrange a meeting between the service user, carers, relatives and other professional workers when an older person experiences crisis in caring for themselves and decisions need to be taken about their future care. In theory everybody may agree that it is for the service user to decide, but there is a danger that other stakeholders, who may have good intentions but overwhelming opinions, may dominate. Power (1989, cited in Dwyer, 2005: 1083) found that 'the scope for service user self determination is often reduced by the influence of others, not only relatives and carers, but also professional workers with whom they are in contact'. When service users take decisions at stakeholders' meetings there is an increased danger that they will experience overwhelming pressure to conform to the wishes of others, and it may be better if the service user takes the decision after the meeting.

Seeking a consensus

Processes for reaching agreement can remain implicit and it is important that all stakeholders are clear about how they are to reach decisions and judge whether this method is appropriate. When a group, as opposed to an individual, needs to make a decision or recommendation, seeking a consensus may be better than a compromise or majority view (Moscovici and Doise, 1994). As well as the desirability of achieving a consensus per se, stakeholders can benefit from the processes of striving to achieve a consensus. Even if members do not achieve a consensus they can still benefit from the process of endeavouring to do so, which includes clarifying the different points of view and differences not being brushed aside.

Schein (1988: 73) states that consensus exists when there is a clear option that most stakeholders subscribe to and 'communications have been sufficiently open, and the group climate has been sufficiently supportive, to make everyone in the group feel that they have had their fair chance to influence the decision'. An important point in this defini-tion is that those stakeholders, who do not enthusiastically support the majority opinion as their first choice, feel they have had their fair chance to influence the decision and are prepared to support it. Hayes and Houston (2007: 988) argue that according to the work of Jungen Habermas, 'when people seek to establish genuine understanding and consensus, in conditions where power is held in check, then moral communication is supposed to unfold'. They identify six imperatives of 'discourse ethics' which are summarized below. They identify that all participants must:

1. be included in the dialogue provided they have the communicative ability to converse meaningfully with others;
2. be allowed to introduce, question and criticize any assertion whatso-ever;
3. be permitted to express their attitudes, desires and needs without restriction;
4. be empathic towards the perspectives of others;
5. hold power in check so that the only legitimate force is the force of argument;
6. strive to achieve a consensus.

Achieving these conditions is a challenge when there are power differ-entials and divisions within stakeholder groups, though with commit-ment and skill progress can be made in moving closer to this goal.

Dangers of conformity

One of the surprising findings of child protection research is the high degree of interprofessional agreement at child protection conferences (Hallett, 1995: 223; Farmer and Owen, 1995: 98). However, there is an important distinction between apparent consensus and true consensus. Apparent consensus occurs when on the surface it appears that all stake-holders agree, but in reality some or all are superficially conforming to a dominant view that they do not actually hold or that they find it convenient to acquiesce with. Such conformity can take the form of silence rather than active support.

Pressure to conform can come from a variety of sources that have little to do with the merits or otherwise of the case being put forward. Individual stakeholders can conform because they feel intimidated, lack sufficient confidence in their own view or believe that they are alone in their opposition, when in fact it is only one or two vocal stakeholders that hold the prevailing view. They can fear conflict or chastisement or that they would upset others or that they would make a fool of themselves. Professional members may not want to be seen disagreeing with colleagues in front of service users, and service users might not want to be seen as uncooperative. Janis (1972) refers to an extreme pressure to conform as 'groupthink', which occurs in insular and cohesive groups in which all disagreement is suppressed.

There is a difference between changing one's mind and conforming to the view of others. Ellen disagrees with the health visitor's suggestions about monitoring arrangements, believing them to be an unwarranted intrusion into family life, but feels under pressure to accept them. Nevertheless she becomes more cautious in her view after listening to what the health visitor has to say about some of the things that had been happening before the family had contact with children's services. Whether this is regarded as conformity or open mindedness will depend on whether she had been convinced of the arguments of the health visitor or conforming to a dominant view. Consensus requires open mindedness, with stakeholders being prepared to move forward in their view, building on the views expressed by others. This contrasts with having rigid inflexible views and not being prepared to change, no matter how convincing the arguments put forward.

By the end of the core group meeting members were able to reach a broad agreement about the details of the child protection plan. When such a consensus is not achieved and no stakeholder has a right or particular responsibility to take the decision, a balance will need to be struck between gaining reluctant agreement by a process of attrition, abandoning the meeting with the matter being left undecided or taking the decision without the support of all the stakeholders.

chapter summary

In this chapter I have argued that sound decision making requires stakeholders to work together and that meetings of various kinds offer the opportunity to do so in practical and effective ways. Social workers have a valuable contribution to make, and I have outlined a number of distinct benefits of working together, including sharing information, developing a fuller picture and integrated plans, engendering commitment, and producing integrated actions. However, working together requires preparation, effective communication, open dialogue, the constructive ⭨

management of conflict and chairing skills. A number of potential barriers to working together exist, including the divisions within society and families, between different professions, and between professionals and service users. Overcoming these barriers will include members of different professions developing an identity as a member of an interprofessional team as well as a member of a profession. When a group decision is required, stakeholders should seek to achieve consensus through a process of open dialogue. However, there is the ever present danger of group conformity.

key practice points: working together

To work together stakeholders need to:

- create the conditions in which constructive discussion and open dialogue can take place;
- collaborate together and integrate their work;
- share information and communicate effectively with each other;
- explain clearly and listen vigilantly;
- acknowledge divisions and develop practices that overcome them.

putting it into practice

1. What reasons might Paul's father have for not attending the core group meeting and how might he be engaged in their work?
2. What are the benefits of the case study core group members working together?
3. What skills do you think the social worker, Ellen, needs to lead the work of the core group effectively in bringing about change in the care of Paul?
4. What barriers might there be to the case study stakeholders working together, and how might they be overcome?
5. What obstacles might there be to the core group achieving a consensus about Paul's child protection plan?

Recommended reading

P. Reder and S. Duncan (2003) 'Understanding communication in child protection networks', *Child Abuse Review*, 12(2) 82–100. This journal article explores some of the problems of communication that haunt professional practice.

M. Lymbery and A. Millward (2009) 'Partnership working', in R. Adams, L. Dominelli and M. Payne (eds), *Practising Social Work in a Complex World*, Basingstoke: Palgrave Macmillan. This chapter discusses the political and professional obstacles to working together and identifies attributes that make it more likely.

G. Barrett and C. Keeping (2005) 'The processes required for effective interprofessional working', in G. Barrett, D. Sellman and J. Thomas (eds), *Interprofessional Working in Health and Social Care*, Basingstoke: Palgrave Macmillan. The chapter explores some of the factors that enable and prevent different professions working together.

5 | Using knowledge and managing emotions

In this chapter I discuss the role of different forms of knowledge, ways of thinking and emotions in social work decision making. A model of professional wisdom is presented in which practitioners make decisions through a combination of intuition and analysis, using multiple sources of knowledge, while competently managing their emotions. Such professional wisdom has an important role in contributing to collaborative decision making with others, including supporting service users and carers to make informed life decisions. Making sound decisions requires critical approaches to using knowledge, different modes of thinking and the management of emotions generated by decision situations. Non-critical approaches can result in unsound decision making, leading to decision regret and bad outcomes.

practice scenario

Mr Richmond is an 81-year-old widower who is in hospital after experiencing a fall and soon will be ready for discharge. His daughter, Gloria, who lives some distance away, is concerned about his safety and care when he returns home. The occupational therapist's assessments have found that it is not safe for Mr Richmond to use a stick. However, he is reluctant to use a Zimmer frame finding it difficult to acknowledge his increasing physical impairment. He has also been assessed as being unable to climb stairs or make a cup of tea for himself. The health authority has informed the local authority of Mr Richmond's need for community services on discharge. Esther, a hospital-based social worker, is working closely with the ward-based care-coordinator who is concerned about the risks Mr Richmond will ↘

face if he returns home. Mr Richmond is finding it hard to make a decision about whether to return home or move to residential care and does not want to cause his daughter further stress. Esther recognizes that he and his daughter have difficult judgements to make and will draw on a number of sources of knowledge in helping them decide whether he would be able to return home reasonably safely or whether he could be happy in residential care. Esther sees her role as enabling him and his daughter to consider the options and their possible consequences, so as to make an informed decision that gives the best chance of achieving the outcomes they want.

Professional wisdom

'Professional wisdom', sometimes referred to as 'practice wisdom' or 'practical wisdom', has been characterized in many ways. Here the term will be defined as the capacity for reflective judgement that involves the ability to make or support sound decisions based on deep understandings in conditions of uncertainty (O'Sullivan, 2005). The concept includes, but is not restricted to, as is often the case, experiential knowledge developed through practice experience. Professional wisdom is a quality of judgement and thinking that can be used to make or support sound decisions, though it is open to question whether particular work environments support or undermine its use. Kitchener and Brenner (1990: 203) identify four aspects of reflective judgement:

- the presence of unavoidable difficult 'thorny' problems inherent in the lives of adults;
- a comprehensive grasp of knowledge characterized by both breadth and depth;
- a recognition that knowledge is uncertain and that it is not possible for truth to be absolutely knowable at any given time;
- a willingness and exceptional ability to formulate sound executable judgements in the face of this uncertainty.

Professional wisdom integrates different types of knowledge, modes of thinking, emotions and action. Every effort will be made to show how these elements integrate with each other, though for the sake of clarity the chapter is divided into three sections: the first on knowledge-based decision making, the second on two modes of thinking and the third on emotional competence.

Knowledge-based decision making

There is considerable confusion and contention over the relationship between knowledge and professional practice. For example, Trevithick (2008: 1212) states that confusion remains about what constitutes knowledge in social work and how it is applied in practice. Different types of knowledge have been identified and the ways they do or should relate to practice debated (Sibeon, 1990; Drury Hudson, 1997; Osmond, 2005; Trevithick, 2008). This section will focus on the knowledge used to make decisions and will be restricted to two related issues: the existence of different sources of knowledge and the question of the validity of knowledge. The argument put forward, simply stated, is that through professional wisdom practitioners use multiple sources of knowledge, both tacitly and deliberatively; and that there is no definitive way of deciding whether knowledge is valid or not.

A key feature of professional wisdom is the selection, integration and use of different types of knowledge to make holistic judgements based on the best combination of knowledge that the practitioner holds or has access to. There is an important distinction between 'tacit knowledge' and 'consciously held knowledge'. Usually knowledge is thought about in terms of consciously held knowledge, that is explicit knowledge, for example a theory, a law or some research findings. In contrast, tacit knowledge is hidden knowledge, hidden from both the observer and possessor of the knowledge. As Eraut (1994: 111) states, tacit knowledge is 'something not easily explained to others or even to oneself'. Tacit knowledge is gained through experience, but also can include knowledge originally acquired through education and training or reading research, that over time has become non-conscious embodied knowledge. An observer of Esther responding in an emergency situation knows that she has knowledge because of the way she rapidly assesses the situation and acts. However, because Esther uses tacit knowledge, she is not consciously aware of the knowledge she is using and has some difficulty explaining the knowledge basis of her actions. Nevertheless, with retrospective analysis she should be able to trace the knowledge she used to identify and interpret significant cues in the situation. Tacit knowledge is part of the development of professional expertise and is related to skilled behaviour and forms the basis of intuition, though not all tacit knowledge is necessarily valid knowledge and it can be a source of errors and mistakes.

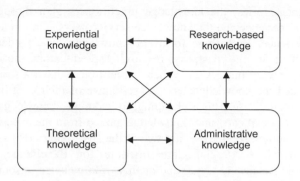

Figure 5.1   Transformation of knowledge

Multiple sources of knowledge

In making and supporting sound decisions, practitioners and service users can draw on multiple sources of knowledge, and over the years there have been a number of attempts to categorize the different types of knowledge that are available in social work (Sibeon, 1990; Drury Hudson, 1997; Osmond, 2005; Trevithick, 2008). Here four categories will be used: experiential knowledge, research-based knowledge, theoretical knowledge and administrative knowledge. These categories and others like them are 'ideal types' and as a consequence there are strong overlaps and interactions between them, meaning that the distinction between the different types are liable to break down on close examination. Knowledge that falls into one category is often transformed into another, for example research-based knowledge is often used in the formulation of social policy, theories are often used as the starting point of research, and the findings of research used to develop theories (Figure 5.1). Despite these limitations the categories may help practitioners to think about the different types of knowledge used within the practice. Both service users and practitioners can and do make contributions to the production of all four categories of knowledge.

Experiential knowledge

Experiential knowledge will be regarded as knowledge gained directly from practice and life experience, rather than, for example, reading a research article, listening to a lecture or taking part in a simulation. In a sense all knowledge that an individual human being possesses has been gained through some type of experience but this category refers to knowledge gained through practice and life experience. There are two main subcategories, the knowledge practitioners gain through their practice experience and the knowledge service users gain through their life experience. Both these forms of knowledge have tended to be undervalued in the past, by researchers, educators, academics, managers, policy makers and others. Practitioners have also at times undervalued the knowledge service users have of their own lives and the services they use. This is changing, for example 'knowledge gained from doing social care' and 'knowledge gained from the experience of and reflection on service use' are two of the five sources of knowledge identified by the Social Care Institute for Excellence (SCIE) Knowledge Review 3, 'Types and quality of knowledge in social care' (Pawson *et al.*, 2003).

Research-based knowledge

Research-based knowledge is produced from the process of planned, systematic and methodical investigation that directly or indirectly collects observational data with the purpose of constructing knowledge. It is common to refer to the use of research knowledge in practice as 'evidence based practice' (Newman *et al.*, 2005). Payne (2005: 56) states that evidence-based practice 'proposes that social workers should practise using the best available evidence of what action will be effective to achieve the intended outcomes'. Esther would like to find research on the outcomes of decisions made by people in Mr Richmond's position, particularly whether factors have been identified that make it more likely a person would be settled and happy in residential care or returning home. As a busy practitioner she has only limited time and is not even sure whether such research has been carried out. A number of issues have been identified in relation to using research-based knowledge in practice, including that often there is a scarcity of research studies carried out in relation to the particular decision in hand and that, where relevant research has been carried out, practitioners may not know about it and, if they do, they may have difficulty applying the findings to the particular situation.

Research-based knowledge is most useful where relevant research studies have been carried out and the findings of which are assessable to practitioners who are able to be integrate them with the other sources of knowledge. Given constraints of time, there are considerable benefits to practitioners having well-developed skills in using electronic databases to find relevant studies and research reviews. Through SCIE's online database Social Care Online Esther finds a literature review published on the Joseph Rowntree Foundation website, 'Improving care in residential care homes: a literature review' (Joseph Rowntree Foundation, 2008).

This confirmed her fear that little research has been done in relation to residential care for older people as distinct from nursing care. In particular little or no research has been carried out in relation to factors influencing the choice of residential care over alternatives and the psychosocial outcomes of this choice. Through discussions with a colleague, who is completing an advance award in social work, she also found some interesting research by Trappes-Lomax *et al.* (2006) which compared the outcomes for older people being discharged home directly from hospital with those who first were transferred to a joint health and social care residential rehabilitation unit. Although she found reading the research review and the journal article generally very helpful, she would like to see specific research carried out that compared the psychosocial outcomes for older people who need to decide whether the time has come to give up the struggle of living in their own home.

Theoretical knowledge

Theory is a contested idea with considerable debate about what a theory is or ought to be (Payne, 2005: 3). Here theoretical knowledge will be regarded as a series of connected concepts that can help explain relationships between different aspects of professional or life processes. It can be produced by theorists through theory building, scholarship and critical thinking. Theories can provide a framework for understanding situations, making decisions and taking action. Sibeon (1990) identifies three types of theory used within social work: theories of what social work is, theories of how to do social work and theories of the client world. In relation to the latter category, there are a number of theories about, for example, ageing, including disengagement theory (Cumming, 2000), continuity theory (Atchley, 2000) and Erikson's model of psychosocial development (Erikson, 1977). These may help Esther and Mr Richmond understand his predicament and situation. For example, psychosocial development theory may help in understanding the struggle Mr Richmond is having in his late life between 'integrity and despair', with him oscillating between accepting and regretting the life that he has lived.

Administrative knowledge

Administrative knowledge is knowledge produced by those who govern, administer or manage the various functions of the state, local authorities and agencies. The practitioner's administrative knowledge will include knowledge of laws, regulations, policies, guidance, procedures and protocols that have been set out in various documents. For example, *Discharge from Hospital Pathway, Process and Practice* (Department of

Health, 2003) states that it was produced 'to assist health and social care commissioners, managers and practitioners working in the statutory and independent sectors to improve local hospital discharge policy and practice'. As is typical of this type of document, it sets out how there should be a locally agreed policy, in this case for good interagency work in the discharge of patients and how the local policy should have various protocols for staff to follow.

Valid knowledge

There has been a tendency for some types of knowledge to be privileged over others, while other categories have been undervalued or ignored. Traditional hierarchies of what constitutes valid knowledge have tended to place knowledge produced by randomized controlled trials at the top and the experience of practitioners, service users and carers at the bottom (Glasby *et al.*, 2007: 433). There is agreement that social work decisions should be based on knowledge rather than ignorance, but there are disputes about what constitutes valid knowledge. One way of looking at this is to regard something as 'valid' if it is considered to be well based or well founded. This means that if knowledge is to be regarded as valid, it needs to be based on evidence and reasoned argument, though what counts as evidence is contested and is often equated with 'research evidence' and sometimes particular types of research evidence. SCIE Knowledge Review 3, 'Types and quality of knowledge in social care' states that 'all types of knowledge deserve equal respect and attention' (Pawson *et al.*, 2003), by which they do not mean all knowledge is equally 'good or useful'. It means that practitioners should give experiential knowledge, research-based knowledge, theoretical knowledge and administrative knowledge equal respect and attention, while equally subjecting them to critical scrutiny.

Drawing on the work of Rodwell (1998: 99) we can judge the validity of knowledge in terms of its credibility. Hence, valid knowledge can be regarded as knowledge that is credible and stands up to critical examination. Credible knowledge is knowledge that both the holder and relevant others find worthy of belief. To know whether knowledge claims are worthy of belief one needs to be able to examine their basis, rather than just accept their validity at face value. This means scrutinizing the basis of knowledge, that is subjecting it to careful examination. Internal scrutiny is what we have already referred to as reflexivity, while external scrutiny is explaining one's reasoning to others so that they can examine its validity. External scrutiny is related to the idea of accountability, which Hunt (1998) defines as 'a preparedness to give an explanation and justification to relevant others, for one's acts and omissions'. Others can include service users, carers, colleagues, managers and other professional workers. Each of the categories of knowledge may have complementary roles in making decisions but each needs to be used in a critical way. It is important to critically evaluate the knowledge being used and to consider whether there are additional sources of knowledge that will help to make a sound decision.

Two modes of thinking

As well as knowledge, cognitive processes are involved in making and supporting sound decisions, namely intuition and analysis, which relate to skilful behaviour and deliberative action, respectively. Skilful behaviour is part of professional expertise and involves doing complex tasks on 'automatic pilot', that is without conscious thought. Deliberative action involves thinking analytically about what you are going to do before doing it. Esther, Mr Richmond and Gloria will be involved in thinking about the decision situation, which involves both deliberative and non-deliberative mental processes, that is both analysis and intuition. There has been rivalry throughout history between these two distinct forms of thinking (Hammond, 1996: 60), though in social work they both need to be used in combination with each other, each being suited to different tasks. For example, Hammond *et al.* (1997) have identified 11 task characteristics, including the degree of certainty, number of cues and time available, which determine whether intuition or analysis will be the most effective form of cognition.

Decision situations in social work are unstructured in the sense that they consist of a potentially unlimited number of elements impacting on each other in an uncertain way. By the very nature of unstructured situations it is not possible to construct effective technical rules for determining the features of the problem and the best course of action. In such circumstances it is tempting for social work theoreticians to maintain that it is only professional intuition that can be used to make such decisions and there is a danger that the argument becomes polarized between intuitive decision making and deliberative decision making. For example, Luitgaarden (2009) argues that the properties of social work decision tasks are more likely to require intuitive than analytical decision-making strategies. In contrast Sheppard (2006: 210) argues that social workers need to be able to carry out practical reasoning that needs a high level of practical intelligence and analytical ability. The argument here is that analysis and intuition provide two valuable ways of thinking that are available to practitioners and service users.

Intuition

Intuition, what Gigerenzer (2007) refers to as an unconscious intelligence, is often seen as an important aspect of professional decision making, but its definition and nature are problematic. Intuition has been variously described as the absence of analysis (Hammond, 1996: 60), the pinnacle of expertise (Dreyfus and Dreyfus, 1986) or the non-conscious processing of data (Hamm, 1988: 81). However, I will simply define it as making judgements and decisions without conscious deliberation. This absence does not mean that intuition is a matter of chance or a guess; rather it means that the basis of the decision is not explicit at the time the decision is made. Intuition uses tacit knowledge, perceived information from the environment and rules of thumb to make judgements and decisions without deliberation. It involves the rapid identification of relevant cues and the making of connections and associations with an empathic sensitivity to what people are feeling. As such it involves sensing rather than deliberative thinking.

The nature of intuitive decision is disputed. Intuition can be thought of as deciding in a relatively holistic way, without consciously breaking down the decision situation into its various elements. In this view intuitive decisions represent a kind of gestalt which retains the wholeness of the complete picture without prior intellectualization (England, 1986). In contrast, Gigerenzer (2007: 38) claims that intuitions 'spring from rules of thumb that extract only a few pieces of information from a complex environment' and uses these to make non-conscious inferences. His view is that human beings have an evolved capacity for intuition which is an economical and effective way of making decisions.

The absence of deliberation means that intuition is a relatively quick way of sensing patterns, filling in gaps and deciding. Professional intuition can be regarded as an ability that develops through experience which cannot be formally taught. Some people may be regarded as having more natural capacity than others to make intuitive decisions. To be reliable and accurate, intuition needs to be based on expertise that has been developed over a period of time and, although having an important role within professional work, intuitive decision making has a number of drawbacks which stem from its implicit nature. The most important of these shortcomings is that the reasons behind intuitive decisions are not readily available for comment and scrutiny, which is necessary for working together with service users and other stakeholders. This contrasts with analysis in which the reasoning of the decision maker is explicit and can be directly assessed. However, although at the time we are not fully aware of the underlying reasons behind intuitions, they can be 'lifted from the unconscious level' (Gigerenzer, 2007: 47) through retrospective deliberation and analysis. The very nature of intuition means that it is particularly prone to distortion and bias, and needs the safeguards of high levels of reflexivity.

Analysis

Hammond (1996: 60) defines analysis as 'a step-by-step, conscious, logically defensible process', and it will be regarded here as a process of breaking down the decision situation into a number of elements and carefully considering those in relation to each other. Analysis involves the capacity to analyse and synthesize information into hypotheses about particular situations. Chapter 6 gives a way of analysing the decision situation in terms of key factors, decision goals and a set of options. Chapter 7 gives different ways of analysing options in order to decide what course of action to take. These processes involve a simplification of the decision situation, using conscious deliberation over the different elements in a systematic and organized way. In this way, analysis uses chosen aspects of the decision situation in a precise manner. This contrasts sharply with intuition in which there is no conscious attempt to break down the decision task, with framing the information and choice of option taking place implicitly. Gloria has not deliberated over the different elements of the decision situation and believes her father to be at an unacceptable risk if he returns home. She could be described as using her intuition to assess the level of risk. Esther suggests that Mr Richmond and Gloria join her in analysing the risks involved in both returning home and going into a residential home. She explains that this would include carefully considering each option in terms of dangers and potential benefits. Although this would take time she believes it would put them in a better position to make an informed decision and be less likely to suffer post-decision regret.

The strength of analysis is that it encourages openness about reasoning and so potentially holds decision making open to scrutiny. Analysis can make explicit the judgements about uncertainty that need to be made within social work; it is an approach that can be formally taught and learnt. Analysis requires intellectual capacity and does take time, although how much time can be exaggerated. A judgement will always be needed as to whether the results of analysis will be worth the investment of time. However, analysing the decision situation can become so complex that it hinders rather than aids sound decision making, a process known as 'paralysis through analysis'. Analysis can encourage a misplaced confidence in the ability to make reliable predictions in conditions of uncertainty. For example, there is a danger of getting caught up in the detail of risk assessment, a form of aided analysis, with decision makers becoming overconfident about their predictions. However, analysis helps make probability judgements about which course of action is most likely to give a good outcome.

Combining intuition and analysis

There is a danger of creating a false dichotomy between the two modes of thought, with a tendency to polarize intuition and analysis into two opposing camps. This obscures their compatibility and complementarity with one being dependent on the other. Some decisions in social work will need breaking down into component parts and given careful consideration, but because social work decision making involves issues of uncertainty and value, intuition is needed within the analysis to make judgements about the significance of information. As will be seen in Chapter 7, professional intuition plays an important role within decision analysis in the making of judgements about the likelihood and the value of possible outcomes. Equally, as we have seen, analysis is required when practitioners and service users need to explain their intuitions, as it is only through analysis that the basis of these decisions can be traced. Combining the explicitness of analysis with the skilled judgements of professional intuition means that intuitive decisions can be explained, while intuition can be used to make some of the component judgements needed within analysis.

Social workers need to develop their capacity for analysis, while at the same time developing their intuitive expertise, as both intuition and analysis have important roles within social work. When experienced and skilled social workers need to make decisions relatively quickly, intuition is most likely to be the best approach. When there is more time to make a decision, they can make a judgement as to whether an analytical approach is indicated, which will tend to be when the potential consequences of the decision justify the investment of time. This is most likely to be in risky, complex or unfamiliar decision situations. Practice teachers are likely to use analysis when explaining to their students how to approach a particular decision, even if it is a decision they would have taken intuitively. When facilitating service-user decision making or making decisions with others, some degree of analysis will be needed as these approaches involve being explicit about the basis of choice. Inexperienced social workers will need to take a more analytical approach to decision making because they will not yet have developed the necessary expertise. There is a danger that they will use their intuition despite their lack of relevant experience, as it tends to be the default thought process used by human beings. Where there is no time for an analytical approach, beginning social workers need to seek the guidance of their supervisor or more experienced colleagues.

Emotional competence

Decision making is often solely associated with thinking, with emotions being seen as irrelevant factors that need to be excluded. However, decision makers not only need to think about the decision situation, they need to be aware of the emotions they and others are experiencing and the impact they are having. Much emphasis has been placed on the important role of reflexivity in relation to knowledge, thinking and beliefs about the decision situation. Equally important is reflexivity about what emotions are being generated, what is triggering them, what impact they are having and whether they are being managed and coped with appropriately. It is not easy to define what an emotion is, there being different perspectives on emotions. Baron (2000: 59) states that the term can roughly be taken to mean 'a state that is subjectively experienced as pleasant or unpleasant, that drives or motivates certain kinds of behaviour specific to the emotion and that tends to be elicited by a certain kind of situation'.

Emotions and social work

The importance of emotional competence, also referred to as 'emotional intelligence', is being increasingly recognized in social work (Morrison, 2007). Salovey and Mayer (1990, cited in Morrison, 2007: 250) were the first to 'use the term "emotional intelligence" to describe a form of social intelligence that involves the ability to monitor one's own and others' feelings and emotions, to discriminate among them, and use this information to guide one's thinking and action'. Salovey *et al.* (2008) organized emotional competence into four branches of abilities: ability to perceive, appraise and express emotion; ability to use emotions to facilitate thinking; ability to understand and analyse emotional information; and ability to regulate emotions.

Social workers have long recognized the need to manage their emotions and have appropriate emotional involvement. One of the casework principles in Biestek's (1961) classic text is 'controlled emotional involvement', and Butrym (1976) states that this involves avoiding the twin dangers of over-emotional involvement, resulting in over-identification with service users, and under-emotional involvement, resulting in a lack of empathy. Emotions are an integral part of social work that need to be acknowledged, understood and worked with. Stevenson (1986: 505) states that social workers need to sustain 'an appropriate professional role when deep emotions are involved and when ambivalence and conflict are integral to the situations within which social workers ... must work'. An important part of appropriate emotional involvement is the capacity to 'contain' one's anxiety, which is discussed further in Chapter 8 on effective supervision.

A wide range of emotions are experienced in social work, such as fear, anxiety, joy, hope and compassion. Furthermore, social workers have to cope with not only their own emotions, but also those of service users and other stakeholders. During an interview Esther experiences fear when Mr Richmond waves his stick at her. She feels anger when she learns that a member of staff has sexually abused a service user who moved to residential care. She feels a sense of loss and sadness when a service user dies while awaiting discharge from hospital. She feels joy when a service user finds the strength to oppose the medical staff and fulfils the wish to return home despite the risks.

The term 'emotion' is being used to refer to emotional states, such as anger, sadness, happiness and fear, which particular situations can elicit. It is important to distinguish between what is being referred to here as 'emotions' and 'moods'. Emotions have object directedness: we are angry about something, afraid of something, happy at something, or sad about something. Parrott (2001: 3) states that moods lack this quality of object directedness: a person in an irritable mood is not necessarily angry about anything in particular. He goes on to state that there is a connection between moods and emotions, with a mood making it more likely that the corresponding emotion will be experienced and that an emotion can sometimes develop into a mood when it spreads beyond its initial object. Many words in the English language represent specific emotions, though it is important to distinguish between the 'emotion words' (words that denote emotions, for example happiness, sadness, jealousy) and the emotional states themselves.

Cultures differ in the number of emotion words they have and it is a contested issue as to how far culture shapes emotions (ibid.: 4). Some theorists emphasize how emotional states are universal, while others emphasize the cultural specificity of emotions. It is generally agreed that the number of emotion words in a language varies between cultures and that the number of emotional states recognized within a culture does not necessarily correspond to the number of emotion words. Parrot (ibid.) gives the example that English speakers sometimes feel pleasure or satisfaction at the misfortune of another person, but their language does not supply a word for this emotion. When English speakers learn the German language has a word for this emotion – *Schadenfreude* – they recognize that they have an emotion for which they lacked a word, and may subsequently borrow *Schadenfreude* from German because it is useful to have such a word. Having sounded a note of caution about equating emotional states with emotion words, the focus now will be on specific emotions that the English language has words for.

Impact of emotions on decision making

People in the grip of high emotions are often accused of not thinking straight, but emotions can promote vigilant thinking as well as undermine it. In fact emotions can impact on thinking and thought in a number of ways (Oatley *et al.*, 2006: 257) with individual emotions either having a positive or negative influence on achieving the decision makers' goals. The experience of an emotion can change priorities – either appropriately or inappropriately – distort thinking or provide the motivation to think carefully about the decision situation.

Until recently social science has emphasized the so-called 'negative emotions' to the neglect of the more 'positive emotions', and the negative impact that emotions can have on decision making. It is now generally believed that emotions have a generally positive role in relation to thinking and the way we act. Oatley *et al.* (2006: 260) state generally that:

> emotions have principled, systematic effects upon cognitive processes, and that emotions lead to reasonable judgements of the world ... Emotions structure perception, direct attention, give preferential access to certain memories, and bias judgement in ways that help the individual respond to the environment in ways we recognise as valuable aspects to our humanity.

Emotions prioritize thoughts, goals and actions and guide interpretation of situations and events. Three positive general effects of emotions on decision making can be identified. They:

1. give information about our environment before we have had time to think about it;
2. guide where to place our attention;
3. are an important motivating force and without them there is a danger that we become complacent or insensitive.

Nevertheless, Oatley *et al.* (ibid.) also state that while emotions generally have a positive effect, intense emotions can interfere with thinking.

The argument will be put forward that in a professional activity like social work, which deals with difficult life situations, intense emotions are generated at times and there is potential for these to distort the thinking process: professional workers need to be critically aware of their emotions and manage them in a positive way. The important point is to be critically aware of the role emotions are having and make sure we are not being unduly swayed by them or our judgement clouded by them.

Theories of emotions

A theory is needed about the nature of emotional states and how they operate to help us to understand the relationship between emotions and decision making. Lazarus's (1991) cognitive-motivational-relational theory is one of many theories of the emotions and is a member of a group referred to as 'appraisal theories'. The features of the theory relevant to this chapter are:

- a decision situation can elicit an emotion if it is perceived to be personally or professionally relevant;
- the particular emotion generated will depend on the decision maker's appraisal of the situation;
- depending on the type generated, an emotion will drive or motivate a particular type of behaviour(s), a phenomenon known as the action tendency;
- the decision maker's coping pattern can override or inhibit the action tendency.

Following the work of Lazarus (1991), specific emotions will be regarded as resulting from an individual's personal appraisal of the situation he or she faces. An emotion, being the result of a person's appraisal, indicates what the person's perception or cognition of the situation is. So rather than being opposed to thinking, emotions and thinking processes are connected to each other. This means that they are not diametrically opposed to each other, as is often thought, but rather inextricably linked. Lazarus (1991: 87) states that appraisal is 'an evaluation of the significance of what is happening in the person–environment relationship for personal well being ... which is influenced by both environmental and personality variables'. Appraisal of the situation involves the rapid non-conscious evaluation of events, that is how one defines and evaluates one's relationship to the situation. It is the process by which the personal emotional meanings of a situation are constructed. According to this theory, our appraisal of the situation determines which specific emotion we experience. For example, if the appraisal is one of threat, loss or achievement this will evoke corresponding emotions of fear, unhappiness or pride.

The part of the theory we are most interested in concerns what Lazarus calls the 'action tendency'. Action tendency is the impulse to act when we experience a specific emotion. Lazarus explains that:

> if the significance of what is happening involves personal harm or benefit, an emotion is generated that includes the action tendency which provides the basis for the unique physiological activity characteristic of the each individual emotion. (1991: 40)

Lazarus (1991: 87) identifies action tendency as one of the defining features of an emotion, with each individual emotion having its own characteristic action tendency. If people perceive themselves as having been demeaned, they experience anger, and the action tendency is to retaliate. If a person feels compassion, the action tendency is to reach out and help. The action tendencies of emotions can have significant impact on thinking about decisions and need to be appropriately managed.

We may or may not act on the action tendency, and whether we do or not depends on the coping process. This is more deliberate than the action tendency and may override it or inhibit it. As Lazarus explains: 'the coping process, which may be consistent with or in conflict with the action tendency and may override or inhibit it, is more psychological, planful and deliberate and it also influences the actions and physiological pattern' (1991: 40).

Figure 5.2 is a schematic representation of how, according to appraisal theory, emotions can be related to decision making. An individual's personal appraisal of a situation generates a specific emotion with its accompanying action tendency which they may or may not act upon depending on their coping processes. The action tendency potentially influences the way the decision situation is analysed and what course of action is taken.

Gloria appraises the situation of her father returning home as one of uncertain threat and risk, and the emotion of anxiety is generated which, according to Lazarus (1991: 237), is the hallmark of uncertainty. Lazarus (1991: 238) states that the action tendency of anxiety is 'escape', but without there being anything specific to get away from, and which is experienced as vague and diffuse, and which can have either positive or negative effects on functioning, depending on the coping processes.

Gloria wants to put an end quickly to the uncertainty in the situation and is pushed towards her father going into residential care, not wanting

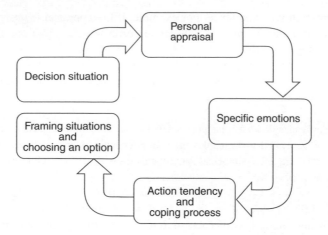

Figure 5.2   Emotions and decision making

to take the time to analyse the decision situation. As a consequence she puts pressure on Esther by continually ringing her up and asking when her father is moving into a home. The daughter makes negative comments on Esther's competence and asks her whether she knows what she is doing. Esther initially appraises the situation as one of Gloria demeaning and personally attacking her, which generates the emotion of anger, whose action tendency is to retaliate. Esther wants to tell Gloria a few 'home truths' but verbally attacking her would be considered unprofessional and so she manages to hold on to her anger until she finishes the telephone conversation. As stated, an emotion depends on the personal appraisal of the situation by the person concerned, and an important way of coping with negative emotions is to reappraise the personal meaning of the situation. Esther initially feels Gloria is demeaning her with her comments and experiences anger, but, while discussing Gloria's attitude with a colleague, she reappraises the situation as one of Gloria being worried about her father and so she ceases to experience anger.

Job satisfaction, stress and coping

Esther is feeling generally under pressure and harassed by her workload and Gloria is a source of further pressure. It could be that this pressure is the last straw and Esther goes off sick; or it might motivate her to put even more energy into thinking through the decision situation with the stakeholders. Comparatively little attention has been paid to the impact of stress on individuals' ability to think about decision situations and make and support decisions. Case-specific stress and general workload stress can be seen as potentially having different kinds of impact on thinking. Stress that emanates from the demands of the decision situation of a specific case is more likely to motivate vigilant thinking, while stress from one's workload and work environment in general is more likely to impair thinking.

There is clear evidence that social workers get job satisfaction and enjoyment from their work, despite the fact that it is a demanding and stressful job (Collins, 2008: 1176). Collins (2007: 263) states that many social workers find a sense of commitment, meaning and purpose in their work, with it being a very significant part of their personal identity. He goes on to explain how there is likely to be a continuing strong motivation to help service users and carers and that the sense of commitment and the internal meaning social workers attribute to their job can facilitate coping and mitigate psychological distress. He adds that the feeling of doing 'a worth while job', and that other professionals see it in a similar light, adds to positive self-esteem and well-being, though it is recognized to be a demanding and stressful job.

Stress

Stress in social work has been the source of some concern (Gibson *et al.*, 1989; Jones *et al.*, 1991; Storey and Billingham, 2001), but 'stress' can be defined in a number of different ways, with there being a distinction between the subjective experience of stress and the external demands on a person. Lazarus (2006: 58) states that a good way of thinking about stressful person–environment relationships is the relative balance of forces between environmental demands and the person's resources for dealing with them. Lazarus and Lazarus (1994) define stress as occurring when there is a subjective imbalance between the perceived demands made on a person and his or her perceived resources to manage these demands. Pressure may be necessary to mobilize the intellectual, emotional, social and physical resources necessary to make sound decisions; but pressure of too great an intensity, over too long a period, can have a detrimental effect. Storey and Billingham (2001: 667) found that there appeared to be a relationship between the level of stress and the worker's perception of the quality of service he or she provided. There was a level of stress that actually improved performance, while, at the same time, too high a level impaired the quality of the service provided.

There are a number of potential detrimental reactions to working under continuous stress and Collins (2008: 1178) identifies two destructive strategies: behavioural and mental disengagement. Behavioural disengagement involves reducing the effort to deal with the source of stress; mental disengagement involves emotional and cognitive disengagement. Satyamurti (1981) found that some workers coped by emotionally distancing themselves from their work and depersonalizing the people they had to deal with. Continual working under stress can result in 'burnout' that is associated with 'emotional exhaustion', 'depersonalisation of service users' and 'a sense of a lack of personal accomplishment in one's work' (Stevens and Higgins, 2002: 325). 'Emotional exhaustion' has been characterized by a lack of energy and a feeling of being worn out, while 'depersonalisation' is a negative approach to others, treating them as objects (Ben-Zur and Michael, 2007: 64). A possible relationship between these three aspects of burnout is that emotional exhaustion resulting from continual working under stress results in depersonalization of service users which in turn leads to a low sense of personal accomplishment in one's work.

Organizational factors

A traditional view is that stress is an individual problem; but within an interactional model of stress, both worker and organizational factors are important in its prevention, causation and management, with a complex interaction between many valuables (Storey and Billingham, 2001). The prevention of stress can be divided into three levels: primary, which actually prevents stress occurring in the first place by providing a good working environment; secondary, that involves detecting and intervening in the workplace when stressors have been identified but before stress is harmful; and tertiary, that promotes the recovery of individuals who are suffering from the negative effects of stress.

Employing agencies have a responsibility for the primary, secondary and tertiary prevention of stress. In terms of primary prevention, Stalker *et al.* (2007: 182) argue that managers can control important factors, such as job autonomy, supportive supervision, workload management, promotional opportunities and perception of personal safety, as well as the effective use of supervision, as discussed in Chapter 8. Secondary prevention is through managers and systems being vigilant for the first signs of undue stress, excessive demands on individuals and teams, and making it as easy as possible for employees to access sources of support and counselling. Tertiary prevention is effected by taking appropriate actions in relation to employees who display signs of 'burnout' or patterns of sickness and absence that reflect the harmful effects of high and continued experience of stress. Storey and Billingham (2001: 667) suggest that staff counselling, structured support, stress management training, staff appraisal, sabbaticals and unpaid leave may be effective strategies to help staff recover from the negative effects of stress.

Worker factors

At the individual worker level, individuals may have different capacities for coping with varying levels of pressure – with what motivates one person being the source of breakdown in another. The concept of 'hardiness' is sometimes employed to denote the quality of being able to cope with pressure. A number of factors are thought to strengthen the capacity to cope with pressure, including the willingness to access sources of support both from colleagues and managers, having supportive social networks outside work, having the ability to exert some control over work, having a clear work/personal-life boundary, and having the ability to relax away from work. Storey and Billingham (ibid.) found there was an inverse relationship between the level of support received from colleagues and managers, and the level of stress experienced, with the more support received the less stress experienced.

Generally a distinction can be made between three types of coping: problem-based coping, emotion-based coping and meaning-based coping (Collins, 2008: 1177; Howe, 2008: 104). Problem-based coping focuses on doing something about the source of stress and tends to be used when something can be done to reduce demands. Emotion-based coping is focussed on reducing or managing emotional distress and tends to be used in situations that are not amenable to change. Meaning-based coping involves the reappraisal of the source of stress and tends to be used when the problem can be reframed. Ben-Zur and Michael's (2007) study of psychological variables associated with burnout found that an important factor was practitioners' appraisal of the demands on them, in particular that the strongest factor militating against burnout at the worker level was appraising pressures in terms of challenge and controllability, rather than as overload and stress.

chapter summary

In this chapter I have presented professional wisdom as a capacity to make reflective judgements using different types of knowledge, modes of thinking and emotions. Decisions need to be made on the basis of valid knowledge, but what is 'valid knowledge' in social work remains contested. It was argued that ⊿

↘ practitioners need to give equal respect to different categories of knowledge while subjecting all of them to critical examination. Two modes of thinking were introduced, intuition and analysis, both of which are important in social work and which can be used in combination with each other. Social workers also need to be emotionally competent, which includes the capacity to contain their emotions. Social work was presented as a potentially satisfying but stressful job, with both frontline workers and managers having responsibilities for the prevention of emotional exhaustion. It was argued that agencies need to provide supportive working environments within which social workers can make and support wise decisions, based on the integration of different types of knowledge, modes of thinking and emotional competence.

key practice points: using knowledge and managing emotions

Practitioners need to:

- use all sources of knowledge critically and only base decisions on valid knowledge;
- only use their intuition when it is based on expertise developed over a period of time and then with a high degree of reflexivity;
- use analysis when working with others or when facing difficult or important decisions;
- be critically aware of and manage their emotions and have appropriate emotional involvement;.
- effectively use sources of support including supervision.

putting it into practice

1. Give some specific examples of the types of knowledge a social worker like Esther would use in her day to day work with service users and identify any difficulties in using these types of knowledge and any precautions he or she might need to take. ↘

2. Do you think Esther is right in trying to get both Mr Richmond and his daughter to analyse the situation in a more systematic way? Give reasons for your answer.
3. In what ways can Esther manage her emotional involvement with Mr Richmond and his daughter Gloria?
4. How can Esther and her agency prevent her from experiencing burnout and emotional exhaustion?

Recommended reading

L. Trinder (2000) 'A critical appraisal of evidence-based practice', in L. Trinder and S. Reynolds (eds), *Evidence-Based Practice: A Critical Appraisal*, Oxford: Blackwell Science, pp. 212–41. This chapter gives a balanced critical appraisal of an evidence-based practice approach, clearly giving the arguments for and against.

Chapter 12, 'Judgement and decision making: practical reasoning, process knowledge and critical thinking', in M. Sheppard (2006) *Social Work and Social Exclusion: The Idea of Practice*, Aldershot: Ashgate. In this chapter Michael Sheppard considers the mental processes by which practitioners reason, judge and make decisions about practice.

S. Collins (2008) 'Statutory social workers: stress, job satisfaction, coping, social support and individual differences', *British Journal of Social Work*, 38(6) 1173–92. This journal article considers the satisfaction social workers feel in their work, healthy and unhealthy coping strategies, the importance of worker resilience and sources of support.

6 | Framing situations

When making a decision, decision makers have a mental image or frame of the decision situation, constructed through the selection, interpretation and organization of information. Framing can take place both consciously and non-consciously and practitioners need to be explicit, purposeful and critical in their framing of decision situations. The framing of the decision situation or problem requires the active involvement of service users and other stakeholders and should include the identification of: key factors, outcome goals, a set of options and ways of improving the chances of the options being successful. The soundness of a decision will depend on whether the frame accurately reflects a full range of factors without the distorting effects of unfounded beliefs and biases. Practitioners need to remain critically alert to the possibility that their decision frames are distorted or biased in some way and so should keep an open mind.

practice scenario

Winston and Alice are both in their late seventies, with Alice assessed as being in the early to middle stages of dementia. During her life she has enjoyed going for walks on her own and has continued to do so. On a number of occasions recently she has been brought back by the police, who found her 'wandering' in a nearby village. Winston has become increasingly concerned that she will get lost and has taken to locking the doors to prevent her going out. The couple's son, Preston, who lives a few miles away, has become very concerned about his father not letting his mother out of the house. Bill, a social worker in the adults' team, is the care manager. The couple have home care assistance five days a week. The home care assistant has reported that Winton is very distressed at Alice's reaction to him keeping ⬦

her in. Bill decides to arrange a conference between the different stakeholders, which include Alice, Winston, Preston, the home care assistant, the community psychiatric nurse (CPN) and himself. The stakeholders are mindful of the *Mental Capacity Act 2005: Code of Practice* (Department of Constitutional Affairs, 2007), particularly of the five key principles. As they discuss the situation they will be engaged in constructing a frame of the decision situation in order to decide what to do, if anything.

Framing processes

Framing processes operate when thinking about a situation, including when assessing and analysing them. Framing is the process of constructing mental or verbal representations of situations. When we think about a decision situation, we have a mental image of it. This will have a very important influence on what we decide. So it is important that we go about constructing our mental representations of decision situations in a systematic and thoughtful way. Through collecting and analysing information, Bill has built up a picture of Alice and Winston's situation and the decisions that may need to be taken. The reliability of the information collected is always open to question, with the possibility that one misinterprets what one is told or observes, or that one is deliberately misled.

People use 'frames of reference' when framing situations, which are pre-existing interpretive schema that can either facilitate or distort decision situations. For example 'assessment frameworks' can be regarded as a kind of 'frame of reference' that are designed to facilitate the selection, organization and interpretation of information, though other frames of reference, like inappropriate biases or beliefs, can produce distorted pictures. The relationship between framing processes and structured assessments is complex. The produced 'assessments', whether written or oral reports, or mental pictures, are constructed through framing processes; but once built they become a frame of reference for future framing of the decision situation. For example, Bill's changing mental picture of Alice and Winston's situation contributed to and draws from the written assessment completed using a common assessment framework for adults.

As stated assessment frameworks can be thought of as tools designed to facilitate the framing of situations, but not everybody agrees that they are successful in doing this. For example, White *et al.* (2009: 1199) claim that they have the potential to disrupt the traditional narrative accounts of professional workers that link context, character, events and process into a coherent story. This disruptive process they refer to as 'descriptive tyranny'. However, they report that as well as disrupting many professional workers' attempts to build coherent stories of situations, other workers were able to defy the descriptive tyranny and construct a coherent story, despite the inflicted categorical structure.

Frames of situations do not only depend on the characteristics of the situations themselves but also the characteristics of decision makers. They will have their own 'frames of reference' within which frames are constructed. Hence, decision frames are always from a particular 'point of view' with each stakeholder having his or her own particular frame. Bill, Alice, Winston, Preston, the home care assistant and the CPN share certain beliefs about the situation, though there are also differences. These differences reflect the different ways they each frame the information they have, which in turn reflects differences in information selection, interpretation and organization. They are all looking at the same decision situation from their particular point of view, using their own frames of reference. Each stakeholder appears preoccupied with a different aspect of the situation. Preston is alarmed at his father's behaviour towards his mother, the CPN is worried about the risk to Alice and others when she is 'wandering', Bill sees Alice's walking as beneficial to her, while the home care assistant is concerned about Winston being so distressed at his wife's behaviour. The aim needs to be that, through collaboration, the stakeholders frame the decision situation in the most accurate, systemic and valid way possible.

There is always a danger that a person's frame of the situation remains vague, implicit or disorganized, and there are advantages in Bill and the other stakeholders explicitly constructing a decision frame together. These advantages include enabling stakeholders to have a critical awareness and reflexivity in relation to the way they are framing the situation, and making each stakeholder's thinking available to the others so that they can assess its validity and together build a critical picture of the situation.

Constructing pictures of situations

Building a picture involves analysing situations by listening to the story people tell and putting these together in terms of the relationships between people, the processes operating and the contexts in which they occur. A systemic perspective attempts to encompass the whole picture, taking into account a wide range of factors on a number of interconnected levels of analysis including the personal, interpersonal, environmental and sociocultural levels. The constructed picture needs to reflect social work's distinctive perspective which stresses the multifaceted nature of social situations, the significance of context, the uniqueness of service users and their living contexts, the importance of their perspectives, and the interconnections between past, present and future possibilities. The picture can never be regarded as finally complete and definitive, and needs to be kept under review.

Social judgement theory (Dowding, 2002: 87) can help us to understand the process by which we make sense of situations and so make judgements about them. The theory simply stated is that human beings build mental representations of social reality by combining environmental factors together to form a coherent picture. The picture depends on what factors are identified, the meaning and weight given to them and how they are put together. The psychologist Egon Brunswik likened the process by which several factors are combined together to form a mental representation of social reality to the way a camera lens collects light together to form an image (Leeper, 1966: 415). Brunswik thereby viewed judgement in terms of the relationship between the real environmental system and the decision maker's mental representation of that system (Hogarth, 1987: 8). Brunswik's depiction of the process became known as social judgement theory. Figure 6.1 depicts the ways people build up an integrated mental representation of the decision situation by combining together a number of relevant factors. These factors are 'fallible' (Hammond, 1996: 87) in the sense that they may only indicate rather than provide evidence of what is happening and so can lead to mistaken inferences.

Key factors

It is easy to get lost in the detail of descriptive information and what is needed is an analysis of this data. This will of necessity involve the identification of key factors, and the ability to do this is an important professional skill. The process of identifying key factors can be problematic as it involves critically examining information and weighing its significance. Perception is of necessity selective, there being far more information potentially available in the environment than can be processed consciously. This means that decision framing involves a series of conscious and non-conscious microdecisions about what information is selected and what meaning is given to it. These microdecisions are shaped by what decision makers believe to be important (their values), their models of how the social universe works (their social understandings and theories) and the emotions that have been generated by their appraisal of

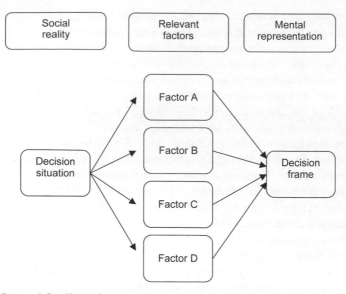

Figure 6.1   Using factors to construct mental pictures of situations
Source: Adapted from Hogarth (1987: 9).

the situation. The tendency of people to have a preoccupation with risk, harm or life problems means they can skew pictures of situations to the negative side of people's lives and explicit efforts are needed to ensure they include service-user resources, strengths and life satisfactions.

It is important that social workers have developed knowledge about life and life issues so as to be able to appreciate the significance of particular factors, though at times there may be a lack of knowledge about what factors are potentially relevant. Social workers also need the interpersonal skills necessary to communicate with people and enable them to tell their own story. For example, at times it is hard to interpret Alice's verbal communications and there is a danger that how she feels will be ignored. Bill needs the skills to interpret what she is feeling, as expressed through her non-verbal communication, including her facial expression, posture, demeanour and indeed her walking; but what is being communicated can easily be missed or misinterpreted and so not taken into account.

The key factors need to be put together to form a coherent picture of the situation, a process Imbrogno and Canada (1988: 21) refer to as building a 'creative synthesis'. This can be problematic, especially when there is ambiguity about what sense to make of the information. For example, does Winston's locking the doors and preventing Alice from leaving the house constitute abuse or care? Notwithstanding the problematic nature of how the factors fit together, they need to be placed in relation to each other to form a coherent integrated picture. There are constraints in obtaining a full picture, including limits on the human capacity to process information, limits on time and the information not being obtainable.

'Objective facts' or 'social constructions'?

Social judgement theory makes a distinction between reality independent of human consciousness and our descriptions and representations of it. Within the philosophy of science many questions have been raised about the nature of the relationship between these two domains, including: does it make any sense to believe that a 'reality' independent of human consciousness exists? What status should our descriptions and representations of reality have? Are some descriptions more accurate than others? For example, the practice scenario in this chapter states that the police 'find Alice "wandering" in a nearly village'. Should this be regarded as an 'objective fact' or a 'social construction'?

Objective facts

When key factors are regarded as *facts*, decision makers endeavour to be 'objective' rather than 'subjective' in their framing of the decision situation, with objectivity being considered possible and subjectivity as something that can be avoided. The existence of an objective reality about which human beings can establish 'the facts' is not questioned. There is a belief in an independent reality external to the mind that can be established through reliable observation. A distinction is made between what are regarded as 'facts' in a taken-for-granted way and what are regarded as 'facts' after careful investigation.

The strength of 'the facts approach' is the emphasis on empirically verifiable evidence that guards against spurious inferences. However, reducing pictures of decision situations to what can be 'objectively' observed will mean important aspects will be missing and that the meaning of those 'facts' are likely not to be as 'objective' as the decision makers may believe. It is hard, if not impossible, to describe objectively the actions of human beings without interpretation. For example, when Algase *et al.* (2007: 697) searched for the concept of 'wandering' in the contents of scientific databases they found that the term had broadly two sets of connotations. They found a high degree of agreement and most concern expressed about 'straying' and 'leaving'. The second set, 'meandering' and 'foraying/exploring' were less prominent in the literature but suggested some possible benefits of 'wandering' as a pastime and a means of addressing needs. The authors had a great deal of difficulty in producing an 'objective' definition of 'wandering' that omitted both sets of connotations.

Social constructions

Within the social constructionist perspective, decision framing is an active process in which the mental picture is socially constructed and is more a cultural story than a mental representation of 'reality'. The existence of an 'objective reality' independent of human language and thought is questioned. This perspective takes a critical stance towards all knowledge, including that regarded as 'facts' (Burr, 2003). The raw materials of the construction of reality are found in the reservoir of cultural meanings embedded in language. Social reality is a cultural product, something that human beings have more or less developed a consensus about within particular cultural contexts (Berger and Luckmann, 1966). Through 'negotiated intelligibility' (Gergen, 1985) certain actions and experiences can become accepted as true – hence describing Alice's behaviour as 'wandering' is part of a cultural story constructed through language and dominant discourses.

This view of the picture emphasizes the power of those who are in positions 'to determine how situations are to be understood and what knowledge is to count as relevant' (Howe, 1994: 526). A social constructionist approach can make all frames of a decision situation problematic – allowing for the possibility of reframing; for example, Bill's endeavours to get the stakeholders to reframe Alice's 'wandering' as 'walking' (Marshall and Allen, 2006). Within this perspective all decision frames are provisional, which is an advantage from the point of view of being open to review and reframing, but it can appear to trivialize the 'real' risks people face, with the danger that the approach descends into extreme relativism.

'Critical interpretations'

It is increasingly recognized that each of these perspectives holds some 'truth', but on their own they are inadequate and the subjectivist and objectivist perspectives on 'reality' need to be integrated (Houston, 2001). For example, 'critical realism' recognizes the existence and importance of both the 'real world' and the 'conceptual' one and does not accept the 'either–or' approach but proposes a 'both–and' perspective (Dannermark et al., 2002). Within what could be called a 'critical interpretations view', there is a 'real world' in which 'real events' happen but true objective knowledge of that world independent of the human mind is not possible. The aim is, through critical analysis, to get as close to this reality as possible. This will involve critical awareness, critical engagement, critical observation, critical listening, critical thinking and critical framing. In particular there is an acute awareness that the best we can hope for is an accurate and valid interpretation about which we still need to keep an open mind. Within this perspective, the police reporting that Alice was found 'wandering' is no longer so 'factual' but merely their interpretation of what they found, and the challenge is to develop this into a more critical interpretation.

No matter how the picture of a situation is regarded, identifying key factors and putting them together should not be a once and for all event, but a process in which the picture is under continual review and development. Decision makers may at first have a relatively open mind about the nature of the decision situation. This soon becomes structured through the framing processes, with the danger of minds becoming closed to the reception of any new information or perspectives that contradict these initial frames. In contrast, decision framing needs to be 'iterative', a term used by Thompson (1996: 173) when discussing the assessment process, which means that it needs to be a cyclic process continually striving to improve the understanding of the nature of the decision situation and the processes operating. It may be best to regard our pictures of situations as hypotheses that are subject to change, either on the basis of new information or as a reinterpretation of existing information that provides opportunities for reframing. It would be easy for Alice's continuing desire to walk to be simply seen as a symptom of her dementia and that her walking is aimless and lacks any purpose. It can be more difficult to reframe her 'wandering' as purposeful 'walking'.

Building a decision frame

Workers can think of analysing decision situations as answering a number of questions, including: what are the key factors in the situation? How can these factors be put together to form a coherent picture? What are our goals? How can we achieve them? What is being suggested is that when people are making important decisions they need to be systematic and reflexive about how they are thinking about the situation facing them. What is needed is a succinct summary of the understandings that have been built by collecting and analysing information through assessment processes. At a minimum, an explicit frame needs to include the:

● identified key factors in the situation;
● outcome(s) decision makers want to achieve;

- options they have to achieve these outcomes;
- ways of improving the chances of a good outcome.

Identifying key factors

As a first step it might be helpful to list the identified factors to form a succinct summary of the decision makers' understanding of the situation. The stakeholders' list of key factors in Alice and Winston's situation included:

- In the recent past Alice has been regularly going on walks and returning safely.
- Recent incidents of Alice not returning and being brought back by the police have alarmed Winston.
- Winston's main concern and priority is Alice's safety.
- At present Winton is confining Alice to the house.
- The home care assistant is concerned about the affect on both Winston and Alice of her being confined to the house.
- Alice does not always give coherent answers to questions and so it is not always possible to ascertain her wishes directly, though from her non-verbal communication she appears to be distressed and agitated at present.
- Winston is also distressed and exasperated by his wife's behaviour.
- Winston wants to remain with his wife in their own home and believes that she wants to stay with him.
- Preston is very concerned about his father trying to confine his mother to the house and the affect it is having on her.
- The GP has found slight bruising on Alice's arms, but is unsure whether this results from Winston holding her. There is no known history of violence between the couple.

The stakeholders in the situation are committed to Alice staying in her own home, as long as either she or her husband do not experience unacceptable levels of distress or harm.

Identifying outcome goals

Outcome goals will be defined as desired or planned outcomes in relation to the service user's own life situation and well-being. The purpose of social work can be framed as helping people to achieve good outcomes, making the identification of desirable outcomes very important. Social workers can have an important role in helping service users to identify the outcomes they would like to achieve, though the various stakeholders potentially have different goals, and the degree to which they can negotiate agreement will depend on a number of factors. Social workers can help to frame outcome goals in such a way that they have the widest possibility of being accepted by all stakeholders, though it is not usual in social work for decision making to proceed with a recognition that the stakeholders have different goals.

Practitioners can have difficulty in clearly identifying outcome goals, possibly as a consequence of confusing 'process' and 'outcome'. When asked to identify outcome goals some practitioners may refer to services, interventions or other processes like 'working together'. These processes of achieving outcomes are very important in their own right, but should not be confused with the desired-for outcomes themselves. In the past social work has been criticized for overemphasizing processes at the expense of outcomes, and partly as a consequence explicit outcome frameworks have been developed within the 'Every Child Matters' and 'Adult Social Care' policy agendas. May-Chahal and Broadhurst (2006) point out how in their research what service users and agencies framed as desirable outcomes differed, and that the former did so in terms of their life relevance, while the latter did so in terms of organizational relevance. They concluded that agencies need to take more account of how service users define what a 'good outcome' would be.

A distinction can be made between shorter-term goals and longer-term goals, with a potential tension existing between immediate concerns and long-term planning. Short-termism involves being preoccupied by the immediacy of the situation and losing sight of longer-term considerations. To make sure there is no neglect, conflict or confusion between shorter- and longer-term outcomes decision makers can explicitly identify both types of goals. Shorter-term goals can be identified by asking: what do we want to achieve in the short term? All the stakeholders agree that the desirable short-term outcome is the easing of the mental distress both Winston and Alice are currently experiencing. Longer-term outcomes tend to relate to people's aspirations for human development, quality of life and states of well-being, which can be lost sight of in the immediacy of the situation. Longer-term outcomes can be identified by asking the question: in the longer-term, how do we want the outcome to be judged? This question gives the decision makers an appropriate time perspective to consider their longer-term outcomes and starts them thinking about desirable outcomes. All those at the meeting agreed that the longer-term outcomes were for both Alice and Winston to have an acceptable quality of life, while remaining in their home environment as long as possible.

Identifying options

The explicit identification of options is a part of sound decision framing. Options are not objective facts waiting to be discovered but rather are constructed by the decision makers within the limitations of their creativity and the contextual parameters in which they operate. This systematic approach to decision making is not as common as might first be thought. Rather than considering a set of options there is a tendency for human beings to take a more pragmatic approach and have only one option in the frame at any one time, with no simultaneous consideration of a range of options, with the search for a solution ending as soon as a minimally satisfactory option is found. Within the decision-making literature, this is referred to as 'satisficing' (Beach, 1990: 106), where decision makers take the first satisfactory solution they come across without comparing it with other options. The order in which the alternatives are examined may be more or less haphazard, which can mean other more appropriate options may not be considered because an apparently satisfactory solution has already been found and the search finished. This is a method of decision making commonly adopted in everyday life: for example, buying the first satisfactory car found despite there being other car dealers to visit.

At the opposite end of the spectrum of 'satisficing' is taking a 'scattergun' approach, where every course of action that the decision makers can think of is included in the decision frame to be either subjected to analysis or 'immediately thrown' at the situation in the hope that something will work. What is needed is an integrated, focused and targeted approach to identifying options. There is a limit to the number of options that can be usefully considered and it may be best to first think in terms of choosing between broad courses of action, for example between 'Alice remains at home' and 'Alice moves to residential care', alongside the different ways these options could be implemented. The stakeholders' outcome goals meant that they quickly moved on to consider what to do about Alice's need to walk and Winston's response. The stakeholders identified two options: 'preventing Alice going out' and 'assisting Alice to go for walks'. When they have decided which of these courses of action to take, they will be faced with other choices.

Imaginative identification of options requires that decision makers are critically aware of possible paths, services and assistive technologies while taking into account contextual constraints and opportunities. Eadie and Lymbery (2007: 671) argue that creativity is not an optional extra but needs to become an integral feature of practice so that service users receive the service and support they need. They go on to argue that this requires professional education and organizations to enable practitioners to develop creative approaches to their practice. Very real constraints are likely to exist within the practice environment and the decision situation, and it is these very constraints that mean social workers need to be creative and see opportunities where others might only see obstacles. A prominent constraint is the level and quality of available resources; however, workers and service users can often use the resources that do exist in creative ways.

Legislation and its associated procedures and guidance also have an important role in the shaping of options. Options can take the form of following different legal or procedural routes, as for example in child care when the options may be whether to seek an Emergency Protection Order or not. Whether legal requirements are met is often an important consideration as to whether a course of action is a viable option. Like resources, legislation is both a constraint and an opportunity for creativity. There can be a tendency to regard the law as a restricting force but it can also be considered as a vehicle for opening-up possibilities rather than closing them down (Dalrymple and Burke, 2006). There is also the issue of how far social workers should just accept the legislative status quo, or campaign for new laws or changes to the existing laws, when these do not work in practice or are a source of injustice, for example the debate about the need for protective legislation for vulnerable adults, similar to that which exists in respect of children (Penhale and Parker, 2008: 37; Blake, 2009: 14).

Improving the chances of the options achieving outcome goals

Success will be measured in relation to whether the chosen option achieves the outcome goals or not, and the decision frame can usefully include ways of improving the chances of the options being successful. There are at least two reasons for this. First, it helps avoid the potential confusion between outcome goals and ways of helping achieve these desirable outcomes. Second, it is important to recognize explicitly that stakeholders can often take supportive actions to increase the chances of an option achieving the planned outcome. It is important when it comes to analysing an option's possible consequences to have in mind any services, technologies and actions that will accompany that option. Workers can draw a distinction between general and specific ways of increasing the chances of a good outcome. Generally anything that improves the soundness of a decision will improve such chances, for example the stakeholders being effectively involved in making the decision. There are also likely to be specific ways of improving the chances of a particular option having a good outcome. For example, there are many ways of improving the chances of helping and supporting Alice to walk being a success.

In fact choosing which combination of actions, services and technologies will be most effective in helping the broad courses of action to achieve the outcome goals may become the next decision within an overall problem-solving process. For example, the professional stakeholders think the use of assistive technologies would be a way of improving the chances of the 'helping Alice to walk safely' having a good outcome. An electronic tracking device would help Winston locate Alice if she did not return home of her own accord. The ways risks can be managed can become the subject of negotiation, with the use of such devices likely to be subjected to ethical reasoning. In Robinson *et al.*'s (2007) study, the people with dementia spoke of the need for independence and had concerns about carer surveillance; while a major theme for carers was the conflict between the prevention of harm and the facilitation of a person's right to autonomy. They explained how such tensions impacted on carers' abilities to provide person-centred care.

Choosing between the options will not be considered here, as this is the subject matter of the next chapter, but it is important to note that considerable uncertainty surrounds what the actual outcomes of the different options will be and the value these outcomes will actually have for service users. To take just one example, the stakeholders do not know what the actual outcome of helping and supporting Alice walking will be and whether they will agree that is a good or bad outcome.

Decision frames and distortion

As has been stated decision framing involves the use of frames of reference that can either facilitate or distort the decision situation. To distort the decision frame is to represent or think about the decision situation in a misleading, biased or less than accurate way. It is true that there is no one correct decision frame, nevertheless the decision situation can be misrepresented through various types of inappropriate beliefs and biases that are used as frames of reference. The work of Russo *et al.* (1996) demonstrates that predecisional distortion can affect the evaluation of information and subsequent choices. Here we will focus on potential biases, distorting beliefs and predispositions. These include confirmation bias, a deficits approach, the rule of optimism and personal beliefs. An important subset of sources of distortion are those that potentially operate when working across difference, namely stereotypes, oppressive beliefs and ethnocentrism. Sources of distortion operate in a number of ways, for example through selective attention, making assumptions and developing a mindset. The existence of potential sources of distortion means that professional workers need to be reflexive in their practice and take a critical questioning approach to constructing their pictures of situations.

Confirmation bias

Confirmation bias is a tendency that human beings have to seek out, emphasize or interpret information that confirms their initial impressions or assumptions. Littell (2008: 1300) defines confirmation bias as a 'tendency to emphasise evidence that supports a hypothesis and ignores evidence to the contrary'. As Sheppard (1995: 183) states, instead of continually questioning whether their interpretations are the most accurate, 'people tend actively to seek out information which confirms their initial interpretations. In the process they have a tendency to ignore observations and evidence which might disconfirm or falsify their interpretation'. For example, if Bill, very early on, forms an opinion that Winston is not abusing Alice, there is a danger that he will seek or emphasize information that confirms his initial opinion and ignore information that sheds doubt on it. As well as seeking to confirm initial hypotheses, the minds of decision makers can become predisposed to seeing the decision situation in a particular way, as when the Orkney inquiry found that the minds of the managers considering the removal of a number of children from their families were predisposed towards confirming allegations of ritual abuse (Clyde, 1992: 229). Decision makers need to be reflexive about the way the decision situation is being framed, with a continuous questioning of the interpretations and assumptions being made, actively seeking information that sheds doubt on these and making any adjustments necessary in the light of this ongoing examination.

Deficits approach

Another potential bias is the way professionals and non-professionals can have a tendency to focus on deficits when assessing situations. In order to counteract this, Saleebey (2009) and others developed and promoted a 'strengths perspective'. McCormack (2007: 7) states that the strengths perspective does not deny that serious problems can exist but rather that they are not the whole story. He argues that it is not as if the 'strengths' are not present in the situation but that they tend not to be recognized as such, and many people do not have a vocabulary to describe strengths and abilities. He gives the example of the difficulty some job applicants have when asked to identify their strengths.

The strengths perspective is important in overcoming the apparent inbuilt bias towards deficits, though there is a danger some practitioners over compensate and neglect difficulties. As Healy (2005: 169) states, the strengths perspective is 'an important corrective to a pathologizing view of human service users, [however] we must be careful of also underestimating the elevated risks facing vulnerable populations'. When framing decision situations, a balanced approach is needed where relevant strengths are included, as well as the needs, problems and difficulties being experienced. In practice social workers need to examine critically the way they are framing key factors to check that strengths have been included. Also, it is quite possible to reframe some 'deficits' more neutrally without any loss of relevant information.

Rule of optimism

There is a danger that social workers fall foul of what has been called the 'rule of optimism', which has been used to explain errors in judgement and decision making. The term was used in the report of the inquiry into the death of Jasmine Brentford (Blom-Cooper, 1985: 216) to refer to the way social workers had a tendency to exaggerate progress and to see it where there had been none. This concept is credited to Dingwall *et al.* (1983) and is still in use. For example, the BBC (2007) had the headline 'Cruelty Missed through "Optimism"'. The so called 'rule of optimism' is a type of wishful thinking, self-deception and unwarranted optimism by which professionals think the best of those they work with, misinterpret or deny signs of harm, minimize concerns and are over-optimistic about the prospects of improvement. Hill (1990: 201) states how Dingwall *et al.* (1983) highlighted a number of pressures on social workers to think favourably of parents, including: the social norm of respecting parental privacy and autonomy; the social work principle of acceptance; the need to enlist cooperation for the sake of the child; and the likelihood of having to work with the parents in future.

There are different perspectives on optimism. For example, Peterson (2000: 44) states that research by a number of psychologists has documented the benefits of optimism and the drawbacks of pessimism. He states that optimism, however it is measured, has links to such desirable characteristics as happiness, perseverance, achievement and health. However, it is important to distinguish between optimism and hope.

Optimism commonly is defined as a *generalized* confident expectancy that good outcomes will occur (Webb, 2007: 73). In contrast, Webb (ibid.) identifies 'estimative hope' as involving a belief that there is a possibility of a positive outcome, coupled with anxiety about the potential for a negative one. Hence, despite the general benefits of an optimistic outlook, when it comes to solving specific life difficulties and problems in conditions of uncertainty, it is important to recognize the danger of unfounded optimism and the necessity of hope.

Less often referred to but equally important is the impact of being unduly pessimistic about the future and failing to recognize the strengths in the situation and a lack in the belief that improvements can be made. Parton (1986, cited in Braye and Preston-Shoot, 1997: 78) refers to a 'rule of pessimism', where decisions to keep neglected children with their families are influenced by concern about poor quality care provision. This moves the concept out of the realm of individual professional attitudes to the organization of services and their quality. Both inappropriate optimism and inappropriate pessimism can negatively impact on what key factors are identified, how outcome goals are formulated, what options are included and eventually what option is chosen. If Bill were to advocate that Alice should be set free to walk as she pleases, without surveillance of any kind, he could potentially be accused of falling into the trap of the 'rule of optimism'.

Personal beliefs

There are arguments for and against social workers separating their personal lives from their professional lives (Banks, 2006: 134). An argument is that personal beliefs can potentially distort the decision situation and that there is a danger that practitioners are unaware of the impact they can have on their professional work. Social workers learn about life issues and processes during their training and through reflective practice, but beliefs about life are also formed through specific personal experiences. Ideas about birth and death, being a child, becoming adult, families, being a parent, the upbringing of children, relationships and growing old are developed through life experience. These potentially can make a positive contribution to professional work, but there is the potential for them to be both conscious and non-conscious sources of distortion. The 'use of self' is considered important in social work, as is being 'authentic' (Dewane, 2006), though there are a number of pitfalls in practitioners using personal life experiences to inform their framing of decision situations, for example over-identification, making assumptions and having rigid views.

Although having direct experience of life events can contribute to sound decision framing it needs to be done without the expectation that others will have a similar experience. This may only be possible if the issue has been worked through in a way that promotes insight and understanding. There is a danger that practitioners over-identify with stakeholders who have experienced similar life events to them. For example, the CPN's father is in a care home, and there is a danger that she over-identifies with Preston who wants his mother to go into residential care. As a defence against guilt, she may overemphasize the positive benefits of residential care and the dangers of staying in one's own home. This is not to say that personal life experiences cannot be a benefit in professional work, and if practitioners have satisfactorily resolved particular life issues they may be in a stronger position to work with people experiencing similar difficulties. For example, former drug users, with the insights and understandings gained, may be in a good position to work effectively with those who want to stop using drugs.

Working across difference

The likelihood of distortion may increase when working across difference. There are a number of dimensions of difference in society, including those of ethnic group, gender, 'race', age, sexuality, disability, religion, class and others – and practitioners will inevitably be involved in working across one of more of these differences. Difference is an important source of social identity for individuals and groups, as well as a source of richness and variety in society. However, difference can also be a source of privilege, oppression, discrimination and inequality. Social workers like other people have been brought up within a particular cultural context and occupy particular social positions, which means they will have been socialized into particular roles and learnt particular beliefs. They will be members of particular social groups yet practice in a multi-cultural and socially diverse society. Hence, there will always be a danger that their framing of decision situations will be distorted in some way.

Stereotypes

Mullaly (2002: 84) argues that one way in which dominant groups maintain their power and privilege is through the use of stereotypes, which he defines as biased, oversimplified, universal and inflexible conceptions of social groups. Gudykunst (1998: 122) states that stereotypes are the pictures we have of members of the various social categories we use. He identifies three aspects of stereotypes:

1. we categorize others based on easily identifiable characteristics;
2. we assume that certain attributes apply to most or all of the people in the category;
3. we assume that individual members of the category have the attributes associated with their group.

Hence, a stereotype is an image or picture of a particular 'person type', for example a stereotype of an 'older person'. Such beliefs about group members can be taken-for-granted and as a consequence we may not be consciously aware of them. 'Stereotyping' is applying the stereotype to a particular person, regardless of his or her own individual characteristics; for example, seeing Alice in terms of a stereotype of a person with dementia who aimlessly wanders without purpose or meaning. By definition all stereotypes, whether positive or negative, statistically true or untrue, have a distorting effect as they are applied without regard to the particular circumstances and characteristics of the individual concerned. There can be some statistical truth in stereotypes; however, even when this is the case, not all members of a group will share any particular stereotypical feature. Hence stereotypes, whether positive or negative, should not be used within the construction of the decision frame – but there is a danger that they are.

Oppressive beliefs

Related to stereotypes are oppressive beliefs and myths about different groups, which also can have distorting effects on decision frames. A number of oppressive belief systems have been identified, including racism, sexism, heterosexism, ageism and ablism (Mullaly, 2002: 162–8). Smith (2008: 43) identifies a process of negative attribution that reinforces the sense of membership of one's own group and at the same time underlines the negative value associated with those who are seen as 'not one of us'. These negative attributions can have a direct impact on the decision frame and so how decisions are made, for example when low priority is given to an older service user's mental-health needs solely on the basis of the preconceptions younger people have about older people's needs.

Oppressive beliefs and myths can also operate in indirect ways. For example, Lord Laming in his report into the death of Victoria Climbie draws attention to how racism can have an expression in ways other than the direct application of prejudice and that this may have allowed the focus to shift from Victoria's fundamental needs. Lord Laming (2003: 245–7) states that:

Victoria was a black child who was murdered by her two black carers. Many of the professionals with whom she came into contact during her life in this country were also black. Therefore, it is tempting to conclude that racism can have had no part to play in her case. But such a conclusion fails to recognise that racism finds expression in many ways other than in the direct application of prejudice.

These included: a fear of being accused of racism stopping people acting when otherwise they would; workers responding differently for fear of being thought unsympathetic to someone of the same 'race'; and misplaced assumptions about Victoria's cultural circumstances. For example, Victoria 'standing to attention' was misinterpreted as reflecting cultural respect and obedience. Social workers and other professionals who are well aware of the negative impact of racism and other forms of oppression still need to be vigilant about the ways these can have more subtle indirect effects.

Ethnocentrism and different ways of life

Gudykunst (1998: 106) argues that everyone is ethnocentric to some extent and the question is simply one of: to what degree? Ethnocentrism is to view one's own group as the centre of everything and to scale and rate others with reference to it. There is a danger that practitioners have an ethnocentric view and regard their own way of life as the natural way of doing things, which leads to the making of assumptions and insensitivity. Professionals have a right to their own way of life, but in a multicultural society there needs to be awareness and appreciation that different people have different ways of living and different ways of doing things. When workers have achieved awareness, understanding and valuing of different ways of life there is a danger of overreliance on cultural explanations of problems and ignoring emotional, interpersonal and structural factors (Ahmed, 1986: 140). Culture sets an important context for understanding decision situations but it is only one of a number of important factors to be taken into consideration.

From particular cultural positions some differences between ways of life are highly controversial, being seen as going against some core value that transcends culture. For example, regarding women in a particular culture as oppressed, or a particular pattern of family life as being irresponsible. There are at least two positions in relation to clashes of cultural values. The first is *cultural relativity*, with all cross-cultural evaluations being seen as invalid. Within this position, actions or lack of actions that may be labelled abuse or neglect by outsiders should only be judged within that culture's own standards. This might involve, for example, accepting a higher level of physical chastisement from a parent because such punishment is thought to be (erroneously or not) part of a particular culture's way of doing things.

The other position is of *value absolutism*, with core values being absolute rather than relative, with some cultural practices being regarded as oppressive or wrong – for example, female circumcision being regarded as child abuse. Within social work both extreme relativism and absolutism are hazardous. There is a need for a balance between sensitivity to different ways of doing things and a clear sense of what is unacceptable (Stevenson, 1989: 201). What is unacceptable is, to some extent, defined by the laws of the nation state in which the social worker is practising, although workers and service users can question the fairness or adequacy of these laws. Lord Laming (2003: 346) repeated the point about defining what is unacceptable when he stated that:

> Every child in this country is entitled to be given the protection of the law, regardless of his or her background. Cultural heritage is important to many people, but it cannot take precedence over standards of childcare embodied in law.

Nevertheless laws need interpretation; of necessity there needs to be areas of discretion: so the twin hazards of cultural superiority on the one hand, and accepting the unacceptable as cultural practice on the other, remain.

chapter summary

Decision framing was presented as a process of selecting, interpreting and organizing information to form a picture of the situation. Framing processes operate in the production of assessments, both in terms of written reports and mental pictures. In the chapter I have focused on three aspects of decision framing: constructing pictures of the situation, formulating outcome goals and building options. It was argued that social workers need to be reflexive in their framing and critically examine the way they are thinking, feeling and acting, if they are to avoid distorting the decision situation. They need to examine critically their own thinking for signs of confirmation bias, a deficits approach and the 'rule of optimism'. When working across difference, practi- ➘

tioners need to be aware of the operation of stereotypes and other oppressive beliefs, including ethnocentrism. A balanced approach is needed that takes account of strengths as well as deficits; in particular practitioners should not be too quick to form firm opinions and should remain critically aware of the need to keep hypotheses under review and look for disconfirming as well as confirming information.

key practice points: framing situations

Practitioners and other stakeholders need to:

- be aware that they have a constructed picture of the situation that needs to be reflexively examined for unfounded assumptions and other forms of distortion;
- be able to identify carefully key factors in the situation, outcome goals and options;
- be aware of confirmation bias and be alert to information that sheds doubt on currently favoured hypotheses;
- be on the look out for the operation of the unfounded optimism while recognizing the need for hope;
- avoid a deficits approach and take care to identify and acknowledge strengths;
- be aware that stereotypes and other oppressive beliefs can distort the decision frame.

putting it into practice

1. How do you think Alice's 'wandering' should be framed: as aimless wandering or purposeful walking? What factors do you think the framing should be based on?
2. Critically examine the key factors of the practice scenario identified in the chapter and suggest improvements to the way stakeholders framed the situation.
3. What do you think are the main potential sources of distortion in the framing of the practice scenario?

Recommended reading

'Introduction: power in the people', Chapter 1, in D. Saleebey (ed.) (2009) *The Strengths Perspective in Social Work Practice*, 5th edn, Boston: Pearson. In this chapter Dennis Saleebey explains how the strengths perspective is a lens through which to view the world.

'Assessment', Chapter 10, in J. Dalrymple and B. Burke (2006) *Anti-Oppressive Practice: Social Care and the Law*, 2nd edn, Buckingham: Open University Press. This chapter presents an informed and reflexive approach to assessment processes which recognizes that they cannot be purely objective.

C. May-Chahal and K. Broadhurst (2006) 'Integrating objects of intervention and organisational relevance: the case of safeguarding children missing from education systems', *Child Abuse Review*, 15(6) 440–55. This journal article is about the potential conflict between professional and service-user framing of problems and why it is important to understand how service users are framing their situation.

7 | Analysing options

Decision making has been defined as making a choice between two or more options, though how such choices should be made is contested. Two broad forms of decision making have been identified – intuitive decision making and deliberative decision making – and it has been argued that both types have a place in social work. In this chapter I will focus on deliberative decision making in which decision makers are explicit about how options are being analysed and choices made.

Standing in contrast to this is 'naturalistic decision making', a term Klein (1999) uses to refer to how practitioners make decisions in field settings using their experience and intuition. He studied experienced decision makers, like fire-fighters under time pressure, making high-stake choices with inadequate information in dynamic conditions. His research shows that these decision makers built mental simulations to make decisions rapidly and non-consciously using situational cues to make comparisons with similar situations they have come across in the past. In relatively routine day-to-day decision making, and when rapid decision making is required, experienced social workers are likely to use naturalistic decision making, though in many situations they need to take a more open, deliberative and analytical approach, particularly when working with others, to make important decisions. However, within this more deliberative analytical approach, stakeholders will need to incorporate their intuitive judgements.

In this chapter I will consider an open, deliberative and analytical approach to making a choice between options. Ethical theory, risk theory and decision theory will be used to analyse courses of action and build arguments as to which is the best option. This explicit integrative approach gives the opportunity for greater openness in decision making and the full involvement of service users and carers. Social workers, together with service users and other stakeholders, can manage uncertainty by making ethical, risk and probability judgements as to which is the best course of action.

> **practice scenario**
>
> Rita has just turned 15 years old, and is a young British Asian woman whose parents emigrated from Bangladesh some time ago. There has been a high level of conflict between Rita and her family, particularly her father, due to what he regards as inappropriate behaviour for her age and cultural background. This included staying out late, having older male friends and under-achieving at school. She was reluctantly accommodated by the local authority when she ran away from home following a major family crisis amidst fears that she was being sexually exploited by older male acquaintances. Rita's parents are pleased that their daughter is safe and are looking forward to when she wants to return home. Joyce, a white British social worker, is involved with Rita and her family. Rita has been placed with a well-respected foster family of similar ethnic background while work towards her reconciliation with her family is undertaken.
>
> The placement is going reasonably well but Rita is engaging in some disruptive behaviour within the foster home and tensions are developing between her and the foster father. However, Rita is attending her new school, seems happy there, is having positive contact with her family, whom she visits most weekends, and family relationships appear to be improving. Joyce is working closely with Rita, the educational psychologist, a local project worker and both families. A scheduled review is imminent which will consider the progress of the rehabilitation plan and whether the time is right for Rita to return home which at present she seems ambivalent about doing.

Ethical theories and making decisions

Given that social workers strive to be ethical in their work it is not surprising that ethics play an important part in deciding between courses of action. Reamer (1993: 78) believes that it is useful for practitioners to have a grasp of ethical theories and their connections to social work. Three broad theoretical approaches to ethical decision making will be considered: *virtue ethics*, concerned with the moral character of the decision maker and what a virtuous person would do; *deontological ethics*, concerned with choosing the course of action that is morally the right thing to do in itself; and *consequentialist ethics*, concerned with choosing the course of action that achieves the best chance of a good outcome. In summary, the three ethical theories respectively concern, the character of the decision maker, the actions they take and the consequences of these actions.

Clark (2000: 69) makes a distinction between 'the ethics of personal service' and 'the ethics of social reform'. He states that the ethic of personal service places the unique human being at the centre of attention, with the prime aim of promoting his or her welfare and best interests. However, one criticism of the ethics of personal service is that it neglects the cause of many social problems and the need to reform society. The primary aim of social reformism is amelioration of the social conditions that are seen as the root cause of many individual, family and community difficulties. In this chapter our concern is with the ethics of personal service, how choices are made within particular decision situations and what are good and right decisions in day-to-day social work practice. However, as has been previously stated, a social worker's ethical obligations do not stop there but extend, at the very least, to drawing to the attention of government and others the root causes of the problems that social workers respond to on behalf of society.

Virtue ethics

Within virtue ethics, it is not the goodness of the action itself or the consequences of the action that we should be looking at in order to decide what is the ethically right or good thing to do, but rather the qualities needed by the individual decision makers: including the nature of their character and the quality of their relationships with others. Hughes and Baldwin (2006) define virtues as inner dispositions that aim to do good, and that within virtue ethics the right action or good decision is what the virtuous person would do. However, there are different conceptions of what human virtues we should be striving for, and different virtue-based frameworks reflect different assumptions, particularly about the nature of human relationships and the kind of society we should be living in (Rhodes, 1986: 42). It is doubtful whether, in a society characterized by diversity, it is possible to identify a universal set of virtues that are outside existing belief frameworks. However, a virtual ethics for social work that depicts the qualities required by the good social worker should be more possible, though still difficult, even within any particular nation state.

Within social work there may be broad areas of agreement about the virtues required to do the work, but important differences in emphasis remain. Hughes and Baldwin (2006: 88) explain that 'if I ought to do what the virtuous person would do, I should show charity, truthfulness, compassion, faithfulness, generosity, prudence and so on'. Rhodes (1986: 42) points to compassion, detached caring, warmth and honesty as virtues to be found in social work texts, and adds moral courage, hopefulness and humility. Bowles *et al.* (2006: 56) state that their approach to 'ethical practice is a virtue approach, because [they] are trying to advance agreement in favour of doing social work in a particular way and in favour of developing certain traits such as moral courage and activism'. McBeath and Webb (2002: 1015) argue that the role of the virtuous social worker is one that requires 'appropriate application of intellectual and practical virtues such as justice, reflection, perception, judgement, bravery, prudence, liberality and temperance'. In Chapter 5 I argued that professional wisdom is necessary to carry out social work, which is the same as saying that social workers require the quality or virtue of practical wisdom: that is the practical ability to understand and respond appropriately to difficult problems and dilemmas.

The weaknesses of virtue ethics are: its vagueness in identifying the virtues that a good person or good social worker should have, and agreeing what having these virtues means; how one acquires them; and how they are to be enacted in specific decision situations. Fitzpatrick (2008: 88) points out that the very vagueness of virtue ethics is also its strength, as it repeatedly draws attention to the inadequacy of looking solely at either consequences of actions or at the goodness of the action itself but that we also need to look at the character of the actor and the nature of his or her relationships with others.

Deontological ethics

Deontological ethics – the ethics of duty – concerns the rightness of a course of action in itself. This is not legal duty but ethical duty, concerned with doing the right thing regardless of what the outcome might be. Baron (2000: 395), when referring to what he calls 'rights theories', states 'that they are deontological because they specify what we can and cannot do to each other regardless of the consequences'. He explains that 'such rules are described in terms of the conditions not the consequences, even though conditions may be correlated with consequences' (ibid.: 394). Fitzpatrick (2008) describes how deontological ethics concerns how moral obligation to take a course of action comes from 'principles that make little or no reference to consequences' and that the resulting ethical decisions are made according to generalizable rules and principles. For example, always telling the truth or always keeping promises, even if the consequences are unwelcome (Clark, 2000: 71).

There are a number of ideas operating in social work that potentially take the form of deontological principles that could have a strong influence on making decisions about Rita's future. These include self-determination, acceptance, non-judgmentality and confidentiality. Banks (2001: 27) states, 'a key theme running through all these principles could be identified as the Kantian theme of respect of the individual person as a self-determining being'. As well as a guide to moral behaviour, all the above principles could also be seen as moral rights: the right to determine one's future, the right to be accepted, the right not to be morally judged, the right to be respected as a unique human being, the right to confidentiality and the right to privacy.

Consequentialist ethics

Consequentialist ethics is not so concerned about doing the morally right thing but achieving an outcome with good consequences. It is concerned with the consequences of taking a particular course of action, not so much the rightness of the action in itself. As Clark (2000: 72) states, 'consequentialist moral theories focus on the outcomes or consequences of actions. For the consequentialist, an action is morally good or bad insofar as it produces good or bad consequences'. In the words of Reamer (1993: 70), 'adherents of the [consequentialist] school of thought argue that certain actions are to be performed not because they are intrinsically good but because they are good by virtue of their consequences'.

Since much of social work is about helping people achieve good outcomes, consequentialist ethics are potentially important in social work. It might be asked: consequences for whom? First of all, consequences for the service user and, when there is more than one client, consequences for the primary client. However, this does not mean that only the consequences for the primary client are considered and that those for others are disregarded. It depends on the particular circumstances: for example, some situations will have consequences for family members or the general public. The uncertainty of the social world means it is not possible to predict confidently what the consequences will be, hence consequentialist ethics necessitate an assessment of the possible outcomes, which are rarely wholly good or wholly bad, but a mixture of positive and negative. As you will see later, this entails considering the balance of the possible consequences of taking a particular course of action.

Ethical theories in practice

Ethical theories produce ethical decisions: it is not the case that in a particular situation one theory produces an ethical decision and another produces an unethical one. Rather, theories provide different ethical bases for deciding what to do. As Macklin (1988: 66–7 cited in Reamer, 1993: 79) states:

> the choice between [consequentialist] ethics and a deontological moral system … is not a choice between one moral and one immoral alternative. Rather, it rests on a commitment to one moral viewpoint instead of another, where both are capable of providing good reasons for acting. Both perspectives stand in opposition to egoistic or selfish approaches, or to a philosophy whose precepts are grounded in privileges of power, wealth, or the authority to technical experts.

In any particular decision each ethical theory may come into play. The professional character of the social worker is important, whether making or supporting decisions. Social workers want to conduct themselves in accordance with their moral duty. This means that the way they go about making decisions is influenced by such principles as 'self-determination' and being 'non-judgemental' about service users' chosen ways of life. As social work is about promoting the welfare of people it is concerned about achieving good outcomes, so choice of actions will be influenced by consequentialist ethics, that is which outcome will produce the most happiness or welfare or prevent most harm. In any particular situation, each set of ethics may influence the choice.

In the adults' field, deontological ethics may have the strongest influence, as adults are deemed to have the right to determine their own future and social work decision making is often focused on enabling the decision maker to make informed choices. However, consequentialist ethics will be influential, as informed choice includes knowing the consequences of the different courses of action and the adult service users want to produce self-defined good outcomes in their lives. In children and family work, consequentialist ethics may have the edge as the welfare of the child is the paramount importance and the consequences of the course of action for the child will be the important consideration. Nevertheless principles and rights, like self-determination of parents to bring up their children and young people to have increasing control over their own lives, will still have an important influence.

Many situations in social work involve what are termed ethical dilemmas which can be regarded as conflicts between ethical obligations.

Bowles *et al.* (2006: 65) state that dilemmas 'involve the likelihood that we have to sacrifice some moral obligation', for example whether Rita should have self-determination or be protected from the detrimental consequences of her actions. As Reamer (1995: 4) states:

> ideally of course the social worker would act in accord with all these values simultaneously. What social worker would not want to simultaneously respect service users' right to self-determination, protect service users from harm, obey the law, and protect her- or himself? The problem, however, is that situations sometimes arise in social work when core values in the profession conflict, and this leads to ethical dilemmas. An ethical dilemma is a situation where professional duties and obligations, rooted in core values, clash. These are the instances when social workers must decide which values – as expressed in duties and obligation – will take precedence.

Banks and Williams (2005: 1012) explain that:

> in resolving a dilemma, a choice is made, usually after much thought and agonizing, and one alternative is judged to be less bad/unwelcome than the other. But because the choice made still involves violating some moral requirement or principle, moral agents may nevertheless feel remorse or regret at the decision made or action taken.

There are a number of limitations to application of ethical theories to real world situations. Stakeholders cannot consistently rely on virtue, deontological or consequentialist theories always to give the morally right course of action in a particular situation. On their own none of these provides clear guidance. It is also true that, even though virtue, deontological and consequentialist theories are based on incompatible first principles, they can often lead to the same course of action. However, equally they can lead to contrasting conclusions. Despite these limitations it is argued that awareness and use of the ethical theories will sharpen thinking about the ethical issues involved. As Reamer (1993: 78) states:

> the process of debate and scrutiny of these perspectives is likely to produce the kind of thoughtful judgement that is always more valuable than simplistic conclusions reached without the benefit of careful, sustained reflection and discourse.

In the real practical world of social work decision making, decision makers cannot afford to choose one theory over another, but rather they

need to use theories to help analyse the ethics involved in particular decisions. As Clark (2000: 74) states, in real life ethical problems 'thoughtful decision-makers are usually willing to abandon neither the moral
insights of deontology nor the real world arguments of [consequential-
ism]'.

Risk and risk taking

Making decisions involves an element of risk when there is ambiguity
about what is happening in a situation or when there is uncertainty about
what the outcome of a course of action will be. For example, it is not
possible to predict for certain how any of the options in the practice
scenario will actually turn out: whether Rita stays in her present foster
home or returns to the family home. From what we know about young
people, families, foster care, being looked after and Rita and her specific
situation, each of these options could either have a good or bad outcome.
Hence each option involves risk taking, that is following a course of
action that exposes Rita to the chance of a loss in order to achieve the
benefit of having a stable base in which she can successfully negotiate
her transition to adulthood. Risk management endeavours to assess the
level and nature of risk so stakeholders can make informed decisions
about minimizing the chances of losses and harms, while enhancing the
chances of achieving the benefits sought.

Managing risk

When faced with a choice that involves uncertainty, decision makers
anticipate the dangers and turn to how the risks can be managed. The
practice scenario decision making will rightly be influenced by the
potential to manage the risks entailed in both 'the returning home' and
'the remaining in foster care'. Some stakeholders may be *risk averse* and
in danger of taking an overcautious approach in which issues of protection predominate. Fear can induce this defensive risk avoidance
approach that involves a preoccupation with caution and safety. Risk
avoidance is more likely to occur in a 'culture of fear' (Furedi, 1997)
where practitioners may fear being blamed, being sued, being castigated
by the media, being the subject of a complaint or being reprimanded or
unsupported by management (Taylor, 2006).

The alternative to 'risk avoidance' is 'risk taking' which can take the
form of either 'informed risk taking' or 'reckless risk taking'. 'Reckless
risk taking' entails risks that could severely harm self or others, without
full knowledge of the possible consequences or without due care and

attention to the safety of others. In contrast, an informed risk-taking approach is when risks are taken to achieve particular benefits with full knowledge of the possible consequences. It potentially involves balancing the chances of benefits and harms, and how the former can be maximized and the latter minimized. Risk management consists of the steps which increase the likelihood of achieving positive outcomes and reduces the chances of the feared harms occurring (Carson and Bain, 2008: 151). Important components of risk management include ongoing risk assessment, hazard reduction, capacity building and providing support and services. It can develop opportunities to take informed, acceptable and fair risks, rather than restrict self-determination.

Whether a risk is taken may hinge around the issue of risk acceptability, which Brearley defined as 'whether the benefits of a course of action are such that the risks can be borne' (1982: 23). Decision makers also need to decide on the fairness of the risk, defined as 'how far actions taken by one or more people are likely to impose the possibility of loss on others and therefore with how far such actions are to be taken or avoided' (ibid.). Risk fairness recognizes that risks are not taken in social isolation and one person's risk taking can be another person's hazard, as when a potentially violent person is discharged from psychiatric hospital. Different stakeholders may have different attitudes towards risk taking and some will have more power than others to determine the course of action and so the degree of risk taking that is acceptable.

Risk assessment

There are likely to be differences in attitudes to risk between Rita, her parents and the professionals working with them. How they view and assess the risks will influence their decisions and future actions. However, knowledge of service-user and carer ideas about risks and their preferred management strategies is often absent from official and professional discourses of risk. Mitchell and Glendinning (2008: 310) argued that this reflects the state's role and continuing preoccupation with danger management rather than exploring and seeking to understand service-user and carer perspectives on risk and risk taking. In this context risk assessment has become a major aspect of professional practice in many field settings.

Risk assessment concerns the collection and analysis of information for the purpose of estimating the degree of risk of a targeted event happening, for example the likelihood and degree of harm of Rita's placement breaking down. Risk assessment usually identifies factors in the present situation and the past, which help to predict the chances of the targeted event occurring in the future. 'Risk factors' increase the chances of it happening, while 'protective factors' decrease the chances. For example, a risk factor might be the absence of a supportive relationship, while a protective factor is having such a relationship. Methods of risk assessment vary, with predictive factors being identified by actuarial research, by establishing a professional consensus or by the professional judgement of practitioners working in specific situations.

Predictive factors fall into a number of different categories and there are different classification schemes (Schwalbe, 2008: 1460), though the simplest is the twofold classification of 'static factors' and 'dynamic factors'. These are sometimes referred to as 'fixed' and 'fluid' respectively. Static factors are not subject to change and tend to be demographic or historical in nature, for example age or history of violence, while dynamic factors are more contemporary and can change with circumstances, for example family dynamics (ibid.). Risk management can be centred on reducing dynamic risk factors and strengthening dynamic protective factors (Heilbrun, 2003: 128). It may be better to see the degree to which factors are changeable as being located on a spectrum with 'static' at one end and 'dynamic' at the other.

Ward and Patel (2006) state that the risk factors for sexual exploitation of young women are commonly cited as social and economic deprivation, family conflict and discord, educational under-achievement and a history of being in care. The most static of these factors is a history of being looked after, and perhaps the most potentially dynamic is family conflict and discord. It is important to remember that the statistical association between actuarial risk factors and the future occurrence of the targeted event is not evidence of a causal link. For example, Biehal (2007: 813) argues that the statistical association between 'length of time being looked after' and returning home has been wrongly interpreted by policy makers as a causal link, confusing the descriptive level with the explanatory level.

Approaches to assessing risks

It is common to think in terms of two broad approaches to assessing risk: 'clinical' and 'actuarial'. Clinical risk assessment refers to practitioners using their professional expertise to assess the degree of risk on the basis of factors they identify in the particular situation, while actuarial risk assessment refers to practitioners using predictive factors identified through actuarial research. There is considerable interconnection between the two approaches, with a clinical approach being able to take into account any actuarial data that is available, while it is recognized that professional expertise needs to be exercised when using actuarial risk assessment tools. Both approaches have their supporters and dissenters, and each has limitations, which to some degree can be compensated for when they are used in combination with each other.

The limitations of clinical risk assessment are that it is largely subjectively based and liable to individual bias and errors, meaning that both its reliability and validity can be questioned. That is, whether different practitioners assessing the same situation would determine the same level of risk (reliability) and whether the method can identify those 'truly' at risk (validity). However, supporters of clinical risk assessment argue that it is better at identifying dynamic or situational factors that are more useful for predicting what will happen in relation to specific individuals and to identifying unmet needs, future planning and risk management (Grubin and Wingate, 1996).

In contrast, actuarial risk assessment tends to be more heavily weighted towards 'static factors' and it commonly identifies whether a person or situation falls within a statistically low, median or high risk group. Assessments using such factors have been subjected to criticisms, including that they cannot accurately predict what will happen in an individual case. In addition, many actuarial tools have not been appropriately tested and when they have their accuracy is considerably lower than 100 per cent. The 'face validity' of risk assessment tools, which is the degree to which factors identified appear relevant to practitioners, can affect the willingness of practitioners to use them. When practitioners are required to complete risk assessments as a matter of agency policy, they may see them as a bureaucratic chore rather than as an aid to professional decision making. However, it can be argued that such tools are often subjected to unrealistic expectations and do provide a standardized way of assessing risk that brings some consistency between practitioners and ensures that information is collected in relation to known risk factors. It is also true that actuarial risk assessment has been consistently found to be more accurate than clinician risk assessment (Shlonsky and Wagner, 2005: 411).

Risk assessment tools

The number of agencies using risk assessment tools is increasing and there can be considerable variation in what these tools set out to achieve, ranging from simply aiding the collection of relevant data to providing a score of the degree of risk. Pressure on agencies to avoid mistakes may be leading them to place an unwarranted degree of confidence in risk assessment tools, partly as a means of avoiding individual blame

(Munro, 2004: 873). Having some knowledge of the 'validity' issues that surround this type of assessment can help practitioners to have realistic expectations of what risk assessment tools can and cannot do. The issue of validity is relevant to both clinical and actuarial risk assessment and those forms of risk assessment that fall in-between, but the danger of practitioner overconfidence makes it most relevant to those tools that give a risk score.

Risk assessment research has tended to focus on assessing the risk of specific future target events happening and amongst the most well researched are those designed to help predict suicide (Cooper and Kapur, 2004), reoffending (Kemshall, 2003), violence and mental disorder (Blumenthal and Lavender, 2001) and falls (Scott et al., 2007). Practitioners have the problem of (i) knowing whether or not a tool has been properly validated; (ii) if it has, having access to information about the tool's validity; and (iii), if they do, making sense of this information. The following section gives the basics of how researchers measure tool validity in the hope that practitioners can have realistic expectations of them and not be overconfident in their use. The belief is that if practitioners are fully aware of the true predictive value of a tool they will treat the results with appropriate caution and keep an open mind about the true level of risk.

Tool validity

Levels of risk are best thought of in terms of the probability of the targeted event happening and not as a dichotomous variable, for example as 'high risk' or 'low risk' (Heilbrun, 2003: 128). Nevertheless, in terms of validity, the result of the assessment is often classified as 'positive' or 'negative', in a similar manner as a diagnostic test in medicine. If the result shows 'high risk', it is referred to as 'positive', whereas if it shows 'low risk', it is referred to as 'negative'. For example, the result of a risk assessment in the practice scenario in relation to the degree of risk of Rita's foster placement breaking down could be 'positive' (a high risk of breaking down) or 'negative' (a low risk of breaking down). When a risk assessment identifies 'high risk' this could either turn out to be correct (a true positive) or incorrect (a false positive). When a risk assessment identifies 'low risk', this could either turn out to be correct (a true negative) or incorrect (false negative). Figure 7.1 shows the relationship between assessed risk and the actual outcome.

At the time an assessment is carried out, the notion of 'true' and 'false' are theoretical constructs because it is only the passage of time that will show the accuracy of the prediction. A 'false negative' could come to

	High risk (positive test result)	Low risk (negative test result)	
Target event occurs	True positives 60	False negatives 40	**Sensitivity** 60/100 (60%)
Target event does not occur	False positives 30	True negatives 870	**Specificity** 870/900 (96.7%)
	Positive predictive value 60/90 (66.7%)	**Negative predictive value** 870/910 (95.6%)	

Figure 7.1   The validity of risk assessment tools

light if Rita's placement breaks down after being put in a 'low risk' group. In comparison 'false positives' are more problematic as it may never be known whether the danger would have occurred if evasive action had not been taken. For example, if the placement is assessed as 'high risk', and as a result Rita was moved or some extra intervention was undertaken, it would never be known for sure whether or not in fact the placement would have actually broken down. Risk assessment tools that produce a high number of false positives can result in an overcautious approach and unnecessary interventions into people's lives.

Researchers usually measure the validity of risk assessment tools in terms of specificity, sensitivity, positive predictive value and negative predictive value. Using fictitious data, Figure 7.1 illustrates how these values are calculated from the findings of prospective research undertaken to validate a tool. The sensitivity of the fictitious tool is 60 per cent, meaning that it was found to predict accurately 60 per cent of the target events. Its specificity is 96.7 per cent, meaning that it was found to predict accurately almost 97 per cent of those cases in which the target event did not occur. The positive predictive value of the tool was found to be 66.7 per cent, meaning that almost 67 per cent of those cases predicted to be high risk turned out to be so. The negative predictive value of the tool was found to be 95.6 per cent, meaning that almost 96 per cent of those cases predicted to be low risk turned out to be so. When using this tool, practitioners are most likely to be interested in the positive predictive value because they know that when properly used, within an appropriate population, cases assessed as high risk have been found to have a 67 per cent chance of being correct and so a 33 per cent chance of being wrongly placed in the high risk group.

The problem for the practitioner who wants to know how much confidence to have in the result in a particular case is that even journal articles reporting the findings of research into the validity of a particular tool often do not give enough information to know what the predictive value of the tool is. Scott *et al.* (2007: 136) found that most of the studies they reviewed, all of which had passed a strict eligibility test, provided validation measures based on sensitivity and specificity alone, with no consideration of the positive and negative predictive values. The sensitivity and specificity of a tool can be misleading without knowledge of the base rate of the targeted event in the population being considered. However, Munro (2004; 2008b) gives a method of calculating the predicted value of a tool from the sensitivity and specificity when the base rate is known. Nevertheless it would be better if there was an agreed taxonomy for reporting validation measures that included the predictive values of the tool and that these were on every copy of the tool.

Base rates

The base rate of the targeted event in the population is very important from a number of points of view. The base rate of the target event of our fictitious tool is 10 per cent, that is the target event occurs in 10 out of every 100 cases. This is a comparatively high base rate compared with many adverse events of interest in social work, such as child abuse, which can be considerably less than 1 per cent. The lower the base rate the harder it is to design an accurate risk assessment tool. For example, Williams and Pollock (1993: 13) quote a study of 1,000 parasuicides in which only 10 went on to kill themselves over the next year, a base rate of 1 per cent. They state that low base rates make specificity a particular problem, with risk assessment tools giving very large numbers of false positives.

The base rate of a targeted event will be different for different populations, for example in the general population, among new referrals to an agency and those that have already been initially assessed. So the predictive values of a tool of a given specificity and sensitivity may differ if used for general population screening, the initial risk assessment of new referrals or the comprehensive risk assessment of an existing case. Base rates also vary between practice settings which may require different risk assessment tools to assess risk in the community, hospitals, foster homes or care homes. For example, Scott *et al.*'s (2007: 136) study of fall risk assessment tools found that no tool could be reliably applied across different settings.

Munro (2004: 880) argues that a critical mindset is needed in using the results of risk assessment tools as they are only an estimate and need to be kept under constant critical review. In fact a danger of such tools is that they can contribute to confirmation bias where the practitioners are predisposed to only seeing information that confirms the result of risk assessment and slow to see information that contradicts it. If the result of an assessment was a 'low risk' of the foster placement breaking down, there is a danger that Joyce might be predisposed to seeing the placement as 'low risk' and so fail to see the warning signs of a breakdown. This is equally true if the result is 'high risk' when a self-fulfilling prophecy may start to operate.

In summary, when using a risk assessment tool the practitioner should:

● use the results with appropriate caution and keep an open mind about the level of risk;
● check the predictive value of the tool and take this into account when interpreting the risk score;
● be critically aware of the populations the tool has been validated for and their base rates;
● think of the risk score not so much as a prediction but as placing the case in a higher or lower risk group, which may be the best estimate but not accurate;
● if the tool has not been validated or this information is not available, use the tool as an aide-memoire in the collection and organization of information;
● see the tool as an aid to professional practice, not a substitute for it.

Decision theory and decision analysis

Decision theory proposes that the best option is the one that has the best balance between the probability of events occurring and their value in terms of benefit and harm. Hence, decision theory features the two components of risk that we have already come across in Chapter 1: 'likelihood' and 'possible outcomes'. Decision analysis is a way of practically applying decision theory in specific situations and can be used to help decide which option gives the best chance of a good outcome. Both decision analysis and decision theory are concerned with achieving good outcomes and as a consequence can be thought of as solely taking a consequentialist approach to decision making. However, through their appropriate use, important principles can be upheld and virtues practised; for example openness, honesty, self-determination, wisdom, foresight, reflective judgement and the opportunity for the practical implementation of evidence-based practice.

The component steps of decision analysis are:

1. constructing a decision tree, which entails identifying options, the paths that events might take and the possible outcomes of these paths;
2. estimating the probability of events taking a particular path;
3. giving a numerical score to the possible outcomes of the various paths;
4. calculating the expected utility value of each option;
5. identifying the option with the highest expected utility value as the one that gives the best chance of a good outcome.

Constructing a decision tree

Decision trees are diagrams used within decision analysis to represent visually the options available and the possible paths they may take. Decision trees are useful in their own right, as they help to structure the decision and clarify thinking about possible courses of action and what might happen. Constructing a decision tree involves structuring the decision in terms of options, possible paths and possible outcomes. Figure 7.2 shows a relatively simple decision tree with two options, each having two branches or paths representing the different things that can happen if that option is taken. This gives four possible outcomes. However, decision trees can be much more complex than this one, with more options and more paths, some of which may subdivide and as a consequence yield more possible outcomes. It is important that the paths or branches that come out of an option are framed in a way that they cover all possibilities and do not include those that can occur together. In Figure 7.2 this is done in terms of the options being framed as successful or unsuccessful, but this could have been done differently. For example, it might be thought that an outcome of an option could be middling or neutral, that is neither successful nor unsuccessful, in which case a third path would need to be added.

Estimating probability

Baron (2000: 94) states that probability is 'a numerical measure of the strength of a belief in a certain proposition' and that probability judge-

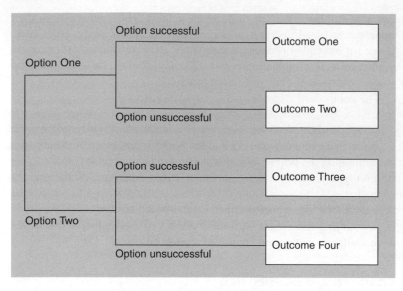

Figure 7.2   A simple decision tree

ment or estimate is the assignment of a number to that belief. Hence probability is a number that represents the chance or likelihood of an event happening. The probability of an event can be expressed in words; for example, Joyce might say there is a very high probability that the placement home will breakdown. The trouble with using words to describe the degree of likelihood is that they are imprecise and people may mean different things by terms like low, median and high probability. For example, two people may agree the probability is very high but when asked what percentage chance this represents, one may say a 95 per cent chance, while the other says a 60 per cent chance. So, despite both agreeing that the probability is very high, they are talking about very different probabilities. When carrying out decision analysis, probability needs to be expressed in numerical form, either in the form of a percentage (for example 60%) or a decimal fraction (for example 0.6).

Conventionally the probability of an event occurring ranges from 0 to 1. When the event will definitely not happen then 0 is assigned; when the event will definitely happen then 1 is assigned. The proportions between 0 and 1 represent the varying degrees of likelihood that the event will happen, so the nearer the probability is to 0 the less likely the event will happen, and the nearer it is to 1 the more likely the event will happen.

The first and most important thing to know about probability is that the probabilities of possible paths of an option add up to 1 or 100 per cent. In the example, if it is judged that there is a 0.2 chance of Rita running away, the chances of her not running away will be 0.8. According to the rules of probability this will only be true if the paths of the options have been framed to be both exclusive and exhaustive, that is 'running away' and 'not running away' are regarded as covering all the possibilities, and that she cannot 'run away' and 'not run away' at the same time.

There are a number of perspectives on the nature of probability, but we will restrict ourselves to two. The first is an objectivist perspective in which probability is seen as a property of the frequency at which events occur in the 'real world' (Dowie, 1992: 36). Within this view the probability of an event happening can be known from research into the frequency of that event happening over a period of time. For example, the probability of a particular surgical operation being successful can be found by recording the outcomes of a large sample of such operations over a period of time. The proportion of successful operations to unsuccessful ones can then be calculated, for example that 63 per cent of the operations were successful. The objectivist perspective is an actuarial approach to probability which is related to the actuarial approach to risk assessment that has already been discussed. Within social work the 'objectivist perspective' has the limitation that valid statistical data are not always available.

A second perspective on probability is the 'subjectivist perspective', in which probability is a matter of judgement based on decision makers' beliefs about how likely an event is. Baron (2000: 99) states that this personal theory of probability proposes that 'a probability judgment can be based on any of a person's beliefs and knowledge, including knowledge about frequencies or about the set of logical possibilities, but also other knowledge as well'. Within this perspective probability estimates are 'mental constructs' inside the heads of decision makers. The subjectivist perspective applied to professional work means that probability estimates are seen as judgements based on studying the particulars of the situation but which can take into account any actuarial data that is available. An important point about this perspective on probability is the distinction between well-justified judgements and those that lack sound reasoning.

Brearley (1982) used the terms situational strengths and hazards to denote the predictive factors identified through the professional expertise of the practitioner. Strengths and hazards are similar to risk factors and protective factors, already considered in relation to risk assessment, but they are situationally specific rather than being factors identified through actuarial research or professional consensus. The identification of strengths and hazards is an opportunity for the practical implementation of evidence-based practice. There has been research on both returning home (Biehal, 2007) and successful foster care (Sinclair *et al.*, 2005). Although there are not definitive lists of factors that predict success or failure in either of these options, the literature does provide useful insights into valid predictive factors that might be operating. Table 7.1 shows a grid of identified hazards and strengths in relation to the practice scenario options.

There were no risk assessment tools available to Joyce to help her estimate the probabilities of either option being successful. On the basis of the situationally specific hazards and strengths identified, and the available statistical information, Joyce with the other stakeholders estimated the chances of the foster care placement breaking down to be 0.4. Joyce was familiar with Farmer *et al.* (2005: 251), finding that 'strain on foster carers reduces their capacity to parent well and has an adverse impact on placement outcomes', and that foster-care strain can precede the placement as well as arise as a consequence of it. Key factors were that the foster carers were still suffering from the effects of a difficult ending to a placement prior to Rita's arrival and have ongoing difficulties with neighbours. This strain appears to have reduced their capacity to cope with Rita's uncooperative and 'acting out' behaviour.

The chances of Rita's placement back home breaking down were estimated at 0.5. From their study, Sinclair *et al.* (2007: 104) considered the best estimate of the proportion of children in the English Child Care System that had been looked after more than once was 40 per cent. Joyce with the other stakeholders judged that there was a greater chance of Rita's return home being unsuccessful due to the presence of a history of a fraught relationship between Rita and her father, her previous poor school attendance, her previous association with older males and her being at best ambivalent about returning home.

It is known from research into human judgement that when asked to estimate probabilities people do not tend to obey the rules of probability or take into account base rates but rely on heuristics or short cuts in thinking (Hardman, 2009). Caution is needed in interpreting this research, as most of it was undertaken in the artificial setting of the research laboratory, where ordinary members of the public, with no knowledge of the rules of probability, were asked to perform artificial tasks that had no personal relevance for them. The availability heuristic is an example of one of these short cuts to making frequency or probability judgements. Tversky and Kahneman (1982: 164) state that the availability heuristic is a 'valid clue for the judgment of frequency

Table 7.1 *Hazards and strengths identification*

Options	Predictive factors	
	Hazards	*Strengths*
Returning home	History of fraught relationship between Rita and her father	The positive contact Rita is having with her family
	Her history of poor school attendance	Her parents' willingness to make changes
	Rita's previous association with older males	Her parents appear well motivated in relation to being involved in a return plan
	Rita at best being ambivalent about returning home	
Remaining in foster care	Rita's uncooperative and 'acting out' behaviour	Rita is going to her new school and is happy there
	Foster carers' ongoing difficulties with neighbours	Rita is responding well to age-appropriate boundaries provided by her foster parents
	Foster carers still suffering the effects of a prior difficult placement breakdown	Foster carers have a network of very supportive friends and family

because, in general, frequent events are easier to recall or imagine than infrequent ones'. However, they go on to state that it can lead to biases, such as when a person's estimate of the likelihood of an event happening is based on recent experience, or when the event has a personal salience or vividness for that person. For example, if Joyce had recently experienced a return home going very wrong, this might lead her to overestimate the chances of this happening in Rita's case.

Scoring possible outcomes

Giving a numerical score to a possible outcome has the advantage of being more specific than using words like good, bad or middling. Quantifying the degree of goodness or badness of the different possible outcomes helps people communicate the value they place on particular outcomes more precisely, though there is considerable controversy as to what such judgements are based on. As with probability, objectivist and subjectivist perspectives are possible, but in social work what people find desirable and undesirable is likely to be regarded as a matter of belief and value and so by definition subjective. There are a number of methods measuring the desirability of a possible outcome (Dowding and Thompson, 2002: 137), though one of the simplest is placing them in rank order and giving each points out of 10 or 100. Such judgements are based on a person's expectations and imaginings of what things would be like for him or her if events took a particular path. A person may overestimate how good or how bad a particular outcome might be when looking into the future, as opposed to what his or her lived experience of the outcome would actually be. It is relevant to ask a person the reasons why he or she gave a specific possible outcome a particular score, so as to encourage critical reflection on the beliefs that lay behind the score.

The scoring of possible outcomes is where service users potentially have the highest levels of involvement, as it is mostly their opinion that counts as to what is a good outcome and what is a bad outcome and the relative harm and benefit associated with the outcomes. Professional workers can have an important role in assisting service users in making an informed opinion about possible consequences. However, considerable differences can exist between the scores given by different stakeholders, for example between professional workers, service users and family members. Knowing that such differences exist is informative and can help promote discussion as to what the differences are based on. As always, it is important to be clear about who the primary client is. In the practice scenario it is Rita who is the primary client and her parents may be regarded as important secondary clients. Although her parents' opinions should be valued and respected they cannot be taken as being able to speak for Rita. Given Rita's age, her scores would be taken into account but might be put alongside the scores of professional workers and her parents.

One way to help the informed scoring of possible outcomes is by constructing a balance sheet of possible consequences. Table 7.2 gives an example balance sheet of the possible consequences of the two options identified in the practice scenario. In constructing such a balance sheet there may not be agreement amongst all the stakeholders about what the possible consequences are and whether a particular consequence is positive or negative. For example, both Rita and her parents identify one of the possible consequences of her return home as Rita's growing autonomy being checked, though Rita sees this as a negative

Table 7.2 *A balance sheet of possible consequences*

	Possible consequences	
	Option successful	*Option unsuccessful*
Returning home	Rita enjoys living with her family again	Father–daughter relationship deteriorates again
	Improvements in family relationships continue	Poor attendance at school recurs
		Rita runs away again and re-enters care
	Rita successfully negotiates her transition to adulthood	
		Rita found to be involved in prostitution
Remaining in foster care	Remains in a relatively positive home environment	Rita's relationship with her foster family deteriorates over time
	Positive contact with family maintained	
		Forced move due to placement breakdown either through foster carers' or Rita's request or Rita running away
	Rita continues to attend school and starts to achieve educationally	

consequence, whereas her parents see it as a positive one. Even when a single stakeholder alone takes a decision, there can be considerable ambivalence about a particular possible consequence, making it difficult for him or her to place a value on it.

Expected utility value

The expected utility value of an option is a number that combines the probability of events taking particular paths and the desirability of the possible outcomes of these paths. For each path, the probability of that possible outcome occurring is multiplied by its outcome score. For each option the resulting figures are added together to give the overall expected utility value of that option. How this is done is shown in Figure 7.3. To take the example of the returning home option, the probability of the option being successful (0.5) is multiplied by the possible outcome score (9) giving 4.5. Similarly the probability of the option being unsuccessful (0.5) is multiplied by the possible outcome score (2) giving 1.0. The results of these multiplications are added together (4.5 and 1.0) giving 5.5 which is the expected utility value of the returning home option.

Decision theory states that the option with the highest expected utility should be chosen, as it gives the best chance of having a good outcome. Decision theory is just that: a theory, and there can be a number of reasons why it is not wise to choose automatically the option with the highest expected utility value. First, decision analysis is only as good as the data put into it, which reflects the beliefs of the decision makers. Second, decision analysis primarily reflects consequentialist ethics and its concern about outcomes, though as we have seen there are other ethical theories that may need to be taken into account. For example, Thomson (1999) advocates always checking whether there are issues of autonomy or social justice that might not have been fully taken into account. Third, when the result of the decision analysis does not fully reflect the service user's preferences he or she may choose an option with a lower expected utility value. Figure 7.3 shows the application of decision theory to the practice scenario. According to the stakeholders' use of decision theory, and their judgements of the value and probability of identified possible outcomes, the best option is for Rita to remain in foster care.

Little research has been carried out into the potential use of decision analysis within social work (O'Sullivan, 2008). Clarke (2002: 461) found that care managers regarded a particular model of risk assessment taught on a training programme to be far too time consuming and complicated to use, given the demands on their time and heavy work-loads. This was particularly in relation to scoring possible outcomes and estimating probabilities, features shared with decision analysis. It is known that human beings are prone to biases when estimating probabilities and professionals can use decision analysis mechanically without due care and attention. There is also a danger that numbers are regarded as somehow more scientific and definitive than words, though they can provide a more concrete basis for comparing judgements of probability and desirability. However, decision analysis can potentially help practitioners and service users to think through difficult decisions and systematically make explicit the judgements that often remain implicit. As Philips (1982 cited in Horlick-Jones *et al.*, 2001: 156) recognized, 'in real-world situations, decision analysis should be regarded as a tool to allow decision-makers to think more clearly about the problem in question, and not as a means to identify an "optimal" or "correct" course of action'.

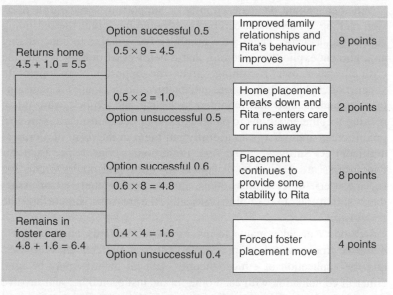

Figure 7.3   Decision analysis of practice scenario

Constructing an argument

Having analysed the options in terms of ethics, risk and the probability and value of possible outcomes, a conclusion can be reached as to which is the best option. There is a danger that the reasons behind the conclusion remain implicit and vague, and there is a need to go back over the analysis to identify and organize the reasons into a clear and explicit argument. Osmo and Landau (2001: 485) argue that there is a need for explicit argumentation in social work and that social workers should lay out in detail their rationale for decisions. The term 'argument', used in this context, means a conclusion supported by a reason or reasons (Thomson, 1999) and has very little in common with its everyday meaning of having a quarrel. The simplest structure of an argument is for a conclusion to be supported by one reason; however, it is more common for there to be a number of reasons that are linked together to form a line of reasoning. A conclusion without supporting reason(s) is known as an 'assertion', which is an unsupported statement of belief. The ability to give reasons for a conclusion is an important professional skill – Joyce needs to be able to construct an explicit argument in support of the stakeholders' conclusion that Rita remaining in foster care is the best option.

Whether making decisions jointly or supporting service-user decision making, an argument can be constructed that gives the reasoning behind the decision. There are a number of advantages to constructing an argument explicitly, including that it helps practitioners to examine critically their own reasoning, gives the opportunity to others to support or challenge a decision, and enables the rationale for decisions to be communicated and recorded in a clear and explicit way. When making recommendations to panels and other decision-making groups, practitioners and others can usefully put them in the form of a critical argument (O'Sullivan, 2004: 49). Practitioners may hope that their conclusions are valid, but the only way they and others (including service users, other professionals, managers and courts) can assess their validity is to examine critically the reasons supporting the conclusion.

Reasons can take many forms including: hazards and strengths; evidence from research on predictive factors and effectiveness studies; and the application of ethical theories. Ethical theories may be used either in combination with each other or against each other and involve deontological principles as well as arguments for a particular option that gives the best chance of a good outcome. In constructing arguments stakeholders need to be clear about why they reached a particular decision. Coming to a conclusion and constructing an argument is at the end of a process that is likely to take the form of:

1. gathering information;
2. analysing this information;
3. coming to a conclusion;
4. identifying the reasons that support the conclusion;
5. constructing an argument.

So an argument can be seen as a summary of the decision makers' analysis of assessment information, including the conclusion they draw as to which is the best option. There are few clear-cut situations where there is absolute certainty about the best courses of action. In such circumstances an argument should include the counter-argument and its rebuttal, which will transform the argument into a critical one. To give a rebuttal is for decision makers to give the reasons why they rejected the counter-argument and supported the argument. A rebuttal is usually an argument that the counter-argument is not valid or not sufficiently strong or is outweighed by the strength of the argument. So a well-structured argument would have the following form:

1. stating the conclusion;
2. giving the reasons supporting the conclusion;
3. stating the counter-conclusion with its supporting reasons and its rebuttal.

The aim is to build an explicit well-reasoned critical argument that clearly sets out the reasoning behind the choice of option. Joyce sets out the argument in favour of Rita remaining in foster care in the following way.

> We have come to the conclusion that Rita remaining in foster care is the best option. The reasons supporting this conclusion are that it is in Rita's best interests that she remains in foster care as this is likely to give her the best chance of a good outcome in terms of her welfare and development. Rita will be continuing to live in a relatively positive family environment with experienced foster carers, maintaining positive contact with her family and continuing to attend school and starting to achieve educationally. It is true that her foster carers were currently experiencing the effects of a difficult ending to a prior placement and have ongoing difficulties with their neighbours and that this strain appears to have reduced their capacity to cope with Rita's uncooperative and acting out behaviour, but these factors are mitigated by the strengths of this particular foster family.
>
> The counter-argument is that Rita returning home will give her a better chance of a good outcome. The supporting reasons for the counter-argument are that Rita will be better off with her own family, with whom she is now experiencing positive contact. Her parents are willing to make changes and appear to be well motivated to be involved in a return plan. However, the history of a fraught relationship between Rita and her father, her previous poor school attendance, her previous association with older male acquaintances and Rita being at best ambivalent about returning home indicates that placement at home has a relatively high chance of breaking down, with Rita re-entering care or running away, possibly to associate with those that would involve her in prostitution. Equally it is judged to be unwise to place Rita back home without her being more clear that this is what she wants to do.

chapter summary

This chapter has focused on how social workers can make and support others in making ethical and well-informed decisions. This requires deliberative decision making in which decision makers are aware of and explicit about how options are being ⬎

analysed and choices made. I have put forward that ethical theories, considerations of risk and the analysis of probability and value, can be combined to build arguments as to which is the best option. I have explained how knowledge of ethical theories, including virtue ethics, deontological ethics and consequentialist ethics, can help practitioners clarify the ethical dimensions of a particular decision. It was stressed how judgements of risk impact on the choice of action and that practitioners need to be critically aware of how these judgements are being made. Decision theory and decision analysis were used as ways of managing the inherent uncertainty of making decisions. The chapter concluded with how stakeholders can build arguments to make explicit the reasons why they have chosen a particular option and rejected others.

key practice points: analysing options

Practitioners need to be able to:

- use ethical theories to analyse the ethics involved in making a particular decision;
- recognize that risk, risk management and risk taking are part of both everyday life and professional practice, and that judgements of risk may vary between stakeholders, particularly between professionals and service users;
- recognize that the results of risk assessment tools are potentially helpful, but treat them with caution and keep an open mind as to the true level of risk;
- recognize that decision analysis can be potentially helpful in thinking through difficult decisions and making explicit the judgements that often remain implicit;
- construct arguments that make clear and explicit the reasons why they have chosen or recommended a particular course of action and rejected others.

putting it into practice

1. Explain how the different ethical theories might help decide whether the time is right for Rita to return home.
2. How do you think approaches to risk and risk taking might differ between Rita, her parents and Joyce?
3. Decide whether you would take issue with any of the estimates of probability or scoring of possible outcomes given on Figure 7.3.
4. Given the strain her foster carers are under, construct an argument as to whether or not Rita should move foster homes.

Recommended reading

'Ethical problems and dilemmas', Chapter 7, in S. Banks (2006) *Ethics and Values in Social Work*, 3rd edn, Basingstoke: Palgrave Macmillan. In this chapter the author explores some of the ethical problems and dilemmas that can arise in decision making in everyday practice.

'Risk Management', Chapter 5, of D. Carson and A. Bain (2008) *Professional Risk and Working with People*, London: Jessica Kingsley. The authors consider how risks can be managed including issues of knowledge, control and resources.

'Making Decisions', Chapter 7, of E. Munro (2008) *Effective Child Protection*, 2nd edn, London: Sage. The author discusses different approaches to decision making, including decision theory and using decision trees.

8 | Using supervision

This chapter presents the potential contribution supervision can make to promoting sound decision making. Supervision has traditionally played a significant part in social work and continues to be seen as necessary to enable workers to carry out their challenging roles. It has an important role to play in enabling frontline practitioners to work effectively with others and to make ethical and informed decisions. There are strong links between the availability and quality of supervision and the quality of decisions and outcomes. The chapter presents the role of the supervisor as critically supportive, enabling the supervisee to think critically about the case and work through the emotions generated. It portrays the supervisee's role as actively seeking to develop their practice, engaging in critical reflection and preparing effectively. A picture is drawn of the supervisor and the supervisee working collaboratively together to produce good outcomes for service users.

Providing and receiving appropriate support and guidance requires contributions from both supervisors and supervisees, though both parties commonly see the lack of supervision as one of the main impediments to effective work with service users (Randall *et al.*, 2000: 350). There has been and continues to be a persistent gap between the expectations of both practitioners and managers, and what actually happens in practice (Hughes and Pengelly, 1997: 186; Kadushin and Harkness, 2002: xvii; Jones, 2004: 16). With equal consistency, the lack of appropriate and effective supervision is pointed to as an important factor in failures in practice (for example, see Laming, 2003: 106).

The picture of supervision that follows may be regarded by some as a somewhat idealized vision that for a number of reasons is not always available, but, as suggested by Kadushin and Harkness (2002: xvii), such pictures can provide an ideal against which experience and practice can be compared and possibly reveal a direction in which changes can be made. I will consider how supervision can support and guide decision making to produce good outcomes. I will explain how effective supervision depends on having a good understanding of: what 'supervision' is; the different forms it can take; the importance of organizational and team contexts; the processes involved in giving and receiving supervision; and the roles that 'power' and 'authority' can play.

practice scenario

Kim is returning to the office after a difficult home visit to see Amy Kirk, aged three years. There are concerns about the care Amy is receiving and Kim is working with her family and the other agencies to ensure she is not being harmed or her development impaired. As agreed in Amy's child protection plan, the nursery school have alerted Kim to the fact that Amy has not been at school that week. Kim had experienced a tense and antagonistic atmosphere in the Kirk household, particularly in relation to ensuring that Amy was safe and well. On the surface things were fine but underneath Kim didn't feel comfortable, sensing hostility and feeling immobilized. She had found herself metaphorically stuck in a living room chair, unable to move, as a rather quiet Amy played at the other end of the room. Feeling on hostile territory she felt unable to approach and talk to Amy, and she didn't get a good look at her. Delroy Miller was present, Mrs Kirk's boyfriend, who Kim found a particularly menacing presence.

Kim was relieved to get back to her car and as she drove back to the office she had both an uneasy feeling and a concern that she had not done her job properly. She hoped that some of her colleagues would be in to discuss the situation and wondered whether she should trouble Susan her supervisor. She had found her recent supervision session both challenging and helpful in developing her work with the Kirk family and the other members of the core group.

When Kim arrived back at the office she discussed with her colleagues what had happened and how she felt intimidated and didn't really get to see that Amy was all right. Her colleagues were very supportive and suggested she see Susan who was in her office. She had a snatched conversation with Susan that helped her to clarify her thinking and emotions. Susan pointed to the specifics of Amy's child protection plan, to which Mrs Kirk had agreed, that an absence from nursery school would trigger a ↘

> visit to check on her well-being. Susan helped Kim to clarify that neither Amy's mother nor her boyfriend had ever actually been violent or overtly aggressive and that they were very defensive and engaged in what Reder *et al.* (1993: 106) called 'disguised compliance'. Kim decided to return to the Kirk household to explain that she had not earlier spoken to Amy. Susan, recognizing the realities of violence towards social workers and the negative impact that threats of violence can have, including perceived threats (Littlechild, 2005), suggested that someone goes with Kim. However, Kim felt confident and instead took the precaution of arranging to be contacted if she had not reported in after 30 minutes from the start of the visit. Kim and Susan make a record of the conversation on the case file and a note to discuss, at the next scheduled supervision session, the planned consideration of curtailing involvement with the family at the forthcoming Review Child Protection Conference and Kim's unsubstantiated but uneasy feeling that Mrs Kirk and her boyfriend were hoodwinking her into thinking everything is all right.

Supervision and decision making

It is generally recognized that decision making in social work is intellectually and emotionally challenging (Munro, 2008b: 101) and workers need support in relation to their case-specific reasoning and emotional involvement. Supervision has an important role to play in making difficult decisions, including 'signing off' decisions taken. All the aspects of the decision-making framework developed in this book can feature in supervision discussions. Case-based discussion can help to clarify and develop critical awareness of the practice context in which decisions are being taken. It can help to identify whether service users and carers are being involved to the highest possible level and whether any limits on their involvement are fully justified. Issues in working collaboratively with others, including service users, carers and other professionals, can be discussed. Clear thinking can be promoted and help given with the management of emotions. In particular supervisors can help supervisees have clear and accurate frames of decision situations, as free from distortion as possible, and analyse options and make decisions based on well-reasoned arguments.

Case-based supervision needs to emphasize the development of the reasoning of frontline workers through the promotion of critical thinking and the nurturing of reflexivity, with the aim of building capacity and increasing confidence, with both challenge and support likely to be involved. It has developed as a process by which the weight of uncertainty can be shared and help received to clarify and make decisions. The supervisory process can provide an opportunity to share risk taking and accountability, and move away from individual blame when things go wrong. The worker can give an account to his or her supervisor, who in accepting this gives the organization a shared accountability for the social worker's actions and inactions.

The nature of organizations, and teams within which frontline workers and managers are located, can impact on their capacity to provide and receive effective supervision. For agencies to promote sound decision making, they will need to provide a safe environment in which supervision can take place, giving workers space and time to think through issues and manage their emotions. For example, Noble and Irwin (2009: 351) argue that in the 'increasingly complex fields of practice, supervision can provide a valuable space for review, reflection and action'. Whether the supervisor can provide such a space, and whether supervisees feel sufficiently trusting and confident in their supervisor to use this space positively, is another matter (Brown and Bourne, 1996: 12). It is open to question whether all organizations and teams are able to offer a space in which effective supervision can take place.

There is likely to be a spectrum of organizations, with functional ones at one end and dysfunctional ones at the other. Where an organization and team fit along this spectrum will affect their capacities to offer frontline workers effective 'supervision', which becomes more difficult as the dysfunctional end is approached. Phillipson (2009: 190) suggests that while there are great expectations of supervision, and that some good quality supervision is experienced, many people are disappointed by what they can either offer or receive. Jones (2004: 16) found that in ever-busy working environments, commitment of time to supervision to allow more in-depth examination of practice was fragile. Continual change has become a characteristic of many of the organizations that employ social workers, creating environments in which providing and receiving supportive supervision can be more difficult. However, there is much that frontline supervisors and supervisees can do to provide and receive effective supervision.

What is 'supervision'?

Supervision can take many forms, including individual supervision, group supervision, peer supervision and autonomous practice supervision (Tsui, 2005: 23), and each of these forms can have a distinctive role in supporting sound decision making. Social work as a profession is unusual in the emphasis it places on supervision, particularly the importance placed on its supportive functions. The term 'supervision' can be seen as a misnomer, often being associated with an overseeing control, something that should be anathema to professional work. 'Administrative overseeing control' is not what professional social workers tend to mean by 'supervision'. Rather social work 'supervision' is an interactional process by which frontline workers receive the support and guidance they need from their agency supervisor who carries out their agency responsibilities. As Kadushin and Harkness (2002: 215) state, supervision is a highly interactional situation in which the supervisee responds to the supervisor's actions, which in turn affect the supervisor's response.

It can be helpful to make a distinction between 'supervision' and 'consultation', although the ways the terms are used and differentiated can differ. Brown (1984: 3) describes 'consultation' as occurring when, in a professional context, one person seeks help and advice from another, who has a contribution to make to the resolution of a particular practice issue. He points out that 'supervision' entails a supervisor who carries some agency responsibility for the supervisee's work, whereas in 'consultation' the consultant does not carry any such responsibility, which remains entirely with the consultee. So in supervision decision making is a shared responsibility, whereas in consultation responsibility for decisions rest with the consultee. Both supervision and consultation are potentially important in supporting sound decision making, although many authors do not make a clear distinction between the two.

Individual supervision

The most common format of supervision is based on a one-to-one relationship between the supervisor and supervisee (Tsui, 2005: 23) and contrasts with group supervision and peer group support. The frequency, duration and style of individual sessions can vary and can include both regular planned sessions and unplanned impromptu face-to-face contacts or communication by telephone or some other form of technology. Phillipson (2009: 189) argues that workers like Kim often 'depend on "on the hoof" supervision in the corridor or office', one that is rarely formally recorded or used to expand notions of 'supervision'. Recognizing the important role that 'corridor conversations' can have should not detract from the need for planned scheduled sessions in which important decisions are analysed and reviewed before being taken. Lord Lamming (2003: 211) was critical of the way a number of important decisions about Victoria Climbie's case would seem to have been taken during the course of informal, ad hoc discussions in the corridor between social worker and supervisor.

It can be useful to think of processes occurring within individual supervision between supervisor and supervisee as having a parallel with the processes operating between worker and service user. Having insight into these 'parallel processes' can promote more effective supervision, either as a model of social work practice or as a way of detecting unhelpful processes. In the former supervisee and the supervisor see the processes and skills operating in supervision as models of the processes and skills involved in working with service users (Tsui, 2005: 6). For example, the support and guidance Susan gives to Kim's decision making can provide a model for how Kim supports and guides Mrs Kirk's decision making as regards her parenting of Amy and her relationship with Delroy Miller. The idea of 'parallel processes' may also help to identify unhelpful processes such as those Lord Laming (2003: 206) points to in which the supervisor's passive acceptance of what the social worker said effectively mirrored the way the social worker had passively accepted what she was told by Victoria's carers.

Peer supervision

'Peer supervision' involves colleagues discussing a case in order to develop their thinking, formulate plans and make decisions. This process, more accurately referred to as 'peer consultation', can occur both through impromptu exchanges in the office and in organized 'peer supervision' meetings. Much significant supervision takes place spontaneously among peers with social workers commonly relying on colleague support, guidance and discussion in relation to their work with specific cases. Such peer supervision can be seen as a context and process in which transformative learning takes place through membership and participation in a 'community of practice' (Wenger, 1998: 6). That is, a group of people with a common interest in a particular field, who through a process of sharing experiences, transform themselves.

Social workers are usually based in a team and can see their team colleagues as their main source of support. Payne (2000: 5) makes the point that the idea of 'team' is a contested one and distinguishes 'workgroups' from 'teams', with 'team' representing an aspiration of cooperation, collaboration and coordination, qualities particularly required by multidisciplinary teams working with the same family or service user; for example, the core group Kim is a member of. Successful peer supervision may partly depend on these qualities but it is more dependent on the existence of a positive and supportive team culture, including positive team relationships and dynamics, qualities that may depend more on sharing the same office and developing what Brashears (1995) refers to as a 'mutual aid group' that has the common purpose of delivering effective services.

Organized peer supervision involves group members presenting a case, followed by colleagues asking questions to clarify points and giving feedback. For this to occur there needs to be a safe and respectful atmosphere where everyone's ideas are valued. In such a group Thomasgard and Collins (2003: 315) claim that members may be less defensive upon hearing the comments of others: there may be increased sharing of personal vulnerabilities or an enhanced ability to identify and build upon strengths. Members can benefit from hearing different perspectives and alternative viewpoints as well as receiving emotional support from colleagues. There is the potential for the presenter to reap many of the benefits of supervision, including the development of critical thinking, a more open mindset and emotional containment in relation to a particular case.

Group supervision

Supervisors can provide supervision in a meeting of team members, in which the focus can be on team development and/or individual workers' handling of specific cases and decision making. Brown and Bourne (1996: 163) state that group supervision has great potential. However, for this to be harnessed and realized its complexities demand careful consideration, though, provided the supervisor is aware of the dangers, they can be effectively managed. Group supervision requires additional group work skills from the supervisor which they may or may not possess. It is not known how common group supervision is but in case-work-oriented teams it is likely to be in addition to individual supervision. Group supervision is particularly suited to residential, day care and community project teams and can be valued and appreciated when it is the only form of supervision available, which can be the case in domiciliary care and volunteer settings.

Brown and Bourne (ibid.) describe two of the potential benefits of group supervision as, firstly, how 'hearing the struggles of others and sharing their own, supervisees may feel less isolated and more able to gain a more balanced view of their own practice. Secondly, the group can act as a secondary source of experience, enabling group members to learn from the experience of others, thereby accelerating their own professional development'. This ability of one supervisee to make vicarious use of another's experience is regarded as one of the principles upon which effective group supervision is based. Brown and Bourne (ibid.) describe how one member might describe a decision with which they are struggling, in the hope that others will help them explore it further. However, other group members may seize the material for themselves and begin to explore how they would respond if they faced a similar issue. Meanwhile the member who initiated the discussion seems to take a back seat, apparently detached from the discussion. The group may appear to have gone off course but the initiating member is being allowed time to think and reflect and, later, perhaps well after the discussion has moved on, may return from his or her silence having developed a deeper understanding of the issues involved in making the decision.

Brown and Bourne (ibid.: 162) assess the advantages and disadvantages of group supervision as being balanced and dependent on the setting and purpose. From both the points of view of the supervisor and supervisee they identify a number of disadvantages that seem particularly pertinent to case-based supervision. From the supervisee point of view, there are greater opportunities for critical feedback that may inhibit those who lack confidence; there can be pressure to conform in highly cohesive groups; and the communications and interventions that may assist one member may create problems for another. From the supervisor point of view, they are more exposed in group supervision; they will require greater self-assurance, knowledge of group dynamics and skills in group work; they may find it more difficult to restore the focus should the group follow a non-productive line; and they may experience the dual focus of 'group' and 'individual' as demanding. Group supervision is likely to be more effective for team development, addressing team issues and continuing professional education, but less so in relation to discussing individual case decisions which may be more effectively achieved through individual supervision and peer consultation.

Giving and receiving supervision

The experience of giving and receiving supervision at least partly depends on how the different functions of supervision are balanced and carried out. It is generally recognized that supervision has a number of complementary and overlapping functions which Kadushin and Harkness (2002) identify as administrative, educative and supportive. This gives three interlocking supervision roles: organizational, professional and personal (Tsui, 2005: 14), though there is considerable variation in how these functions and roles are envisaged. There are tensions between the three strands with a danger that one can come to dominate at the expense of the others, whether this is the administrative, educative or supportive components. Ruch (2007b: 665) argues that supervision's supportive and educative functions are being gradually stripped away and asks how, in such a context, practitioner anxiety generated by practice can be appropriately 'contained' in order for them to respond reflectively and effectively. Jones (2004: 16) found that 'the administrative aspects of supervision (associated with the accountability, compliance and organisational procedures and oversight of task performance) were viewed by participants as having increasingly squeezed out educational and supportive aspects'. He found that this is what most staff had come to expect from supervision, though this expectation diverged greatly from what most staff thought supervision still ought to be providing.

The argument is that a combination and integration of the three identified functions could potentially provide social workers with the guidance and support to make sound decisions. However, as Tsui (2008: 350) rightly argues, to do this, supervision needs to be viewed comprehensively as a multiparty process, including the service users, the organization, the supervisor, the frontline worker and the team (including interprofessional colleagues). Seeing supervision as involving multiple parties, even though only two may be present, helps shed light on some of the dynamics and tensions within supervisory and case processes. Despite these dynamics and tensions, few would disagree with Kadushin and Harkness's (2002: 20) description of the ultimate objective of supervision as being to provide, in the context of a positive relationship, efficient and effective services to service users.

Supporting

Kadushin and Harkness (ibid.) state that the short-range objective of supportive supervision is helping the worker feel good about doing his or her job and that the main concern is with the prevention and management of stress and burnout. Important as this is, the supportive function can be conceived as being much wider than this. Supervision needs not only to be concerned with the emotional well-being of the worker but the impact emotions generated in relation to specific cases can have on their case-specific thinking and decision making. In addition, the notion of support should not be restricted to the emotional dimension, but extended to the thinking one. The supportive function should include helping the worker develop his or her thinking about the case. This does not only include helping the worker overcome some of the dangers associated with shoddy thinking, for example vagueness and unfounded assumptions, but also helping him or her to analyse complex situations and decisions.

Rushton and Nathan (1996) identify an 'inquisitorial function' and an 'empathic-containment function' as dual functions in child protection work supervision. The concept 'inquisitorial function', as originally formulated by these authors, does not necessarily sound supportive. However, they see seeking clarification as an important aspect of this function and state that:

> by clarification we mean that supervisors will have to check and challenge the information the worker volunteers (and does not volunteer), to feel they have a clear understanding of the case and, where necessary, to confront the staff member who might be vague, evasive or defensively aggressive.

Their 'inquisitorial function' can be positively reframed as 'supportive critical questioning' in which the supervisor seeks clarification and does not accept vagueness, with the aim of promoting critical thinking. In the second function identified by Ruston and Nathan, the supervisor helps the worker contain the intense emotions that can be generated by difficult decision situations. They argue that the 'empathic-containment function' has to be provided if the worker is to be enabled to operate in emotionally charged areas of work and that the worker is searching for a person who is available to help with difficult feelings. Despite the obvious tensions between the two functions they are committed to one person carrying out both roles as they relate to the dual concerns of the worker.

Empathic-containment

Ferguson (2009: 474) argues that to think that social workers can just make up their minds rationally to do something and just get on and do it is to ignore the emotional dimension of their work. He argues that supervision needs to give workers space to talk openly, be still, process their feelings and get to know their experiences, and make sense of what is reverberating within them. 'Containment' is a key concept in achieving, what he describes as, the healthy management of anxiety, which involves supervisors emotionally attending to the worker's inner chaos and conflicting emotions to help them contain their feelings safely.

Hughes and Pengelly (1997: 178) describe the qualities of 'containment' as the experience of being in a 'bounded, safe place' with a supervisor who has the capacity to apply understanding to anxiety-laden experiences which become 'contained'. These feelings are attended to by the supervisor, not only to be supportive but to explore them so as to discover the information they provide. The authors state that containment thus provides a concept for the capacity both to be appropriately supportive and to challenge effectively. In the first instance, it is the supervisor that becomes 'the container' for the worker's anxieties by listening, asking and tolerating the worker's account of his or her feelings (ibid.). This offers a model for supervisees to develop this capacity in relation to their work with service users, which in turn offers a model to service users in relation to their own feelings.

Critical supportive questioning

Supervisors have an important role in helping frontline workers to improve their reasoning and decision making about cases; and a means of achieving this is by asking critical supportive questions. Through asking such questions Susan could promote the standards of thought set out by Paul and Elder (2007b: 32) involving clarity, precision, accuracy, relevance, depth, breadth, logicality and fairness. This requires an open and honest dialogue to develop between supervisor and supervisee, enabling alternative explanations and interventions to be explored. In Chapter 5 I discussed how both intuitive reasoning and analytical reasoning were important in social-work decision making and how analytical reasoning is required when making decisions with others. Such analytical reasoning needs to be encouraged and workers enabled to crystallize what they are worried about. Seeking clarification and not accepting vagueness can help frontline workers to think more clearly and more deeply about the situations they are involved with and their responses to them. Unfounded assumptions can be identified and challenged; the plausibility of explanations offered can be critically examined and solutions jointly built.

'Socratic questions' are the types of questions employed by Socrates, the ancient Greek philosopher, aimed at guiding his pupils to clear thinking. They are designed to open up issues and problems, uncover assumptions, analyse the use of concepts, distinguish between what is known from what is not known and follow logical implications (Paul and Elder, 2007a: 36). The following series of questions, based on Paul and Elder's categories, illustrate the sort of questions Susan could ask Kim about her reasoning in relation to working with the Kirk family and Amy:

1. What is the purpose of your involvement in this case?
2. Is this the most pressing issue that you are now responding to?
3. What information/evidence are you basing your assessment/plan/ decision on?

4. What inferences are being made?
5. What ideas, concepts and theories are being used in your reasoning?
6. What assumptions is your reasoning based on?
7. What consequences will follow from this assessment/plan/decision?
8. What point of view is being assumed and are there others that should be considered?

Through such questions supervisors can help frontline workers uncover the hidden distortions that may be affecting their work. Gibbs (2009: 291) points out the danger of decision making and judgements being contaminated by unchallenged and untested assumptions, biases and personal beliefs. Through supportive critical questioning supervisors can detect and counteract the biases and beliefs discussed in Chapter 5, including confirmation bias, deficits approaches, the rule of optimism and stereotypes. They can also uncover the operation of the heuristics encountered in Chapter 6, like using the availability heuristic when judging the likelihood of a plan being successful. Munro (2008a) states that:

> Supervisors need to encourage workers to report their feelings so that they can consider whether they are distorting their work. Once the emotions, whether positive or negative, are out in the open, it becomes possible to predict how they may distort the thinking and counteract the bias. (Ibid.: 5)

> For supervisors, this requires creating a culture in which challenging assessments and decisions is not seen as a personal criticism but an intellectual task that is morally necessary in order to provide the best standard of reasoning for service users. (Ibid.: 8)

Supervisees may not always experience critical questioning as supportive. Trevithick (2005: 254) points out that 'for some practitioners, supervision is not a creative or comfortable experience, perhaps due to personality clashes or because exposing our work to scrutiny in this way feels threatening'. Supervisors taking every opportunity to give positive feedback on the workers strengths may lessen defensiveness and aid the creation of the necessary atmosphere of open dialogue, confidence and trust.

Developing

Developmental models of supervision most typically see the supervisee moving through a series of stages from 'dependence' to 'autonomy'

(Walker *et al.*, 2008: 106). The important stages in professional development can be described as 'being a student', 'being newly qualified', 'growing into an experienced worker' and 'becoming an advanced practitioner' – with the educational needs of each being different. Within such a developmental model, the nature of supervision changes as the supervisee gains experience, knowledge and skills (Hawkins and Shohet, 2006: 70). Hence, the supervision that Kim receives from Susan is different in a number of important ways to the supervision that Kim gives to her social work student. As the supervisee develops, the supervisor is required to change his or her approach. From the supervisor's point of view there is likely to be a progressive move from a prime focus being the development of the worker, to developing the worker's thinking and decision making in a particularly difficult case. From the supervisee's point of view the move may be from a preoccupation with self-performance to one of the dynamics of the case.

As supervisees move from being students to advanced practitioners their supervisory needs are likely to change from a greater to a lesser need for supervisor-imposed structure, didactic instructions, direct feedback on practice behaviour and supervisory support in general (Kadushin and Harkness, 2002: 214). This requires the supervisor to be able to adapt his or her approach of supervision to the development stage of the supervisee. As Kadushin and Harkness (ibid.: 215) state, 'the same intervention by the supervisor may evoke different responses from two different supervisees whose learning needs, styles and preferences are different. Hence, like the good social worker, the good supervisor has to be sensitive to how his and her interventions are being received and modify the approach to optimise the learning situation for the supervisee'.

The student supervisor has two distinct roles, which Ford and Jones (1987: 64) describe as:

> that of supervision and that of practice teacher. The supervisor is accountable to both the agency and the service user; the practice teacher has responsibility to the education establishment and the student. The supervisor has, first, to ensure that a good standard of service is offered to the agency's service users and, second, to develop skills in teaching so as to maximise the learning of the student.

This is most clearly demonstrated when long-arm arrangements split the two aspects between practice educator/teacher and an agency supervisor. The practice educator is accountable for the practice education and assessment of the student, while the agency supervisor is accountable for ensuring agency functions are carried out effectively (Karban, 1999: 60).

Davys and Beddoe (2009) provide a practical model of supervision which recognizes the importance of both facilitative and didactic interventions within effective supervision, meaning that both the promotion of reflective learning and the transfer of knowledge are valuable processes. When Kim explains a relevant procedure to her student, didactic teaching occurs, involving the transfer of knowledge from supervisor to worker. Reflective learning involves the discussion of 'case events' in supervision sessions that takes the supervisee through a transformative process in which mistakes and negative experiences are used as learning opportunities. The process consists of retelling 'the event', followed by discussion of its impact on and implications for the supervisee and what can be learnt from it, and how this learning will be implemented in the future, concluding with an evaluation of whether 'the event' had been successfully addressed in the discussion.

Supervision is also regarded as having a key role to play in helping newly qualified social workers make the transition from student to qualified practitioner, one that can be associated with stress, anxiety and shock (CWDC, 2009). They are likely to need a strong emphasis on support, with both professional and personal development being important in relation to being confronted with the harsh realities of practice, being a member of staff and consolidating what they have learnt on their qualifying course. Dreyfus and Dreyfus (1986) referred to the first two stages of their model of expertise development as 'novice' followed by 'advanced beginners'. Newly qualified social workers are increasingly being recognized as 'advanced beginners', who are not yet fully functional and competent and require appropriate expectations and support, as evident in the Newly Qualified Social Worker (NQSW) Programmes. These introduce appropriate caseloads, tailored development opportunities and access to support, guidance and supervision to help review and develop the skills, knowledge and confidence to operate at increasing levels of complexity (CWDC, 2008).

Unfortunately in the past and in different contexts newly qualified workers have not always been provided with appropriate levels of support and supervision. For example, Gibbs (2009) found that the new recruits in her study of a statutory child protection agency in Victoria, Australia, were left to 'sink or swim', reflecting an organizational culture that lacked compassion and sensitivity to their needs. She goes on to argue that it is important that new recruits experience the supervisory relationship as safe and containing, providing a space to talk about what they find difficult and challenging, so as to learn to stand back, to think and reflect on what is happening.

The more experienced a worker becomes, the more the need for didactic interventions within supervision is likely to diminish with their continuing educational needs being met outside of supervision, for example by post-qualifying training and other continuing professional education activities. However, there is likely to be an ongoing need for the case-specific reflective learning that case-based supervision potentially offers for those working in high risk or complex situations, no matter how experienced and skilled the practitioners are. For example, reflective learning occurs when Susan asks Kim questions about the visit to the Kirk family, which promotes within Kim a process of analysis that transforms the way she is thinking about her visit and through which she learns different ways of thinking, deciding and doing in the situation.

Overseeing

The administrative function entails monitoring the standard of work, ensuring agency policy and national guidance is implemented, that practice is both legal and ethical, that procedures and protocols are followed and that proper records are being kept. As has been stated, there is a danger of over-focusing on the administrative function to the exclusion of the others and it is only through the integration of the three functions that sound decisions will be made and good outcomes achieved. The agency responsibilities of a supervisor can be wide, for example: implementation of the agency's stress policy, lone worker policy or its equality and diversity policy. It will be up to supervisors to handle the situation appropriately and sensitively if during case discussions they discover a worker is under undue stress and in danger of experiencing 'burnout' or that the worker is not valuing diversity or is being oppressive in their practice.

There is a danger that a 'deficits approach' might be taken, only focusing on what isn't there or what is wrong. Necessary as this may be, it can be balanced by recognizing strengths, valuing the worker's contribution, taking every opportunity to give explicit praise and expressing the agency's appreciation of the good work he or she is doing. There is also an increasing danger of seeing social work as only the completion of a series of tasks within a specified time and that success is solely seen as whether the task was completed on time. Gibbs (2009: 291) found that many of the participants in her study described having to cope with little supervision, which, when they did get it, was primarily about task competition and getting the job done. Carrying out tasks such as risk or family functioning assessments or the formulation and implementation of plans can be difficult in many practice areas. There is a danger that administrative supervision is only concerned with whether the report has been completed in time, not the difficulties workers and family members face in working together to achieve a professional standard of work. Having said this, the completion of tasks remains a basic requirement of all professional work, for example the carrying out of action points identified in reviews, conferences and supervision.

Appropriately kept records can increase the effectiveness of supervision, enabling the supervisor and supervisee to engage in meaningful case discussion. Lord Laming (2003: 106) stated that effective supervision involves the supervisor reading the case file and applying some thought to the decisions taken. He pointed out that no manager had thoroughly read Victoria's case file before it was closed, and as a consequence basic omissions such as the failure to speak to her were never picked up and the decision to close was never challenged. Reading entire case files to obtain an overview can take time, but failure to do so was also implicated when occupational therapist, Georgina Robinson, was murdered by a patient at the mental health centre at which she worked (Blom-Cooper et al., 1997).

Case records and reports are an important aid to frontline workers communicating effectively with each other and they need to record clearly issues discussed in supervision and any decisions made. As well as recording decisions, well-kept case records should contain the information and analysis on which decisions are based and the reasoning and justifications behind them. However, O'Rourke (2009) found that many workers described difficulties trying to make sense of other people's recording with basic details missing and many assumptions being made. The puzzle for many of these practitioners was that the files had been 'signed off' by managers, reinforcing the sense of confusion as to what was an adequate record. She argues that if supervisors are going to be able to check that appropriate records are being kept, then both they and their supervisees need to have a good understanding of the attributes of well-kept records.

Supervision can be used to promote the recording of only clear, specific, contextualized information as part of anti-oppressive practice and a first step to improving record keeping. Trevithick (2005: 249) states that 'one of the greatest tensions within record keeping is how much information to record and how best to do this in ways that are accurate, objectively critical and sufficiently detailed yet also succinct'. However, O'Rourke (2009) points to how general statements that records should be 'accurate, relevant, concise and complete are meaningless without practical examples'. If Langan's (2009: 474) research into recording in mental health services is widely applicable, practitioners need to change urgently their recording practices. She found records to be often vague, with non-specific, out of context information recorded, including stigmatizing labels and repeated unsubstantiated second-hand information which over time became established as 'facts'.

Electronic records could in theory improve supervisors' and service users' access to records and reports, and provide a catalyst to raise standards. Unfortunately there is little sign of this happening at present, with IT systems being reported to be hindering professional practice rather than promoting it (Bell, 2008). One source of problems appears to be the imposition of forms-based 'management information systems' (Ince, 2010) rather than systems that aid the documentation of cases in terms of a temporal and analytical narrative.

Supervision, authority and power

If sound decisions are going to be made both supervisor and supervisee need to be comfortable with the authority of the supervisor. Adult attitudes towards those who have authority over them, or to possessing such authority itself, can contribute to the supervisory relationship dynamics. According to Brown and Bourne (1996: 32), 'issues to do with power, and how it is managed, lie at the heart of supervision and the supervisory relationship. When one person is in a position of formal authority over another a dynamic is created that derives from that inequality of power'. In Chapter 1 a distinction was made between 'power' and 'authority', with authority being a legitimate circumscribed source of power, possessed by virtue of occupying a particular role or position in an organization or society. This legitimate source of power can be used appropriately within the limits of the role, but it can also be abused. The authority of the supervisor needs to be used by both the supervisor and supervisee to promote effective practice and sound decision making, though legitimate 'authority' can get entangled with negative power dynamics.

Both the supervisee and supervisor need to respect and value the authority of the frontline supervisor, though both can have problems with the authority aspects of the supervisor's role. Some of these problems are due to a failure to distinguish between being authoritative and being authoritarian. Being authoritative is using proper authority to guide, support and sometimes direct the supervisee in the achievement of agency, professional and service-user identified outcomes. Being authoritarian is controlling the supervisee through the misuse of power and possibly coercion. Hughes and Pengelly (1997: 167) state that many supervisors struggle to act with proper 'authority', by which they mean authority that is thoughtfully and non-oppressively exercised and based on valid sources. They identify three sources of authority: role authority, professional authority and personal authority.

Role authority is the authority that comes with the job and relates to agency responsibilities that the supervisor carries. As Hughes and Pengelly state, the supervisor's role provides the authority to oversee the supervisee's work, while the supervisee's role requires him or her to acknowledge this authority and provide the supervisor with the information needed to fulfil his or her role (ibid.: 168). Professional authority comes from demonstrated competence, knowledge and skills. This is an authority that is carned through the supcrvisor's dcmonstration of practice ability and this being recognized by the supervisee. Personal authority comes from the capacity to establish a natural authority and communicate this to the supervisee and having an attitude to authority that pervades the way that the professional and role authority is exercised.

Hughes and Pengelly (ibid.: 169) state that there are complex connections between the three sources of authority:

> Supervisors and supervisees who rely solely on the authority of role will tend to mechanistic implementation, characterised by coercion and compliance. Those who pursue professional concerns or expertise in a way that exceeds their legitimated authority of role put themselves, their supervisees and service users at risk by abusing the power of their professional status. Sole reliance on personal charisma to influence others, ignoring the nature and limits of role and professional competence, results in the assertion of illegitimate power only.

Of particular importance is what happens when either the supervisor or the supervisee or both solely rely on the role authority of the supervisor, which can lead to oppressive compulsion and thoughtless routinized compliance. When this happens there is a very narrow conception of professional work, with the supervisor feeling compelled to give instructions and workers routinely looking to the supervisor for direction. In such situations supervisees are not developing their practice, and the chances of achieving sound decisions and good outcomes is diminished.

As well as individual attitudes to authority there are issues of commonality and difference. There needs to be recognition that both social differences and commonalities between supervisor and supervisee can have an impact on the supervisory relationship and decision making. Given the multidimensional nature of identity, supervision will usually involve some commonality and difference between supervisor and supervisee. Both consciously and non-consciously the social differences between the two can impact on the relationship dynamics. Difference can be constructed in society in a way that one social group occupies a more privileged position than another. There are many sources of social difference, including ethnic group, 'race', gender, disability and sexuality. Although there are dangers in binary thinking, it is common that one side of a difference occupies a more privileged position in society, while the other side can be subjected to discrimination. Both supervisor and supervisee need to be critically aware of their own identity and the way they are constructing 'the other', so that supervision becomes a collaborative exercise with shared ownership of decisions and mutual respect for each other's expertise.

chapter summary

In this chapter I have identified a number of potential ingredients for effective case-based supervision which helps the worker to practice effectively with service users, carers and interprofessional colleagues in making and supporting sound decisions and achieving good outcomes. Such supervision requires the provision of a well-organized and supportive organization and team context in which the administrative, supportive and educative functions of supervision are effectively integrated. The supervisor needs to have the capacity to be a 'container' for the worker's strong emotions in relation to their involvement in the case and ask critically supportive questions to help review judgements and assumptions and so keep an open mind. The nature of supervision needs to change as the worker develops from 'novice' to 'advanced practitioner'. The effective supervisor is supportive and helps workers to reflect critically on their involvement in the case, as well as checking that they are working effectively with service users and interprofessional colleagues and carrying out agency and professional requirements, including the maintenance of appropriate case records. Both supervisors and supervisees need to respect and be comfortable with the authority aspects of the supervisory role and for this to be carried out in a way that enables the worker to develop and function as an effective and confident practitioner who is not in need of constant support, guidance and direction when making decisions.

key practice points: making effective use of supervision

Supervisors and supervisees have a joint responsibility to:

- respect each other's role and expertise;
- be open and honest and engage in critical dialogue;
- be critically aware of the power differential between 'supervisor' and 'supervisee' and issues of working across difference;
- record what was discussed in supervision and any decisions made.

To achieve effective supervision the supervisor needs to:

- create an atmosphere in which open dialogue can take place;
- recognize the dangers of an overemphasis on the administrative function;
- take every opportunity to give positive feedback on the worker's strengths, to praise the worker's standard of work, and value his or her contribution;
- ask questions that promote critical thinking and challenge vagueness and unfounded assumptions;
- read the case file before important decisions are taken.

To achieve effective supervision the supervisee needs to:

- achieve a balance between seeking advice and support and developing his or her own practice confidence;
- prepare effectively for planned supervision sessions;
- seek to develop his or her own practice by engaging in critical discussion;
- not become defensive when asked critical questions;
- keep effective case records;
- when uncertain, seek guidance and help in testing out ideas and thinking.

putting it into practice

1. How might Kim's behaviour and emotions be different if she did not have such a supportive supervisor and colleagues?
2. What factors do you think made it possible for Kim to be open with Susan about her visit to the Kirk family?
3. Do you think Susan should use her authority and insist that Kim takes a colleague with her on the return visit to the Kirk family?
4. In the practice scenario both Kim and Susan are white, British, non-disabled, heterosexual women. What impact might it have on the supervisory dynamics if there was a difference in relation to one or more of these dimensions?

Recommended reading

A.M. Davys and L. Beddoe (2009) 'The reflective learning model: supervision of social work students', *Social Work Education*, 28(8) 919–33. This journal article presents a reflective learning model which identifies the importance of both facilitative and didactic interventions within effective supervision.

M. Jones (2004) 'Supervision, learning and transformative practices', in N. Gould and M. Baldwin (eds), *Social Work, Critical Reflection and the Learning Organisation*, Aldershot: Ashgate, 11–22. In this chapter Martyn Jones considers and critiques models and theories of professional supervision.

J. Phillipson (2009) 'Supervision and being supervised', in R. Adams, L. Dominelli and M. Payne (eds), *Practising Social Work in a Complex World*, Basingstoke: Palgrave Macmillan, 188–95. In this chapter Julia Phillipson asks if the remarkable consistency in ideas about the ingredients of effective supervision is helpful or not in developing critical practice.

9 | Decision making and decision outcomes

This book has been about the processes, knowledge, skills and supports required for sound decision making within social work practice. The argument has been that sound decision making, including assessments, plans and actions, increases the chances of good outcomes. In this concluding chapter I will consider the limitations on what sound decision making in social work alone can achieve and why it cannot consistently ensure good outcomes. The relationship between decision making processes and decision outcomes is problematic. Decision making is just one of a number of factors that contribute to decision outcomes; others include the nature of decision situations, social agencies and societies. Frontline workers, their managers, service users and carers can engage with these factors, but they are often beyond their direct influence.

practice scenario

Kim the social worker from the previous chapter returns to the Kirk household that day and plays and chats with Amy while her mother and Delroy Miller are out of the room. She leaves the house reassured. A fortnight later Amy is in hospital with a serious head injury following blows from Delroy Miller. There is to be a serious case review.

Sound decisions and uncertain outcomes

Social workers and their sound decision making make many contributions to the achievement of good outcomes, though there will be times when bad outcomes occur. It remains open to question who or what is responsible for these bad outcomes and how society can prevent them from occurring. There are many inputs into decision situations in the form of a broad range of antecedent factors that have a potential influence on what happens. The inputs range from cognitive processes to the nature of society. To focus simply on individual decision making as an explanation for a bad outcome, as if this was the sole input, is seriously flawed. If society is to make progress in preventing bad outcomes, the negative inputs themselves need to become the focus of preventative work well before problems develop. The following will briefly describe some potential reasons why sound decision making in social work cannot always end in good outcomes, including: the future cannot be predicted with certainty; risk taking is unavoidable; lack of opportunity; competing claims within decision situations; and decisions not being effectively implemented.

The future cannot be predicted with certainty

We live in a non-linear world of fluid relationships that form an open system where the future is uncertain and the present is often ambiguous. As was discussed in Chapter 7, social workers can, to a degree, manage this uncertainty by making probability judgements based on predictive factors in the decision situation, though this should not be confused with the ability always to be able to predict the future accurately and reliably. However, it is relatively easy to backtrack from an event like a child's death and claim that there were warning signs to see and that the tragedy was preventable. Looking back it is easy to overestimate the predictability of the future and criticize decision makers. Hindsight bias allows investigators to view decision situations from the perspective of knowing that a bad outcome has occurred, which means they can view events as predictable that at the time were difficult to predict.

Risk taking is unavoidable

Taking risks is both part of everyday life and professional work, and it is neither desirable nor possible to eliminate risk. As argued in Chapter 7 there are no completely reliable risk assessment tools that accurately assess the level and likelihood of a danger occurring, and the nature of the social world we live in means that it is unlikely there ever will be. This particularly poses problems for those professionals who work with people who pose a danger to others. Many of those identified as falling in a 'high risk' group will be false positives and some of those placed in a 'low risk' group' will turn out to be false negatives. This means that

professional workers mechanically following the results of risk assessment tools would mean subjecting large numbers of people to unnecessary intervention, while others who are denied intervention will go on to
cause harm. It needs to be recognized that social work is a balancing act
between risk and safety in which frontline workers cannot avoid taking
informed risks and that on occasions the feared event will happen.

Lack of opportunity

Service users and social workers may not have the opportunity, through
lack of resources or their position in society, to have the radical impact on
life circumstances that may be needed for service users to have a good
outcome. Life circumstances can be constraining and the lack of opportunity to bring about improvements can seriously affect the service user's
life chances, meaning that many of his or her aspirations remain beyond
reach. People's lives are embedded in the structures of society, and at
times within these contexts the cards are stacked against achieving a good
outcome. In these circumstances achieving good outcomes would require
a transformation of society. For example, Mullaly (1997: 133) identifies
the goal of structural social work as twofold: '(1) to alleviate the negative
effects on people of an exploitative and alienating social order; (2) to
transform the conditions and social structures that cause these negative
effects'. The latter aspiration may appear unrealistic, yet, if social work is
serious about preventing bad outcomes, its commitment to the elimina-
tion of poverty, discrimination, oppression and lack of opportunity would
need to be more forthrightly put into action.

Competing claims within decision situations

There can also be the issue of 'outcome for whom', when one person's
good outcome is another's bad outcome. For example, when there are
primary and secondary clients, an increase in the quality of life for one
can be a decrease in the quality of life for the other. Neglectful parents
may regard their children flourishing in short-term foster care to be a bad
outcome, since it points to the inadequacies of their parenting, but
professional workers are likely to regard this as a good outcome. An
older person enjoying staying in their own home regards it as a good
outcome, but carers may regard the stress this puts them under as a bad
outcome. Given the competing interests within decision situations,
sound decisions may mean that some stakeholders experience a good
outcome while others in the same decision situation regard it as a bad
one.

Decisions not being effectively implemented

This book has been about making decisions and judgements, including assessments and plans, and so far there has been little specific mention of implementing these decisions. Obviously implementation is equally important and itself involves decision making, as do all aspects of the social work process. However, when things go wrong, the cause may have been a failure to implement a previously well-made decision rather than the making of the decision itself. For example, sound decisions made at reviews, conferences or in supervision sessions may be left unimplemented, partially implemented, shoddily implemented or allowed to lapse, particularly when it is judged that there are more immediately pressing matters to deal with. If workers and managers do not pick up implementation problems or situational changes by monitoring and review, and make appropriate adjustments to assessments and plans, situations can deteriorate or drift, leading to bad outcomes, despite having previously made sound decisions.

Decision making and decision outcomes

As can be seen, the relationship between decision making and decision outcome is not a straightforward one. However, for the sake of clarity, decision making will be regarded as either 'sound' or 'unsound' and outcomes regarded as either 'good' or 'bad'. Even though this is a gross oversimplification, hopefully it will help to identify some issues in the relationship between decision making and decision outcomes. Within this limited view, Table 9.1 shows the four possibilities in the relationship between decision making and decision outcome: an effective decision, bad fortune, good fortune and a culpable decision. A *sound decision* may have a *good outcome* and be regarded as an effective decision, or it may have a *bad outcome* and be regarded as bad fortune. An *unsound decision* may have a *good outcome* and be regarded as good fortune, or it may have a *bad outcome* and be regarded as a culpable decision.

Table 9.1 *Decision making and decision outcomes*

| | | Decision making | |
		Sound	Unsound
Decision outcome	Good	Effective decision	Good fortune
	Bad	Bad fortune	Culpable decision

Effective decisions

These situations are a neglected aspect of decision evaluation and public debate, with emphasis being placed on decisions that have bad outcomes. When a sound decision is linked to a good outcome, decision makers, including frontline professionals and service users, should be given some credit and lessons learnt about what made the decision making effective. Focus needs to be on finding out what components of decision making link with good outcomes, so that the criteria for a soundly made decision can be adjusted in the light of what turns out to be effective decision making. The absence of a simple link between decision making and decision outcome means that it is not possible to come up with a formula that will produce good outcomes time after time, but what is regarded as good practice in decision making and decision implementation could be refined and developed.

Bad fortune

When decision makers make sound decisions there still can be a bad outcome, and there has been a debate within social work as to whether they can still be blamed. The question is whether decision makers, who having made a sound decision, can still be held accountable for the bad outcome (Hollis and Howe, 1987; Macdonald, 1990). The argument that they cannot hinges on the acceptance that accountability is for the making and implementation of decisions, and that the belief that decision outcomes depend on other factors as well as decision making. Saying that decision makers who make sound decisions should not be blamed for bad outcomes does not mean that practitioners themselves are indifferent to the outcome and do not experience deep regret, misgivings and self-blame for what has happened. As Banks (2006: 23) states:

> That social workers feel 'guilt' for a bad outcome is not surprising. Yet in the same way that my friends would tell me not to feel guilty for running over a young child who unexpectedly leapt out in front of my car, surely we would say the same to the social worker. We may torment ourselves by blaming ourselves and thinking 'if only I had reacted more quickly; if only I had visited the family an hour earlier', but what we should feel is regret not guilt.

The argument is that, given the number of factors that have been discussed, decision makers can only be held accountable for whether or not they made and effectively implemented *sound* decisions.

The above analysis upholds what, within moral philosophy, is termed 'the control principle', which states that people should only be morally judged for what they have control over (Nelkin, 2008: 2). Not all moral philosophers accept the control principle and argue for the existence of 'moral luck'. This occurs when a person can be correctly morally judged, even though what they are judged for depends on factors beyond their control (ibid.: 3). This would mean that decision makers who make a sound decision but experience a bad outcome can still be correctly blamed for the outcome. Within this analysis, two sets of decision makers would be judged very differently, even though they were equally diligent in decision making and working in very similar situations, the only difference being one case had a good outcome and the other a bad outcome. The argument is that in becoming a social worker, for example, they have accepted this 'moral risk', knowing that they operate in an uncertain world, where not all factors are within their control and that, despite doing their job properly, there will always be the risk of a bad outcome.

Good fortune

Given the lack of a simple link between a decision and its outcome, it is possible for a decision that has been evaluated as 'unsound' to be associated with an outcome that is evaluated as 'good'. In such situations the decision makers may be regarded as lucky, having experienced considerable good fortune. The decision maker's good fortune should not detract from the issue of poor practice, and any feedback, criticism, remedial or disciplinary action should be unaffected by the good outcome. It could be argued that if social workers make decisions in haphazard or ill thought through ways without due regard to the circumstances, this should become the subject of critical attention as much as if it had a bad outcome. This is unlikely to happen in practice, as it is bad outcomes that tend to trigger decision-making evaluation, while good outcomes often are passed over without comment.

Culpable decision

Culpable decisions are when decision makers make unsound decisions and there is a bad outcome; but who or what is culpable needs to be questioned. There will be occasions when decision makers can be blamed for unsound decision making and so for the bad outcome, but it should not be automatically assumed that it is the decision makers that are culpable, there being other possible explanations. Decision makers can be reckless, negligent or incompetent, but careful, vigilant and competent decision makers who are operating in an environment that does not allow this competence to operate can make errors of judgement. Able and skilful practitioners can make unsound decisions, when they are overworked and not provided with appropriate support or guidance. Even when incompetence is located within the level of frontline workers, their agencies and their society may need to share some of the responsibility, particularly in relation to the education and training made available to them.

Learning from bad outcomes

It is bad outcomes that tend to trigger decision evaluation, particularly high profile bad outcomes, like a child being killed by his or her parents through neglect or abuse, or when an individual is randomly murdered by a person with a serious mental health problem. The tendency had been to take a person-centred approach that involves finding who is to blame for the bad outcome. Munro (2005: 531) has criticized this approach for taking 'human error' as its end point rather than the starting point – there is a need 'to understand *why* the mistake was made, by studying interacting factors operating within and between frontline practitioners, resources available and the organisational context'.

In many fields it has become increasingly common to take a systems-centred approach to learning from bad outcomes as opposed to the traditional person-centred approach (Fish *et al.*, 2008). It has been argued that the reasons for bad outcomes are complex, with the whole notion of linear cause and effect being open to question, with events happening without a single direct cause. Many interacting, mutually influencing factors on different levels can be implicated as playing a part in bringing about the life events and 'states of being' that are regarded as decision outcomes. As a consequence, learning from bad outcomes requires an open systems approach where inquirers consider the workings of the whole system and not just single actors. Advances are being made to developing systems-centred approaches to learning from bad outcomes in social work and these aim not just to examine 'cases with tragic outcomes but for conceptualising how services routinely operate and for learning about what is working well and where there are problematic areas' (ibid.: 1).

Preventing bad outcomes

For the reasons outlined, sound decision making alone will not stop all bad outcomes occurring, so how can a greater proportion be prevented?

Prevention is commonly thought of as falling on a continuum, first set out by Caplan (1964), consisting of three levels: primary prevention, secondary prevention and tertiary prevention. The different levels relate to what it is the preventative efforts are trying to prevent, and they are linked to successive stages of problem development, which in turn depend on theories of problem formation and theories of change. Preventive interventions can be targeted at different levels and different stages. They can be targeted at the personal, interpersonal, community or societal levels, and at the different stages of problem formation, such as 'pre-problem', 'in danger of developing a problem', 'experiencing early relatively minor effects of a problem' and 'the development of a severe problem'.

Primary prevention is generally thought of as being aimed at the general population before problems arise, for example public education programmes, and can include targeting an entire population considered 'at risk', for example teenage girls. However, at its most radical it promotes social change and can take the form of improving social conditions and reforming society so that all can have the opportunities to achieve good life outcomes. Secondary prevention is intervention timed at the first signs of difficulty, with the aim of preventing more serious problems from developing. Tertiary prevention intervenes when serious problems have developed and is aimed at limiting the damage done and promoting recovery.

The neat divisions between the different levels of prevention are liable to break down in practice, but they do enable important distinctions to be made between levels of services and interventions. Social workers make important contributions to primary, secondary and tertiary prevention, though limited resources, prioritization and targeting those most in 'need' or who pose the most serious 'risks' have moved social work more and more towards tertiary prevention. If greater strides are to be made towards preventing bad outcomes, there needs to be more early intervention before serious problems arise and a re-engagement with activities that promote the development of individuals, families and communities and the reform of society. The integrated multilevel interventions, advocated by France et al. (2010), are needed that reflect the multilevel interactional developmental processes that bring about and maintain social problems.

All these levels of intervention require the development of skills and knowledge in making judgements and decisions. Chapter by chapter this book has built a picture of critically wise practice in making and supporting sound decisions. This has involved:

- being critically aware of the practice context with its constraining and enabling forces;
- involving service users to the highest level, recognizing their strengths and working with them to build their capacities;
- effectively communicating with others to make integrated assessments and plans based on sound judgements and decisions;
- making critical use of different sources of knowledge, combining professional intuition with well-developed skills of analysis and competently managing emotions;
- reflexively framing and analysing situations to be alert to potential sources of distortion;
- analysing options to make decisions that have the best chance of producing good outcomes;
- using and giving critically supportive supervision in which the supervisor and supervisee positively work together for the benefit of service users.

This systemic view of decision making in social work means seeing frontline social workers as embedded in a wider system of mutually influencing parts. Critically wise practice would be more achievable when the whole system operates in a way that is supportive of sound decision making. Minimizing bad outcomes would require the different domains of the multilayered nested system, including the personal, interpersonal, techno-organizational and sociocultural levels, to be geared to supporting frontline practice.

chapter summary

In this final chapter I have considered why sound decision making will not always lead to good outcomes. Although it is an important ingredient in achieving good outcomes, it is not sufficient in itself to ensure consistently their occurrence. Social situations are complex systems with many interacting factors, including those that operate at the structural levels of society, which means that bad outcomes can occur despite sound decision making. Focusing on the quality of decision making and judgement in social work is important, but other parts of the decision-making system need to operate in a way that supports social workers and other frontline professionals to practice in a way that they can make and support critically wise decisions. There is much frontline

↘

practitioners and their managers can do to bring about good outcomes, however the wider techno-organizational and socio-cultural contexts in which they work need to support rather than hinder their work.

References

Abramson, M. (1985) 'The autonomy–paternalism dilemma in social work practice', *Social Casework*, 66(7) 387–93.

Adams, R. (2008) *Empowerment, Participation and Social Work*, 4th edn, Basingstoke: Palgrave Macmillan.

Ahmed, S. (1986) 'Cultural racism in work with Asian women and girls', in S. Ahmed, J. Cheetham and J. Small (eds), *Social Work with Black Children and their Families,* London: B. T. Batsford, 140–54.

Aldgate, J. (1989) *Using Written Agreement with Children and Families*, London: Family Rights Group.

Aldridge, J. (2008) 'All Work and No Play? Understanding the Needs of Children with Caring Responsibilities', *Children and Society*, 22(4) 253–64.

Algase, D.L., Moore, D.H., Vandeweerd, C. and Gavin-Dreschnack, D.J. (2007) 'Mapping the maze of terms and definitions in dementia-related wandering', *Aging and Mental Heath*, 11(6) 686–98.

Arnstein, S. R. (1969) 'A Ladder of Citizen Participation in the USA', *Journal of the American Institute of Planners*, 35(4) 216–24.

Atchley, R. C. (2000) 'A Continuity Theory of Normal Aging', in J. F. Gubrium and J. A. Holstein (eds), *Aging and Everyday Life*, Malden, MA: Blackwell, 47–61.

Axelsson, S. B. and Axelsson, R. (2009) 'From Territoriality to Altruism in Interprofessional Collaboration and Leadership', *Journal of Interprofessional Care*, 23(4) 320–30.

Bamford, T. (1990) *The Future of Social Work,* Basingstoke: Macmillan.

Banks, S. (2001) *Ethics and Values in Social Work*, 2nd edn, Basingstoke: Palgrave Macmillan.

Banks, S. (2006) *Ethics and Values in Social Work*, 3rd edn, Basingstoke: Palgrave Macmillan.

Banks, S. and Williams, R. (2005) 'Accounting for Ethical Difficulties in Social Welfare Work: Issues, Problems and Dilemmas', *British Journal of Social Work,*. 35(7) 1005–22.

Barber, J. G. (1991) *Beyond Casework,* Basingstoke: Macmillan.

Baron, J. (2000) *Thinking and Deciding*, 3rd edn, Cambridge: Cambridge University Press.

Baron, R. S., Kerr, N. L. and Miller, N. (1992) *Group Processes, Group Decision, Group Action*, Buckingham: Open University Press.

Barrett, G. and Keeping, C. (2005) 'The Processes Required for Effective Interprofessional Working' in G. Barrett, D. Sellman and J. Thomas (eds), *Interprofessional Working in Health and Social Care*, Basingstoke: Palgrave Macmillan, 8–31.

BASW (British Association of Social Workers) (2002) *The Code of Ethics for Social Work*, Birmingham: British Association of Social Workers.

BBC (2007) *Cruelty Missed through 'Optimism'*, London: BBC. http://news.bbc.co.uk/1/hi/england/london/6344783.stm, accessed 10 October.

Beach, L. R. (1990) *Image Theory: Decision Making in Personal and Organisational Contexts*, Chichester: John Wiley.

Beckett, C. (2006) *Essential Theory for Social Work Practice*, London: Sage.

Bell, M. (2008) 'Put on ICT: Research Finds Disquiet with ICS', *Community Care*, 5 June, 18–19.

Ben-Zur, H. and Michael, K. (2007) 'Burnout, Social Support, and Coping at Work Among Social Workers, Psychologists, and Nurses: The Role of Challenge/Control Appraisals', *Social Work in Health Care*, 45(4) 63–82.

Beresford, P. and Croft. S. (2004) 'Service Users and Practitioners Reunited: The Key Component of Social Work Reform', *British Journal of Social Work*, 34(1) 53–68.

Berg, I. K. and De Jung, P. (1996) 'Solution-Building Conversations: Co-Constructing a Sense of Competence with Clients', *Families in Society*, 77(6) 376–91.

Berger, P. and Luckmann, T. (1966) *The Social Construction of Reality*, Harmondsworth: Penguin Books.

Biehal, N. (2007) 'Reuniting Children with their Families: Reconsidering the Evidence on Timing, Contact and Outcomes', *British Journal of Social Work*, 37(5) 807–823.

Biestek, F. P. (1961) *The Casework Relationship*, London: Unwin University Books.

Blake. D. (2009) 'Why No Secrets Must Not Mean No Laws', *Professional Social Work*, Birmingham: BASW, 14–15 March.

Blewett, J. (2008) 'Social Work in New Policy Contexts: Threats and Opportunities', in S. Fraser and S. Matthews (eds), *The Critical Practitioner in Social Work and Health Care*, London: Sage, 238–53.

Blom-Cooper, L (1985) *A Child in Trust: The Report of the Panel of Inquiry into the Circumstances Surrounding the Death of Jasmine Beckford*, Middlesex: London Bough of Brent.

Blom-Cooper, L., Hally, H. and Murphy, E. (1997) *The Falling Shadow: One Patient's Mental Health Care 1978–1993*, London: Duckworth.

Blumenthal, S. and Lavender, T. (2001) *Violence and Mental Disorder: A Critical Aid to the Assessment and Management of Risk*, London: Jessica Kingsley.

Bowles, W., Collingridge, M., Curry, S. and Valentine, B. (2006) *Ethical Practice in Social Work: An Applied Approach*, Buckingham: Open University Press.

Boyle, D., Clark, S. and Burns, S. (2006) *Co-Production by People Outside Paid Employment*, York: Joseph Rowntree Foundation.

Brammer, A. (2007) *Social Work Law*, 2nd edn, Harlow: Pearson.

Brandon, M., Schofield, G. and Trinder, L. (1998) *Social Work with Children*, Basingstoke: Macmillan.

Brashears, F. (1995) 'Supervision as Social Work Practice: A Reconceptualisation', *Social Work*, 40(5) 692–99.

Braye, S. (2000) 'Participation and Involvement in Social Care', in H. Kemshall and R. Littlechild (eds), *User Involvement and Participation in Social Care*, London: Jessica Kingsley, 9–28.

Braye, S. and Preston-Shoot, M. (1997) *Practising Social Work Law*, 2nd edn, Basingstoke: Macmillan.

Braye, S. and Preston-Shoot, M. (2010) *Practising Social Work Law*, 3rd edn, Basingstoke: Palgrave Macmillan.

Brayne, H. and Broadbent, G. (2002) *Legal materials for social workers*, Oxford: Oxford University Press.

Brearley, C. P. (1982) *Risk and Social Work: Hazards and Helping*, London: Routledge.

Bristow, K. (1994) 'Liberation and Regulation? Some Paradoxes of Empowerment', *Critical Social Policy*, 14(3) 34–46.

Brown, A. (1984) *Consultation: An Aid to Successful Social Work*, London: Heinemann Educational Books.

Brown, A. and Bourne, I. (1996) *The Social Work Supervisor*, Buckingham: Open University Press.

Brown, G. and Atkins, M. (2006) 'Explaining', in O. Hargie (ed), *A Handbook of Communication Skills*, 3rd edn, London: Routledge, 195–205.

Burr, V. (2003) *Social Constructionism*, 2nd edn, London: Routledge.

Butrym, Z. T. (1976) *The Nature of Social Work*, London and Basingstoke: Macmillan.

Caplan, G. (1964) *Principles of Preventive Psychiatry*, London: Tavistock Publications.

Carr, S. (2004) 'Has service user participation made a difference to social care services?', SCIE Position Paper, London: SCIE/Policy Press.

Carr, S. (2007) 'Participation, Power, Conflict and Change: Theorizing Dynamics of Service User Participation in the Social Care System of England and Wales', *Critical Social Policy*, 27(2) 266–76.

Carr, S. (2008) *Adult Services Report 20, Personalisation: A Rough Guide*, London: SCIE.

Carson, D. and Bain, A. (2008) *Professional Risk and Working with People*, London: Jessica Kingsley Publishers.

Clark, C. L. (2000) *Social Work Ethics: Politics, Principles and Practice*, Basingstoke: Macmillan.

Clark, P. G. (1997) 'Values in Health Care Professional Socialization: Implications for Geriatric Education in Interdisciplinary Teamwork', *The Gerontologist*, 37(4) 441–451.

Clarke, N. (2002) 'Training Care Managers in Risk Assessment: Outcomes of an In-Service Training Programme', *Social Work Education*, 21(4) 461–76.

Clyde, J. J. (1992) *The Report of the Inquiry into the Removal of Children from Orkney in February 1991*, Edinburgh: HMSO.

Collins, S. (2007) 'Social Workers, Resilience, Positive Emotions and Optimism', *Practice*, 19(4) 255–69.

Collins, S. (2008) 'Statutory Social Workers: Stress, Job Satisfaction, Coping, Social Support and Individual Differences', *British Journal of Social Work*, 38(6) 1173–92.

Cooper, J. and Kapur, N. (2004) 'Assessing Suicide Risk', in D. Duffy and T. Ryan (eds), *New Approaches to Preventing Suicide*, London: Jessica Kingsley, 20–38.

Coulshed, V. and Mullender, A. (2006) *Management in Social Work,* 3rd edn, Basingstoke: Palgrave Macmillan.

Cree, V.E. and Wallace, S. (2009) 'Risk and Protection', in R. Adams, R. Dominelli and M. Payne (eds), *Practising Social Work in a Complex World*, Basingstoke: Palgrave Macmillan.

Critcher, C. (2006) 'Introduction: More Questions than Answers', in C. Critcher (ed.) *Critical Readings: Moral Panics and the Media*, Maidenhead: Open University Press, 1–24.

Croft, S. and Beresford, P. (1993) *Getting Involved: A Practical Manual,* London: Open Services Project and the Joseph Rowntree Foundation.

Cumming, E. (2000) 'Further Thoughts of the Theory of Disengagement', in J. F. Gubrium and J. A. Holstein (eds), *Aging and Everyday Life*, Malden, MA: Blackwell, 25–39.

Cupitt, S. (1997) 'Who Sets the Agenda for Empowerment?', *Breakthrough*, 1(2) 15–28.

CWDC (Children's Workforce Development Council) (2008) *Newly Qualified Social Worker Pilot Programme 2008–2011: Outcome Statement and Guidance*. Children's Workforce Development Council. http://www.cwdcouncil.org.uk/assets/0000/2508/NQSW_Outcome_Statements_0809.pdf, accessed 26 October 2009.

CWDC (Children's Workforce Development Council) (2009) *Supervision Guide for Social Workers: Newly Qualified Social Workers Pilot Programme*. Workforce Development Council. http://www.cwdcouncil.org.uk/nqsw/pilot-programme, accessed 26 October 2009.

Dalrymple, J. and Burke, B. (1995) *Anti-oppressive Practice: Social Care and the Law,* Buckingham: Open University Press.

Dalrymple, J. and Burke, B. (2006) *Anti-Oppressive Practice: Social Care and the Law,* 2nd edn, Buckingham: Open University Press.

Dannermark, B., Ekström, M., Jakobsen, L. and Karlsson, J. C. (2002) *Explaining Society: Critical Realism in the Social Sciences*, London: Routledge.

Davys, A. M. and Beddoe, L. (2009) 'The Reflective Learning Model: Supervision of Social Work Students', *Social Work Education*, 28(8) 919–33.

D'Cruz, H., Gillingham, P. and Melendez, S. (2007) 'Reflexivity, its Meaning and Relevance for Social Work: A Critical Review of the Literature', *British Journal of Social Work*, 37(1) 73–90.

Department of Constitutional Affairs (2007) *Mental Capacity Act 2005: Code of Practice*, London: The Stationery Office.

Department of Health (1989) *An Introduction to The Children Act 1989*, London: HMSO.

Department of Health (1990) *The Care of Children: Principles of Practice in Regulations and Guidance*, London: HMSO.

Department of Health (1991) *The Children Act 1989: Guidance and Regulations, Volume 4: Residential Care*, London: HMSO.

Department of Health (2003) *Discharge from Hospital Pathway, Process and Practice*, London: Department of Health.

Department of Health (2005) *Independence, Well-being, and Choice: Our Vision for the Future of Social Care for Adults in England*, Cm. 6499, London: The Stationery Office.

Department of Health (2007) *Independence, Choice and Risk: A Guide to Best Practice in Supported Decision Making*, London: Department of Health.

Department of Health (2008) *Transforming Social Care: Local Authority Circular, LAC (DH) (2008) 1*, London: Department of Health.

Dewane, C. J. (2006) 'Use of Self: A Primer Revisited', *Clinical Social Work Journal*, 34(4) 543–58.

DfES (Department for Education and Skills) (2004) *Every Child Matters: Change for Children in Social Care*. London: Department for Education and Skills.

Dingwall, R., Eekelaar, J. and Murray, T. (1983) *The Protection of Children*, Oxford: Blackwell.

Dowding, D. (2002) 'Interpretation of Risk and Social Judgement Theory', in C. Thompson and D. Dowsing (eds), *Clinical Decision Making and Judgement in Nursing*, Edinburgh: Churchill Livingstone, 81–93.

Dowding, D. and Thompson C. (2002) 'Decision Analysis', in C. Thompson and D. Dowsing (eds), *Clinical Decision Making and Judgement in Nursing*, Edinburgh: Churchill Livingstone, 131–45.

Dowie, J. (1992) *Professional Judgement and Decision Making D300 Volume 3 Text 6: Assessing Chances*, 3rd edn, Milton Keynes: Open University.

Dreyfus, H. L. and Dreyfus, S. E. (1986) *Mind Over Machine: The Power of Human Intuition and Expertise in the Era of the Computer*, New York: The Free Press.

Drury Hudson, J. (1997) 'A Model of Professional Knowledge for Social Work Practice', *Australian Social Work*, 50(3) 35–44.

Dustin, D. (2006) 'Skills and Knowledge Needed to Practise as a Care Manager: Continuity and Change', *Journal of Social Work*, 6(3) 293–313.

Dwyer, S. (2005) 'Older People and Permanent Care: Whose Decision?', *British Journal of Social Work*, 35(7) 1081–92.

Eadie, T, and Lymbery, M. (2007) 'Promoting Creative Practice Through Social Work Education', *Social Work Education*, 26(7) 670–83.

England, H. (1986) *Social Work as Art: Making Sense for Good Practice,* London: Allen and Unwin.

Eraut, M. (1994) *Developing Professional Knowledge and Competence,* London: The Farmer Press.

Erikson, E. (1977) *Childhood and Society,* revised edn, St Albans: Triad Granada.

Evans, T. and Harris, J. (2004) 'Street-Level Bureaucracy, Social Work and the (Exaggerated) Death of Discretion', *British Journal of Social Work,* 34(6) 871–95.

Farmer, E. and Owen, M. (1995) *Child Protection Practice: Private Risks and Public Remedies,* London: HMSO.

Farmer, E., Lipscombe, J. and Moyers, S. (2005) 'Foster Care Strain and its Impact on Parenting and Placement Outcomes for Adolescents', *British Journal of Social Work,* 35(2) 237–53.

Farnham, D. and Horton, S. (eds) (1996) *Managing the New Public Services,* 2nd edn, Basingstoke: Macmillan.

Ferguson, H. (2009) 'Performing Child Protection: Home Visiting, Movement and the Struggle to Reach the Abused Child', *Child and Family Social Work,* 14(4) 471–80.

Ferguson, M. (1987) 'A Feminist Interpretation of Professional Incompetence in the Beckford Case', in G. Drewry, B. Martin and B. Sheldon (eds), *After Beckford,* London: Social Policy Institute, 33–9.

Fish, S., Munro, E. and Bairstow, S. (2008) *Learning Together to Safeguard Children: Developing a Multi-Agency Systems Approach To Case Review,* London: Social Care Institute and Excellence.

Fitzpatrick, T. (2008) *Applied Ethics and Social Problems,* Bristol: Policy Press.

Flynn, D. (2005) 'The Social Worker as Family Mediator: Balancing Power in Cases Involving Family Violence', *Australian Social Work,* 58(4) 407–18.

Folgheraiter, F. (2004) *Relational Social Work: Toward Networking and Societal Practices,* London: Jessica Kingsley.

Fook, J. (2002) *Social Work: Critical Theory and Practice,* London: Sage.

Ford, K. and Jones, A. (1987) *Student Supervision,* Basingstoke: Macmillan.

Forrester, D., Kershaw, S., Moss, H. and Hughes, L. (2008) 'Communication Skills in Child Protection: How do Social Workers Talk to Parents?', *Child and Family Social Work,* 13(1) 41–51.

France, A., Freiberg, K. and Homel, R. (2010) 'Beyond Risk Factors: Towards a Holistic Prevention Paradigm for Children and Young People', *British Journal of Social Work,* 40(4) 1192–210.

Furedi, F. (1997) *Culture of Fear: Risk Taking and the Morality of Low Expectation,* London: Cassell.

Garrett, P. M. (2001) 'Interrogating "home alone": the critical deconstruction of media representations in social work education', *Social Work Education,* 20(6), 643–58.

Gergen, K. J. (1985) 'The Social Constructionist Movement In Modern Psychology', *American Psychologist,* 40(3) 266–75.

Gert, B. and Culver, C. M. (1979) 'The Justification of Paternalism', *Ethics,* 89 199–210.

Ghate, D. and Hazel, N. (2002) *Parenting in Poor Environments: Stress, Support and Coping*, London: Jessica Kingsley.

Gibbons, J., Conroy, S. and Bell, C. (1995) *Operating the Child Protection System*, London: HMSO.

Gibbs, G. (1988) *Learning by Doing: A Guide to Teaching and Learning Methods*, London: FEU.

Gibbs, J. (2009) 'Changing the Cultural Story in Child Protection: Learning From the Insider's Experience', *Child and Family Social Work*, 14(3) 289–99.

Gibson, F., McGrath, A. and Reid, N. (1989) 'Occupational Stress in Social Work', *British Journal of Social Work*, 9(1) 1–16.

Gigerenzer, G. (2007) *Gut Feelings: The Intelligence of the Unconscious*, New York: Viking.

Glasby, J. (2005) 'The Future of Adult Care: Lessons from Previous Reforms', *Research Policy and Planning*, 23(2) 61–9.

Glasby, J., Walshe, K. and Harvey, G. (2007) 'Making Evidence Fit for Purpose in Decision Making: A Case of the Hospital Discharge of Older People', *Evidence and Policy*, 3(3) 425–37.

Glisson, C. and Hemmelgarn, A. (1998) 'The Effects of Organizational Climate and Interorganizational Coordination on the Quality and Outcomes of Children's Services Systems', *Child Abuse and Neglect*, 22(5) 401–21.

Gorell Barnes, G. (1991) 'Ambiguities in Post-divorce Relationships', *Journal of Social Work Practice*, 3(2) 143–50.

Grubin, D. and Wingate, S. (1996). 'Sexual Offence Recidivism: Prediction Versus Understanding', *Criminal Behaviour and Mental Health*, 6 349–59.

Gudykunst, W. B. (1998) *Bridging Differences: Effective Intergroup Communication*, 3rd edn, Thousand Oaks, CA: Sage.

Hallett, C. (1995) *Interagency Co-ordination in Child Protection*, London: HMSO.

Hamm, R. M. (1988) 'Clinical Intuition and Clinical Analysis: Expertise and the Cognitive Continuum', in J. Dowie and A. Elstein (eds), *Professional Judgement: A Reader in Clinical Decision Making*, Cambridge: Cambridge University Press, 78–105.

Hammond, K. R. (1996) *Human Judgement and Social Policy: Irreducible Uncertainty, Inevitable Error, Unavoidable Injustice*, New York: Oxford University Press.

Hammond, K. R., Hamm, R. M., Grassia, J. and Pearson, T. (1997) 'Direct Comparison of the Efficacy of Intuitive and Analytical Cognition in Expert Judgment', in W. M. Goldstein and R. M. Hogarth (eds), *Research on Judgement and Decision Making: Current, Connections and Controversies*, Cambridge: Cambridge University Press, 144–80.

Hardman, D. (2009) *Judgement and Decision Making: Psychological Perspectives*, Chichester: BSP Blackwell.

Harlow, E. (2004) 'Protecting Children: Why Don't Core Groups Work? Lessons from the Literature', *Practice*, 16(1) 31–42.

Harlow, E. and Shardlow S. M. (2006) 'Safeguarding Children: Challenges to the Effective Operation of Core Groups', *Child and Family Social Work*, 11(1) 65–72.

Harris, R. and Timms, R. (1993) *Secure Accommodation in Child Care: Between Hospital and Prison or Thereabouts?*, London: Routledge.

Hawkins, P. and Shohet, R, (2006) *Supervision in the Helping Professions*, Maidenhead: Open University Press.

Hayes, D. and Houston, S. (2007) '"Lifeworld", "System" and Family Group Conferences: Habermas's Contribution to Discourse in Child Protection', *British Journal of Social Work*, 37(6) 987–1006.

Healy, K. (2005) *Social Work Theories in Context: Creating Frameworks for Practice*, Basingstoke: Palgrave Macmillan.

Heilbrun, K. (2003) 'Violence Risk: From Prediction to Management', in D. Carson and R. Bull (eds), *Handbook of Psychology in Legal Contexts,* 2nd edn, Chichester: Wiley, 127–42.

Hemmelgarn, A. L., Glisson, C. and James, L. R. (2006) 'Organizational Culture and Climate: Implications for Services and Interventions Research', *Clinical Psychology: Science and Practice*, 13(1) 75–89

Hill, M. (1990) 'The Manifest and Latent Lessons of Child Abuse Inquiries', *British Journal of Social Work*, 20(3) 197–213.

Hill, M. (1997) *The Policy Process in the Modern State,* 3rd edn, Hemel Hempstead: Prentice Hall/Harvester Wheatsheaf.

HM Government (2006) *Working Together to Safeguard Children: A Guide to Inter-Agency Working to Safeguard and Promote the Welfare of Children*, London: The Stationery Office.

HM Government (2008) *Information Sharing: Guidance for Practitioners and Managers*, London: Department for Children, Schools and Families.

Hogarth, R. M. (1987) *Judgement and Choice: The Psychology of Decision*, 2nd edn, Chichester: John Wiley.

Holland, S., Scourfield, J., O'Neill, S. and Pithouse, A. (2005) 'Democratising the Family and the State? The Case of Family Group Conference in Child Welfare', *Journal of Social Policy*, 34(1) 59–77.

Hollis, M. and Howe, D. (1987) 'Moral Risks in Social Work', *Journal of Applied Philosophy*, 4(2) 123–33.

Horlick-Jones, T., Rosenhead, J., Georgiou, I., Ravetz, J. and Lofstedt, R. (2001) 'Decision Support for Organisational Risk Management by Problem Structuring', *Health, Risk and Society*, 3(2) 142–65.

Houston, S. (2001) 'Beyond Social Constructionism: Critical Realism and Social Work', *British Journal of Social Work*, 31(6) 845–61.

Howe, D. (1994) 'Modernity, Postmodernity and Social Work', *British Journal of Social Work*, 24(5) 513–32.

Howe, D. (2008) *The Emotionally Intelligent Social Worker*, Basingstoke: Palgrave Macmillan.

Hudson, B. (2002) 'Interprofessionality in Health and Social Care: The Achilles' Heel of Partnership', *Journal of Interprofessional Care* 16(1): 8–17.

Hudson, B. (2005) 'Information Sharing and Children's Services Reform in England: Can Legislation Change Practice?', *Journal of Interprofessional Care*, 19(6) 537–646.

Hughes, J. C. and Baldwin, C. (2006) *Ethical Issues on Dementia Care: Making Difficult Decisions*, London: Jessica Kingsley.

Hughes, L. and Pengelly, P. (1997) *Staff Supervision in a Turbulent Environment: Managing Process and Task in Front-line Services*, London: Jessica Kingsley.

Hugman, R. (1991) *Power in Caring Professions*, Basingstoke: Macmillan.

Hunt, G. (1998) 'Introduction: Whistleblowing and the Crisis of Accountability', in G. Hunt (ed.), *Whistleblowing in the Social Services: Public Accountability and Professional Practice*, London: Arnold, 1–15.

IFSW (International Federation of Social Workers) (2000) *Definition of Social Work*. http://www.ifsw.org/en/p38000208.html, accessed 14 January 2009.

Illich, I., Zola, I. K., McKnight, J., Caplan, J. and Shaiken, H. (1977) *Disabling Professions*, New York: Marion Boyars.

Imbrogno, S. and Canada, E. (1988) 'Social Work as an Holistic System of Activity', *Social Thought*, 14, Winter, 12–29.

Ince, D. (2010) 'Computer Says: "Misery"', *Professional Social Work*, 12–13 March.

Janis, I. L. (1972) *Victims of Group Think*, New York: Harcourt Brace Jovanovich.

Janis, I. L. and Mann, L. (1977) *Decision Making: A Psychological Analysis of Conflict, Choice and Commitment*, New York: The Free Press.

Johnson, D. W. and Johnson, F. P. (1982) *Joining Together: Group Theory and Group Skills*, 2nd edn, Englewood Cliffs, NJ: Prentice-Hall.

Jones, F., Fletcher, B. C. and Ibbetson, K. (1991) 'Stressors and Strains amongst Social Workers: Demands, Supports, Constraints, and Psychological Health', *British Journal of Social Work*, 21(5) 443–69.

Jones, M. (2004) 'Supervision, Learning and Transformative Practices', in N. Gould and M. Baldwin (eds), *Social Work, Critical Reflection and the Learning Organisation*, Aldershot: Ashgate, 11–22.

Joseph Rowntree Foundation (2008) *Improving Care in Residential Care Homes: A Literature Review*, York: Joseph Rowntree Foundation.

Kadushin, A. and Harkness, D. (2002) *Supervision in Social Work*, 4th edn, New York: Colombia Press.

Karban, K. (1999) 'Long-Arm Practice Teaching for the Diploma in Social Work: The Views of Students and Practice Teachers', *Social Work Education*, 18(1) 59–70.

Kempson, E. (1996) *Life on a Low Income*, York: Joseph Rowntree Foundation.

Kemshall, H. (2003) *Understanding Risk in Criminal Justice*, Maidenhead: Open University Press.

Kitchener, K. S. and Brenner, H. G. (1990) 'Wisdom and Reflective Judgement: Knowing in the Face of Uncertainty', in R. J. Sternberg (ed.), *Wisdom: Its Nature, Origins and Development*, Cambridge: Cambridge University Press, 212–27.

Klein, G. (1999) *Sources of Power: How People Make Decisions*, Cambridge, MA: MIT Press.

Laming, Lord (2003) *The Victoria Climbie Inquiry: Report of the Inquiry by Lord Laming*, CM 5730, London: The Stationery Office.

Langan, J, (2009) 'Mental Health, Risk Communication and Data Quality in the Electronic Age', *British Journal of Social Work*, 39(3), 467–87.

Lazarus, R. S. (1991) *Emotion and Adaptation*, Oxford and New York: Oxford University Press.

Lazarus, R. S (2006) *Emotion and Stress: A New Synthesis*, New York: Springer Publishing.

Lazarus, R. S. and Lazarus, B. N. (1994) *Passion and Reason: Making Sense of Our Emotions*, Oxford and New York: Oxford University Press.

Leadbetter, J. (2008) 'Learning in and for Interagency Working: Making Links between Practice Development and Structured Reflection', *Learning in Health and Social Care*, 7(4) 198–208.

Leeper, R. W. (1966) 'A Critical Consideration of Egon Brunswik's Probabilistic Functionalism', in K. R. Hammond (ed.), *The Psychology of Egon Brunswik*, New York: Holt, Rinehart & Winston, 405–54.

Leonard, P. (1996) 'Three Discourses on Practice: A Postmodern Re-appraisal', *Journal of Sociology and Social Welfare*, 23(2) 5–26.

Lipsky, M. (1997) 'Street-level Bureaucracy: An Introduction', in R. Hill (ed.), *The Policy Process: A Reader*, 2nd edn, Hemel Hempstead: Prentice Hall/Harvester Wheatsheaf, 389–92.

Littell, J. H. (2008) 'Evidence Based or Biased? The Quality of Reviews of Evidence-Based Practice', *Children and Youth Services Review*, 30(11) 1299–317.

Littlechild, B. (2005) 'The Nature and Effects of Violence against Child Protection Social Workers: Providing Effective Support', *British Journal of Social Work*, 35(3) 387–401.

Lloyd, L. (2003) 'Caring Relationships: Looking Beyond Welfare Categories of "Carers" and "Service Users"', in K. Stalker (ed.), *Reconceptualising Work with 'Carers'*, London: Jessica Kingsley, 37–55.

López, J. and Scott, J. (2000) *Social Structure*, Buckingham: Open University Press.

Luitgaarden, G. M. J. van de (2009) 'Evidence-Based Practice in Social Work: Lessons from Judgement and Decision-Making Theory', *British Journal of Social Work*, 39(2) 243–60.

Lupton, C. (1998) 'User Empowerment or Family Self-Reliance? The Family Group Conference Model', *British Journal of Social Work*, 28(1) 107–28.

Macdonald, G. (1990) 'Allocating Blame in Social Work', *British Journal of Social Work*, 20(6) 525–46.

Maden, A. (2003) 'Standardised Risk Assessment: Why All the Fuss?', *Psychiatric Bulletin*, 27(6) 201–4.

Manthorpe, J., Rapaport, J. and Stanley, N. (2008) 'The Mental Capacity Act 2005 and Its Influences on Social Work Practice', *Practice*, 20(3) 151–62.

Marshall, M. and Allen, K. (2006) (eds) *Dementia: Walking not Wandering,* London: Hawker Publications.

May-Chahal, C. and Broadhurst, K. (2006) 'Integrating Objects of Intervention and Organisational Relevance: The Case of Safeguarding Children Missing from Education Systems', *Child Abuse Review,* 15(6) 440–55.

McBeath, G. and Webb, W (2002) 'Virtue Ethics and Social Work: Being Lucky, Realistic, and not Doing Ones Duty', *British Journal of Social Work,* 32(8) 1015–36.

McCormack, J. (2007) 'Recovery and strengths based practice', SRN Discussion Paper Series, Report 6, Glasgow: Scottish Recovery Network.

Mendes, P. (2001) 'Blaming the Messenger: The Media, Social Worker and Child Abuse', *Australian Social Work,* 54(2) 27–35.

Minty, T. (1995) 'Social Work's Five Deadly Sins', *Social Work and Social Sciences Review,* 6(1) 48–63.

Mitchell, W. and Glendinning, C. (2008) 'Risk and Adult Social Care: Identification, Management and New Policies. What does UK Research Evidence Tell Us?', *Health, Risk and Society,* 10(3) 297–315.

Morrison T. (2007) 'Emotional Intelligence, Emotion and Social Work: Context, Characteristics and Contribution', *British Journal of Social Work,* 27(2): 245–63.

Moscovici, S. and Doise, W. (1994) *Conflict and Consensus: A General Theory of Collective Decisions,* London: Sage.

Mullaly, B. (1997) *Structural Social Work,* 2nd edn, Toronto: Oxford University Press.

Mullaly, B. (2002) Challenging Oppression: A Critical Social Work Approach, Ontario: Oxford University Press.

Mullender, A. and Ward, D. (1991) *Self-Directed Groupwork: Users Taking Action for Empowerment,* London: Whiting & Birch.

Munro, E. (2002) *Effective Child Protection,* London: Sage.

Munro, E. (2004) 'A Simpler Way to Understand the Results of Risk Assessment Instruments', *Children and Youth Services Review,* 26(9) 873–83.

Munro, E (2005) 'A Systems Approach to Investigating Child Abuse Deaths', *British Journal of Social Work,* 35 531–46.

Munro, E. (2008a) 'Improving Reasoning in Supervision', *Social Work Now,* 40 3–10 August, http://www.scie-socialcareonline.org.uk/profile.asp?guid=53e7e578-460a-4380-9fb0-a29bfeb3dae6.

Munro, E. (2008b) *Effective Child Protection,* 2nd edn, London: Sage.

Nelkin, D. K. (2008) *Stanford Encyclopedia of Philosophy,* 'Moral Luck', http://plato.stanford.edu/entries/moral-luck/, accessed 1 October 2009.

Newman, T., Moseley, A., Tierney, S. and Ellis, A. (2005) *Evidence-based Social Work: A Guide for the Perplexed,* Lyme Regis: Russell House.

Noble, C. and Irwin, J. (2009) 'Social Work Supervision: An Exploration of the Current Challenges in a Rapidly Changing Social, Economic and Political Environment', *Journal of Social Work,* 9(3) 345–57.

Oatley, K., Keltner, D. and Jenkins, J. M. (2006) *Understanding Emotions,* 2nd edn, Malden: Blackwell Publishing.

O'Neill, T. (2001) *Children in Secure Accommodation*, London: Jessica Kingsley.

O'Rourke, L. (2009) 'Practitioners Demand More Guidance and Training in Record-Keeping', *Community Care*, 16 April, 16–19.

Osmo, R. and Landau, R. (2001) 'The Need for Explicit Argumentation in Ethical Decision-Making in Social Work', *Social Work Education*, 20(4) 483–92.

Osmond, J. (2005) 'Knowledge Spectrum: A Framework for Teaching Knowledge and its use in Social Work Practice', *British Journal of Social Work*, 35(6) 881–900.

O'Sullivan, T. (2004) 'Inputs to an Adoption Panel: A Case Study', *Adoption and Fostering*, 28(3) 41–51.

O'Sullivan, T. (2005) 'Some Theoretical Propositions on the Nature of Practice Wisdom', *Journal of Social Work*, 5(2), 221–42.

O'Sullivan, T. (2008) 'Using Decision Analysis: Connecting Classroom and Field', *Social Work Education*, 27(3) 262–78.

Parrott, W. G. (2001) 'Emotions in Social Psychology: Volume Overview', in W. Gerrod Parrott (ed.), *Emotions in Social Psychology: Essential Readings*, Philadelphia, PA: Psychology Press.

Parton, N. (2001) 'Risk and Professional Judgement', in L. Cull and J. Roche (eds), *The Law and Social Work: Contemporary Issues for Practice*, Basingstoke: Palgrave Macmillan.

Paul, R. and Elder, L. (2007a) 'Critical Thinking: The Art of Socratic Questioning', *Journal of Developmental Education*, 31(1) 36–7.

Paul, R. and Elder, L. (2007b) 'Critical Thinking: The Art of Socratic Questioning, Part II', *Journal of Developmental Education*, 31(2) 32–3.

Pawson, R., Boaz, A., Grayson, L., Long, A. and Barnes, C. (2003) 'Types and Quality of Knowledge in Social Care', SCIE Knowledge Review 3, London: Social Care Institute for Excellence.

Payne, M. (1989) 'Open Records and Shared Decisions with Clients', in Steven Shardlow (ed.), *The Values of Change in Social Work*, London: Tavistock/Routledge, 114–35.

Payne, M. (1997) 'Government Guidance in the Construction of the Social Work Profession', in R. Adams (ed.), *Crisis in the Human Services: National and International Issues*, Kingston upon Hull: University of Lincolnshire and Humberside, 381–90.

Payne, M. (2000) *Teamwork in Multiprofessional Care*, Basingstoke: Macmillan.

Payne, M. (2005) *Modern Social Work Theory*, 3rd edn, Basingstoke: Palgrave.

Penhale, B. and Parker, J. (2008) *Working with Vulnerable Adults*, London: Routledge.

Peterson, C. (2000) 'The Future of Optimism', *American Psychologist*, 55(1) 44–55.

Phillipson, J. (2009) 'Supervision and Being Supervised', in R. Adams, L. Dominelli and M. Payne (eds), *Practising Social Work in a Complex World*, Basingstoke: Palgrave Macmillan, 188–95.

Postle, K. and Beresford, P. (2007) 'Capacity Building and the Reconception of Political Participation: A Role for Social Care Workers?', *British Journal and Social Work*, 37(1) 143–58.

Preston-Shoot, M., Roberts, G. and Vernon, S. (2001) 'Values in Social Work: Strained Relations or Sustaining Relationships?', *Journal of Social Welfare and Family Law*, 23(1) 1–22.

Randall, J., Cowley, P. and Tomlinson, P. (2000) 'Overcoming Barriers to Effective Practice in Child Care', *Child and Family Social Work*, 5(4) 343–52.

Reamer, F. G. (1993) *The Philosophical Foundations of Social Work*, New York: Columbia University Press.

Reamer, F. G. (1995) *Social Work Values and Ethics*, New York: Columbia University Press.

Reder, P. and Duncan, S. (2003) 'Understanding Communication in Child Protection Networks', *Child Abuse Review*, 12(2) 82–100.

Reder, P., Duncan, S. and Gray, M. (1993) *Beyond Blame: Child Abuse Tragedies Revisited*, London: Routledge.

Rhodes, M. L. (1986) *Ethical Dilemmas in Social Work Practice*, Boston, MA: Routledge & Kegan Paul.

Richardson, S and Asthana, S. (2006) 'Inter-agency Information Sharing in Health and Social Care Services: The Role of Professional Culture', *British Journal of Social Work*, 36(6) 657–69.

Robinson, L., Hutchings, D,. Corner, L., Finch, T., Hughes, J., Brittain, K. and Bond, J. (2007) 'Balancing Rights and Risk: Conflicting Perspective on The Management of Wandering in Dementia', *Health, Risk and Society* 9(4) 389–406.

Rodwell, M. K. (1998) *Social Work Constructivist Research*, New York: Garland Publishing.

Ruch, G. (2007a) '"Thoughtful" Practice: Child Care Social Work and the Role of Case Discussion', *Child and Family Social Work*, 12(4) 370–9.

Ruch, G. (2007b) 'Reflective Practice in Contemporary Child-care Social Work: The Role of Containment', *British Journal Social Work*, 37 (4) 659–80.

Rushmer, R. and Pallis, G. (2003) 'Inter-Professional Working: The Wisdom of Integrated Working and the Disaster of Blurring Boundaries', *Public Money and Management*, 13(1) 59–66.

Rushton, A and Nathan, J. (1996) 'The Supervision of Child Protection Work', *British Journal of Social Work*, 26(3) 357–74.

Russo, J. E., Medvec, V. H. and Meloy, M. G. (1996) 'The Distortion of Information During Decisions', *Organisational Behaviour and Human Decision Processes*, 66(1) 102–10.

Saleebey, D. (ed.) (2009) *The Strengths Perspective in Social Work Practice,* 5th edn, Boston, MA: Pearson.

Salovey, P., Detweiler-Bedell, B. T., Detweiler-Bedell, J. B. and Mayer, J. D. (2008) 'Emotional Intelligence', in M. Lewis, J. M. Haviland-Jones and L. F. Feldman Barrett (eds), *Handbook of Emotions,* 3rd edn, New York: Guilford Press, 533–47.

Satyamurti, C. (1981) *Occupational Survival: The Case of the Local Authority Social Worker,* Oxford: Basil Blackwell.

Schein, E. H. (1988) *Process Consultation: Volume 1, Its Role in Organisation Development,* Reading, MA: Addison-Wesley.

Schwalbe, C. S. (2008) 'Strengthening The Integration of Actuarial Risk Assessment with Clinical Judgement in an Evidence Based Framework', *Children and Youth Services Review,* 30(12) 1458–64.

Scott, V., Votova, K., Scanlan, A. and Close, J. (2007) 'Multifactorial and Functional Mobility Assessment Tools for Fall Risk Among Older Adults in Community, Home-Support, Long-Term and Acute Care Settings', *Age and Ageing,* 36(2) 130–9.

Scutt, N. (1995) 'Child Advocacy: Getting the Child's Voice Heard', in C. Cloke and M. Davies (eds), *Participation and Empowerment in Child Protection,* London: Pitman.

Seden, J. (2008) 'Organisations and Organisational Change', in S. Fraser and S. Matthews (eds), *The Critical Practitioner in Social Work and Health Care,* London: Sage, 169–85.

Sheppard, M. (1995) *Care Management and the New Social Work: A Critical Analysis,* London: Whiting & Birch.

Sheppard, M. (2006) *Social Work and Social Exclusion: The Idea of Practice,* Aldershot: Ashgate.

Shlonsky, A. and Wagner, D. (2005) 'The Next Step: Integrating Actuarial Risk Assessment and Clinical Judgement into Evidence-Based Practice Framework in CPS Case Management', *Children and Youth Services Review,* 27(4) 407–27.

Sibeon, R. (1990) 'Comments on the Structure and Forms of Social Work Knowledge', *Social Work and Social Sciences Review,* 1(1) 29–44.

Simmonds, C. (2008) 'Secure Accommodation: Out of Sight, Out of Mind', *Family Law,* 38(1033).

Sinclair, I., Baker, C., Lee, J. and Gibbs, I. (2007) *The Pursuit of Permanence: A Study of the English Care System,* London: Jessica Kingsley Publishers.

Sinclair, I., Wilson, K. and Gibbs, I. (2005) *Foster Placements: Why They Succeed and Why They Fail,* London: Jessica Kingsley Publishers.

Smith, R. (2008) *Social Work and Power,* Basingstoke: Palgrave Macmillan.

Spafford. M. M., Schryer, C. F., Campbell, S. L. and Lingard, L. (2007) 'Towards Embracing Clinical Uncertainty: Lessons from Social Work, Optometry and Medicine', *Journal of Social Work,* 7(2) 155–78.

Sserunkuma, J. and Sin, J. (2010) 'Joined Up Thinking', *Professional Social Work,* 12–13 February.

Stalker, C. A., Mandell, D., Frensch, K.M., Harveys, C. and Wright, M. (2007) 'Child Welfare Workers who are Exhausted yet Satisfied with their Job: How do they do It?', *Child and Family Social Work,* 12 (2) 182–91.

Stalker, K. (2003) 'Managing Risk and Uncertainty in Social Work: A Literature Review', *Journal of Social Work,* 3(2) 211–33.

Stanley, N. and Manthorpe, J. (eds) (2004) *The Age of the Inquiry: Learning and Blaming in Health and Social Care,* London: Routledge.

Stevens, M. and Higgins, D. J. (2002) 'The Influence of Risk and Protective Factors on Burnout Experienced by Those who work with Maltreated Children', *Child Abuse Review*, 11(5), 313–31.

Stevenson, O. (1986) 'Guest Editorial on the Jasmine Beckford Inquiry', *British Journal of Social Work*, 16(5) 501–10.

Stevenson, O. (1989) 'Multi-disciplinary Work', in O. Stevenson (ed.), *Child Abuse: Public Policy and Professional Practice,* Hemel Hempstead: Wheatsheaf, 173–203.

Storey, J. and Billingham, J. (2001) 'Occupational Stress and Social Work', *Social Work Education*, 20(6) 559–670.

Taylor, B. J. (2006) 'Risk Management Paradigms in Health and Social Services for Professional Decision Making in the Long-Term Care of Older People', *British Journal of Social Work*, 36(8) 1411–29.

Taylor, C. and White, S. (2000) *Practicing Reflexivity in Health and Welfare: Making Knowledge*, Buckingham: Open University.

Tew, J, (2006) 'Understanding Power and Powerlessness: Towards a Framework for Emancipatory Practice in Social Work', *Journal of Social Work*, 6(1) 33–51.

Thomasgard, M. and Collins, V. (2003) 'A Comprehensive Review of Cross-Disciplinary, Case-Based Peer Supervision Model', *Family, Systems & Health*, 21(3) 305–19.

Thompson, N. (1996) *People Skills: A Guide to Effective Practice in the Human Services,* Basingstoke: Macmillan.

Thompson, N. (2003) *Promoting Equality: Challenging Discrimination and Oppression*, 2nd edn, Basingstoke: Palgrave Macmillan.

Thomson, A. (1999) *Critical Reasoning in Ethics: A Practical Introduction*, London: Routledge.

Trappes-Lomax, T., Ellis, A., Fox, M., Taylor, R., Power, M., Stead, J. and Bainbridge, I. (2006) 'Buying Time 1: A Prospective, Controlled Trial of a Joint Health/Social Care Residential Rehabilitation Unit for Older People on Discharge From Hospital', *Health and Social Care in the Community*, 14(1) 49–62.

Trevithick, P. (2000) *Social Work Skills: A Practice Handbook*, Maidenhead: Open University Press.

Trevithick, P. (2005) *Social Work Skills: A Practice Handbook,* 2nd edn, Maidenhead: Open University Press.

Trevithick, P. (2008) 'Revisiting the Knowledge Base of Social Work: A Framework for Practice', *British Journal of Social Work* 38(6) 1212–37.

Tsui, M. S. (2005) *Social Work Supervision: Contents and Concepts*, Thousand Oaks, CA: Sage.

Tsui, M. S. (2008) 'Adventures in Re-searching the Features of Social Work Supervision in Hong Kong', *Qualitative Social Work*, 7(3) 349–62.

Tversky, A. and Kahneman, D. (1982) 'Judgment Under Uncertainty: Heuristics and Biases', in D. Kahneman, P. Stovic and A. Tversky (eds), *Judgement Under Uncertainty: Heuristics and Biases*, Cambridge: Cambridge University Press.

Walker, J., Crawford, K. and Parker J. (2008) *Practice Education in Social Work: A Handbook for Practice Teachers, Assessors and Educators*, Exeter: Learning Matters.

Ward, J. and Patel, N. (2006) 'Broadening the Discussion on "Sexual Exploitation": Ethnicity, Sexual Exploitation and Young People', *Child Abuse Review*, 15(5) 341–50.

Wattam, C. (1995) 'The Investigative Process', in K. Wilson and A. James (eds), *The Child Protection Handbook,* London: Baillière Tindall, 70–187.

Webb, D. (2007) 'Modes of Hope', *History of the Human Sciences*, 20(3) 65–83.

Wenger, E. (1998) *Communities of Practice: Learning, Meaning and Identity*, Cambridge: Cambridge University Press.

White, S., Hall, C. and Peckover, S. (2009) 'The Descriptive Tyranny of the Common Assessment Framework: Technologies of Categorization and Professional Practice in Child Welfare', *British Journal of Social Work*, 39(7) 1197–217.

Williams, J. M. G. and Pollock, L. R. (1993) 'Factors Mediating Suicidal Behaviour: Their Utility in Primary and Secondary Prevention', *Journal of Mental Health*, 2(1) 3–24.

Woodhouse, D. and Pengelly, P. (1991) *Anxiety and the Dynamics of Collaboration,* Aberdeen: Aberdeen University Press.

Zugazaga, C. B., Surette, R. B., Mendez, M. and Otto, C. W. (2006). 'Social Worker Perceptions of the Portrayal of the Profession in the News and Entertainment Media: An Exploratory Study', *Journal of Social Work Education*, 42(3) 621–36.

Author index

Subject index